T0329606

Trade Like
a Casino

Founded in 1807, John Wiley & Sons is the oldest independent publishing company in the United States. With offices in North America, Europe, Australia, and Asia, Wiley is globally committed to developing and marketing print and electronic products and services for our customers' professional and personal knowledge and understanding.

The Wiley Trading series features books by traders who have survived the market's ever-changing temperament and have prospered—some by reinventing systems, others by getting back to basics. Whether a novice trader, professional, or somewhere in between, these books will provide the advice and strategies needed to prosper today and well into the future.

For a list of available titles, visit our Web site at www.WileyFinance.com.

Trade Like a Casino

Find Your Edge, Manage Risk, and Win Like the House

RICHARD L. WEISSMAN

WILEY

John Wiley & Sons, Inc.

Published by John Wiley & Sons, Inc., Hoboken, New Jersey.
Published simultaneously in Canada.

For general information on our other products and services or for technical support, please contact our Customer Care Department within the United States at (800) 762-2974, outside the United States at (317) 572-3993 or fax (317) 572-4002.

Wiley also publishes its books in a variety of electronic formats. Some content that appears in print may not be available in electronic books. For more information about Wiley products, visit our web site at www.wiley.com.

Library of Congress Cataloging-in-Publication Data:

Weissman, Richard L.
  Trade like a casino : find your edge, manage risk, and win like the house / Richard L. Weissman.
     p. cm. — (Wiley trading series)
  Includes bibliographical references and index.
  ISBN 978-0-470-93309-1 (cloth); ISBN 9781118137949 (ebk);
  ISBN 9781118137956 (ebk); ISBN 9781118137963 (ebk)
  1. Speculation. 2. Investment analysis. 3. Risk management. 4. Portfolio management. I. Title.
  HG6015.W346 2011
  332.64′5—dc22

                                                                      2011016573

Printed in the United States of America.

10 9 8 7 6 5 4 3 2 1

For my wife, Pamela Nations-Weissman, who laughed when I swore I would never write another book.

Contents

Preface

You cannot beat a roulette table unless you steal money from it.

—Albert Einstein

A year ago, I was talking with a struggling trader about the profession of speculative trading. He asked a question that ultimately culminated in the publication of this book. That question was "Can someone really earn a living as a speculator?" This person was putting his life's savings on the line every day and yet did not know for certain whether anyone could actually earn a living through speculative trading. Then, on thinking back to my own start in this business, it occurred to me that I had done the same thing. If you have picked up this book and have been asking yourself that same question, there is good news and bad news. The good news is that the answer to the question is "Yes." Yes, professional speculative trading is a valid career path. Yes, not only can it be done, but it has been, and continues to be accomplished by many professional traders. It is not a matter of luck or chance. The bad news is that it is one of the most difficult careers known to humankind. It is difficult because it requires us to consistently do that which is psychologically uncomfortable and unnatural (we revisit why trading is so difficult in great detail throughout the course of this book).

So how do we transform the dicey game of speculative trading into a valid career path? We do not start from scratch. No need to reinvent the wheel. No need for luck, chance, or even prayers. Instead, what is required is the adaptation of an existing successful business model to the career of speculation. That model is the *casino paradigm*.[1] How do casinos make money? Although each and every spin of a roulette wheel is random, the casino remains unconcerned because probability is in their favor. In trading, we call this the development of *positive expectancy* trading models. Positive expectancy means that after deducting for liquidity risk—for example, the risk of price differences between our model's hypothetical entry or exit price and the actual entry or exit price—and commissions, our model is profitable.

But what if some multibillionaire walks into the casino with a cashier's check for a billion dollars? She finds the cashier quite happy to change her check into chips . . . no questions asked. But when she walks her wheelbarrow of chips over to the roulette wheel and tells the croupier, "Put it all on red," she is politely told that there is a maximum table limit bet size of $10,000 per spin of the roulette wheel. Why does the casino need table limits if probability is skewed in their favor? Because they know that despite the odds being in their favor, on any particular spin of the wheel it could come up red, and if it did, our multibillionaire would own their casino. By using table limits, they force the player to limit her bet size, thereby ensuring that as they keep playing, the casino's probability edge will eventually swallow up the entire billion dollars. In speculative trading we call table limits *price risk management.*

The final prerequisite to the casino model was actually implicitly stated in both of the preceding paragraphs. The specific sentence that addressed this third prerequisite most clearly was ". . . the casino remains unconcerned because they have probability in their favor." Casino owners do not become despondent or close the casino when players win. Instead, they continue playing the probabilities and managing the risk. They adhere to this paradigm 24 hours a day, seven days a week, and 365 days a year. They never abandon the paradigm irrespective of how good or how bad their results are on any given day, week, or month. In trading, we call unwavering adherence to positive expectancy trading models and price risk management *trader discipline.*

Of course, the model for successful speculative trading is more complex than the casino paradigm and throughout this book we explore these various complexities in great detail. Nevertheless, now the book's title makes more sense. Successful traders can walk under ladders, have trading accounts ending in the number 13, you name it . . . it makes absolutely no difference because successful speculation has nothing whatsoever to do with luck. Luck is what the gamblers hope for. By contrast, professional speculators consistently play the probabilities and manage the risk.

This book progresses in a linear fashion from basic, rudimentary concepts to those of greater complexity. Chapter 1 explores the casino paradigm of trading with respect to the development of positive expectancy models in exhaustive detail. First, we look at why technical analysis helps in the development of positive expectancy trading models as well as the flaws in fundamental analysis as a standalone methodology for the development of positive expectancy models. Then we examine the limitations of technical analysis and how fundamental analysis can be used to minimize these limitations.

Chapter 2 examines the casino paradigm of trading as it relates to price risk management. This chapter specifically introduces the reader to what I call the risk management pyramid. The base of the risk management pyramid includes traditional tools of price risk management such as stop loss placement and volumetric position sizing. Within the middle tier of the pyramid are tools used by the portfolio school of risk management, value-at-risk and stress testing. At the pyramid's apex is qualitative analysis by experienced risk managers that I call management discretion.

Chapter 3 concludes our introduction to the casino paradigm with an in-depth exposition of trader discipline. It begins by defining discipline as it relates to speculative trading and explaining why adherence to a disciplined approach is difficult. Then we see how discipline relates to developing, implementing, and adhering to positive expectancy trading models and price risk management. Next is an examination of how the lack of discipline can undermine a positive expectancy trading model. No matter how robust a model is, there are times when the odds do not favor that model's employment. Standing aside during such periods requires patience and discipline, specifically the discipline not to trade until the market again displays the kind of behavior in which the odds are in our favor. The chapter concludes by looking at various types of market action that traders can exploit, as well as pitfalls to avoid in attempting to capitalize upon that type of action.

Chapter 4 explores the best-kept secret in trading, the cyclical nature of volatility. No one can guarantee whether markets will trend, revert to the mean, go up, or go down. The only guarantee is that they will cycle from low volatility to high volatility and vice versa. This chapter examines all of the commonly employed tools for measuring volatility as well as showing how to incorporate them into a comprehensive variety of positive expectancy trading models.

Chapter 5 looks at a problem that can undermine even the most robust of positive expectancy trading models. I call it *trading the money*. Inexperienced traders are always thinking about the money. In 2008, when crude oil dropped from $147 a barrel to $135 a barrel, that was a $12, or $12,000, move per contract. Traders who were thinking about the money took profits and then watched from the sidelines as the market moved another $100,000 per contract over the course of a couple of months. Trading the market and not the money means forcing the dynamics of the price action to dictate decisions to close out trades instead of making emotional decisions based on how much money you are making or risking.

Chapter 6 focuses on different techniques to minimize emotions of regret. The greatest feelings of regret occur when we allow significant unrealized profits to turn into significant realized losses. We minimize these feelings of regret by not allowing unrealized profits to turn into realized losses and by taking partial profits at logical technical support or resistance levels. The other major source of regret for the trader is taking small profits only to see the market make huge moves. We minimize this feeling of regret by taking partial profits at logical support or resistance levels and allowing the remainder of the position to be held through the use of trailing stops.

Chapter 7 discusses the importance of timeframe analysis. First, we look at the traditional approach to this analysis, namely, the simultaneous examination of multiple timeframes to better understand the market's trend, as well as multiple levels of technical support and resistance. Next is an introduction to one of the most valuable tools used by professional speculators, which I call *timeframe divergence*. Timeframe divergence occurs when shorter-term timeframes are out of sync with longer-term timeframes, and it enables traders to enjoy a low risk–high reward entry point in the direction of the longer-term trend. This chapter helps readers use technical analysis so they can better identify these trading opportunities.

Chapter 8 examines a wide array of positive expectancy trend-following and mean reversion trading models. It also explores hybrid models that combine mean reversion technical indicators with longer-term trend-following tools, so that traders can enjoy low risk–high reward entry points taken in the direction of the longer-term trend.

Chapter 9 introduces the reader to another psychological trap that can derail positive expectancy trading models. I call it *anticipating the signal*. Anticipating the signal occurs because traders tend to focus on selling at a high price—or buying at a low price—as opposed to selling only after there is evidence that a market top is in place (or buying only after there is evidence that a bottom is in place). In contrast to anticipating the signal, this chapter shows the benefits of waiting for evidence that it is time to sell or time to buy and explores some simple technical tools to help traders avoid this costly mistake.

Chapter 10 examines common trading pitfalls and how to transcend them. By exploring characteristics of market behavior, the chapter offers traders techniques to aid in systematically stripping away delusional beliefs that can derail or impede performance. Then it explores various emotional states that can subvert or limit success in trading, and helps speculators develop a wide array of techniques to overcome various irrational trading biases.

Chapter 11 offers a wide variety of techniques for analyzing and improving trader performance. The chapter begins with a comprehensive questionnaire to aid in highlighting strengths and weaknesses of speculators in areas such as trading edge identification, performance record analysis, trading methodologies, risk management methodologies, and trade execution considerations as well as research and development. Then I present one of the most powerful and underused tools for improving trader performance, the creation and maintenance of a trading journal.

Chapter 12 explores the psychological mindset required to succeed with a positive expectancy model. I call it *even-mindedness*. Successful traders shouldn't care about the result of any specific trade because they consistently employ positive expectancy models combined with robust risk management techniques. Since that is the case, if they do care, then they (a) haven't done enough research to be certain that it is a positive expectancy trading methodology, (b) are not managing the risk, (c) are letting previous negative trading experiences sabotage their edge, or (d) are addicted to the gambler's mentality of needing to win as opposed to knowing that they will succeed.

In this final chapter, we look at various tools and techniques to get traders off the emotional euphoria-despondency roller coaster.

Richard L. Weissman

Acknowledgments

I believe that all of an individual's accomplishments are integrally linked to the totality of his or her life experiences. As such, all acknowledgments necessarily fall short of their goal. Having said this, I would like to thank family, friends, and colleagues for their support and encouragement in the writing of this book.

In addition, I would like to thank my wife, Pamela Nations-Weissman; Richard Hom, who continues to act as an unparalleled sounding board for many of my trading ideas; my friends and colleagues Dr. Alexander Elder, Konchog Tharchin, and James W. Shelton III; Stan Yabroff and Doug Janson at CQG; Stephen Gloyd, J. Scott Susich, Dominick Chirichella, and Salvatore Umek of the Energy Management Institute, who are tremendous advocates and supporters of my work; and my editorial team at John Wiley & Sons, Kevin Commins and Meg Freeborn.

I also wish to acknowledge my indebtedness to all the authors listed in this book's reference list. If this book has added anything to the fields of trading system development, trader psychology, risk management, and technical analysis, it is a direct result of their work. Finally, I would like to acknowledge the depth of my gratitude to my friend and teacher, Drupon Thiley Ningpo Rinpoche, and his teacher, His Holiness Drikung Kyabgon Chetsang Rinpoche, whose works have inspired and transformed my work and my life.

R. L. W.

PART I

The Casino Paradigm

CHAPTER 1

Developing Positive Expectancy Models

In the case of an earthquake hitting Las Vegas, be sure to go straight to the keno lounge. Nothing ever gets hit there.

—An anonymous casino boss

There are some prerequisite elements that are common to all successful trading programs. This and the next two chapters that follow will cover such elements: This chapter is on developing positive expectancy trading models, the second on implementing robust risk management methodologies, and the third on trader discipline. Let's get started.

WHY TECHNICAL ANALYSIS HELPS

Technical analysis is perhaps the single most valuable tool used in the development of positive expectancy trading models. According to technicians, the reason that technical analysis helps in the development of such models is due to the notion that "price has memory." What does this mean? It means that when crude oil traded at $40 a barrel in 1990, this linear, horizontal resistance area would again act as resistance when retested in 2003 (see Figure 1.1). This reality drives economists crazy because, according to economic theory, it makes absolutely no sense for crude oil to sell off at $40 a barrel in 2003, since the purchasing power of the U.S. dollar in 2003 is different from its purchasing power in 1990. Nevertheless, according to technical analysis, the selloff at $40 a barrel in 2003 made perfect sense

3

FIGURE 1.1   Rolling Front-Month Quarterly CME Group Crude Oil Futures Showing
$40 a Barrel Horizontal Resistance
Source: CQG, Inc. © 2010. All rights reserved worldwide.

because price has memory. Price has memory means that traders experienced pain, pleasure, and regret associated with the linear price level of
$40 a barrel. Let's look at this in greater detail.

Price has memory because back in 1990 a group of traders bought oil at
$40 a barrel. They had all sorts of reasons for their purchase: Saddam Hus-
sein had invaded Kuwait, global demand for oil and products was strong,
and so on. However, if these buyers were honest with themselves, as oil
prices tumbled, all these reasons evaporated and were replaced with one
thought and one thought only—usually expressed in prayer form—"Please,
God, let it go back to $40 a barrel and I swear I'll never trade crude oil
again." When it does rally back to $40 a barrel, that linear price represents
the termination of the painful experience of loss for such traders. And so
they create selling pressure at this linear, $40-a-barrel price level.

There is another group of traders that are also interested in crude oil at
the linear price level of $40 a barrel. This is the group that sold futures con-
tracts to the first group. Because they sold the top of the resistance area,
no matter where they covered their short positions, they took profits and
so have a pleasurable experience associated with the linear $40-a-barrel

price. Consequently, when crude oil again rises to $40 a barrel in 2003, they seek a repetition of that pleasurable experience associated with the linear $40-a-barrel price and they, too, create selling pressure.

But of course, most traders neither sold nor bought at $40 a barrel in 1990. Instead, they stood on the sidelines regretting that they missed the sale of the decade. The beauty of the markets is that if you wait around long enough, eventually you will probably get to see the same prices twice. When this happened in 2003, this third and largest group of traders got to minimize the painful feeling of regret by selling the linear resistance level price of $40 a barrel. This is why technical analysis helps, because most humans seek to avoid pain and seek pleasure instead. In the markets, pain and pleasure play themselves out at price levels such as $40 a barrel in crude oil.

However, in April 2011, when I wrote these words, crude oil was trading at $108 a barrel. Obviously, something changed. In fact, things constantly change in the markets. As Chapter 4 shows in great detail, change and the cyclical nature of price action are among the few things that are in fact guaranteed in the markets. What changed was that during 2004, crude oil experienced a phenomenon known as a paradigm shift. A paradigm shift is an intermediate to long-term shift in the perception of an asset's value. Many fundamental factors led to this paradigm shift. The most important one perhaps was unprecedented demand for hydrocarbons from China, India, and other emerging market economies.

The interesting part about technical analysis, and more specifically about price having memory, was that when this paradigm shift occurred, we did not simply leave $40 a barrel on the ash heaps of market history. Instead, during May 2004 when oil broke above $40 a barrel, the psychology of the market shifted and everyone who sold crude oil at $40 a barrel was wrong and everyone who bought at $40 a barrel was right. Consequently, when in December 2004 the market retested $40 a barrel, those who sold had a chance to alleviate the painful experience of loss, those who bought $40 a barrel in May had a chance to repeat the pleasurable experience of profit, and those who regretted missing the opportunity to buy at $40 a barrel had the chance to minimize that feeling of regret by buying at that price. The old resistance price of $40 a barrel had become the market's new support level (see Figure 1.2).

Next, fast-forward the clocks to September 15, 2008. Lehman Brothers is in bankruptcy, credit markets are frozen, and it is obvious that crude oil—along with almost every other physical commodity—is in the throes of a bear market. In fact, crude oil prices have dropped from $147.27 a barrel to $95.71 a barrel. On that day, as on various prior and subsequent days when teaching trading courses to speculators and hedgers, someone asked, "Where do you think the bottom is in crude oil?" My answer seemed

FIGURE 1.2 Rolling Front-Month Weekly CME Group Crude Oil Futures Showing Breakout Above and Retest of $40 a Barrel as Support
Source: CQG, Inc. © 2010. All rights reserved worldwide.

incredible to the roomful of young energy traders: "Forty dollars a barrel." Of course my prediction proved too optimistic as crude oil eventually bottomed out at $32.48 a barrel (see Figure 1.3). Nevertheless, the market had proven over the course of the decades that $40 a barrel was a level at which price had and continues to have memory in the crude oil market.

THE INEFFICIENT MARKET

Incredibly, academics and economists with strong science backgrounds have put forth a theory of an efficient market without any statistical evidence of market efficiency, despite much evidence to the contrary. The markets have always been inefficient, have always cycled from panic to bubble to panic again, and will always continue to do so. In fact, as stated earlier, this cyclical nature of market behavior is one of the few things we as traders can actually count on.

Ludicrous as it sounds, according to efficient market hypothesis there can be no such thing as a bubble because markets are always trading at

FIGURE 1.3 Rolling Front-Month Monthly CME Group Crude Oil Futures Showing $40 a Barrel as Support during Great Recession
Source: CQG, Inc. © 2010. All rights reserved worldwide.

their correct, or efficient, price levels. In other words, according to these theorists, a tulip in Holland that was correctly priced at 2,500 guilders on February 2, 1637, was also correctly priced at 2 guilders on February 3, 1637.[1] I call this an example of the "Napoleon Analogy."

The Napoleon Analogy occurs when we enter a mental institution in which one charismatic patient has thoroughly convinced himself as well as other patients that he is Napoleon. No matter how many psychiatrists struggle to assure these patients that he is not Napoleon, neither the deluded patient nor his loyal admirers can be convinced. One day, our delusional patient escapes from the mental institution and discovers not a single soul who believes him to be Napoleon. This of course is because he never was Napoleon. He was merely deluded and had convinced others of his delusional belief. Perhaps he will never be convinced that he is not Napoleon. Perhaps there are still people who remain convinced that synthetic Collateralized Debt Obligations (CDOs) on pools of subprime mortgages circa 2005 should still be trading at par value. Despite their conviction to the contrary, those synthetic CDOs are still worthless. Furthermore, much like our deluded, Napoleon-impersonating mental patient, despite the temporary delusional valuation of these synthetic CDOs at par by various financial institutions during the 2005 housing market bubble, the synthetic CDOs were, in fact, always worthless.

Nevertheless, just because the majority are delusional and prices are temporarily out of sync with value, this book is for traders, not long-term investors, and traders must wait for evidence that our mental patient has escaped from the hospital before trading against irrational, bubble-induced price levels. We wait for evidence in the form of lower prices because irrationally priced markets tend to become even more irrationally priced—this is the nature of an inefficient, fat-tailed market—before crashing, and no one can know where the top is until after that top has been proved through the printing of lower prices. As John Maynard Keynes said, "Markets can remain irrational a lot longer than you or I can remain solvent," or as I like to say, "Don't anticipate, just participate." Wait for the evidence of a top to start selling and wait for evidence of a bottom to start buying. The history of markets is littered with graves of those who were prematurely right. Being right over the long run is fatal for traders. Speculators need to be right on the markets in the right season. For example, around January 2009, SemGroup started shorting crude oil around $100 a barrel. They correctly surmised that oil prices were unsustainable at such levels and were out of sync with the asset's long-term value. Nevertheless, on July 16, 2008, SemGroup announced that they had "liquidity problems" and sold their CME Group trading account to Barclays. On December 12, 2008, January 2009 crude oil futures on the CME Group bottomed at $32.48 (see Figure 1.4). Of course, this was no help to SemGroup since they had filed for bankruptcy on July 22, 2008.[2]

But why does the inefficiency of markets matter to us as traders? It is this inefficiency that allows us to develop positive expectancy trading models. This inefficient behavior of markets leads to what statisticians call a leptokurtic—as opposed to a normal—distribution of asset prices (see Figure 1.5). This means that prices display a greater propensity toward mean reversion than would occur if markets were efficient, and, when they are not in this mean reverting mode, they have a greater propensity to trending action (statisticians call this propensity for trending action the fat tail of the distribution).

It is because markets display this leptokurtic price distribution that positive expectancy trading models tend to fall into two categories:

1. Countertrend models that capitalize on the market's propensity toward reversion to the mean.
2. Trend-following models that take advantage of those times when markets undergo a fat tail event.

FIGURE 1.4 Rolling Front-Month Weekly CME Group Crude Oil Futures Showing SemGroup's Failure Despite Correct Assessment of Asset's Long-Term Value
Source: CQG, Inc. © 2010. All rights reserved worldwide.

It is no coincidence that two of the three major types of technical indicators are oscillators that signal when markets are—at least temporarily—overbought or oversold and trend-following indicators like moving averages, moving average convergence divergence, Ichimoku clouds, and so on, which signal when markets are displaying bullish- or bearish-trending behavior.

You might be asking yourself, "If markets can do only two things—trend or trade in a range—why are there three major categories of technical indicators?" The third major category is the volatility indicators, and they

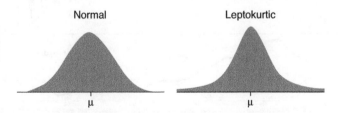

FIGURE 1.5 Leptokurtic versus Normal Distribution of Asset Prices
Source: www.risk.glossary.com.

clue us in to when markets shift from their mean reverting mode to trending action and vice versa. In fact, it is this third category of indicators
that proves most useful in the development of positive expectancy trading models and I have consequently devoted Chapter 4 to the various types
of volatility indicators, how they can be used, and their limitations.

IF IT FEELS GOOD, DON'T DO IT

Well, speculative trading sounds simple enough. Markets can do only two
things, either trade in a range or trend, and volatility indicators can be used
to clue you in to which kind of behavior the market is currently exhibiting.
Why then do almost all speculators lose money? They lose because successful speculation requires that we consistently do that which is psychologically uncomfortable and unnatural.

Why are mean reversion trading models psychologically uncomfortable to implement? In Figure 1.6 (see Figure 1.6) we see that on Friday,
March 6, 2009, the E-Mini S&P 500 futures are not only in a clearly defined bear trend, but that they have once again made new contract lows.

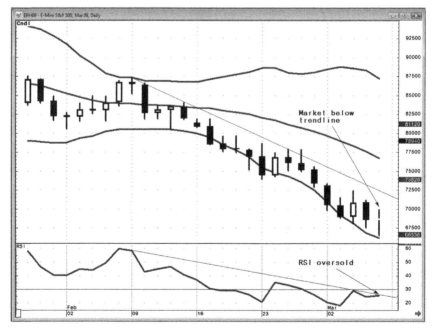

FIGURE 1.6 March 2009 E-Mini S&P 500 Futures Contract Makes New Lows with
Relative Strength Index Oscillator at Oversold Levels
Source: CQG, Inc. © 2010. All rights reserved worldwide.

What the chart cannot show is how overwhelmingly bearish market sentiment was on that day. On Fridays, after finishing my market analysis for the day, I turn off the computer and turn on the financial news, as it is usually entertaining. On this particular Friday, the market had just closed and they were interviewing two market pundits. They will typically have one interviewee advocating the bear argument while their counterpart is bullish. Our first analyst's forecast was 5,000 on the Dow Jones Industrial Average and 500 in the S&P 500 Index. As soon as the words "five hundred" left his lips, the other interrupted, "You are out of your mind." I thought, "Ah, here's the bullish argument." The other analyst then proceeded to berate our bearish forecaster by telling him he was out of his mind because the Dow was going to 2,000 and the S&P 500 to 200. I glanced at the bottom of the screen just to make certain that I had not lost my mind... no, the E-Mini S&P futures had in fact closed at 687.75. Next thought, "When the market is at 687.75 and the bullish analyst is calling for it to drop to 500, this has got to be the bottom." Sure enough, the 2009 stock market bottom occurred on Friday, March 6, 2009 (see Figure 1.7). The trader using a mean reversion model has to consistently buy in to that type of overwhelmingly

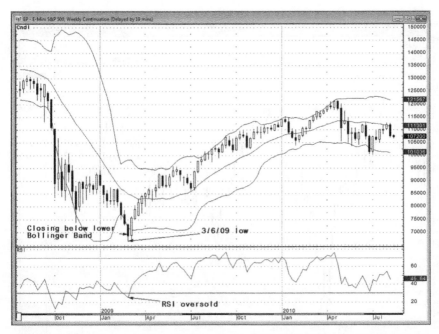

FIGURE 1.7 Rolling Front-Month Weekly E-Mini S&P 500 Futures Contract Showing Close Below Lower Bollinger Band and Oversold Reading on Relative Strength Index

Source: CQG, Inc. © 2010. All rights reserved worldwide.

bearish sentiment or sell in to a 1630s-era tulip—or 2005 housing—bubble-like bullish environment.

Executing a trend-following model is even more psychologically challenging. The market breaks to 1068, all-time new highs. I tell you that the prudent play is to buy these all-time new highs. You glance at a chart and notice that only 12 weeks ago it was trading at 775. You place a limit order to buy 775, figuring you will buy cheaper, experience less risk, and enjoy more reward. By placing the order at 775 you are trading the asset's price irrespective of value (for more details on trading price irrespective of value see Chapters 5 and 10). On November 3, 1982, the Dow Jones Industrial Average hit an all-time new high of 1068.1 (see Figure 1.8). Since that time we experienced market crashes, the bursting of the dot-com bubble, terrorist attacks, the worst credit crisis since the 1930s, and the Great Recession, and as of the writing of this book in 2011, we still have not traded anywhere close to 1068 (see Figure 1.9).

For both mean reversion as well as trend-following traders, the profitable trade is the one that is almost impossible to execute. Or as I like to say, "If it feels good, don't do it." If it feels awful, like a guaranteed loss—more often than anyone could imagine—that is the profitable trade.

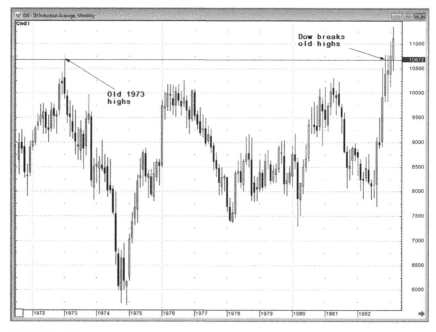

FIGURE 1.8 Quarterly Cash Dow Jones Industrial Average Chart Breaks to All-Time New Highs in 1982

Source: CQG, Inc. © 2010. All rights reserved worldwide.

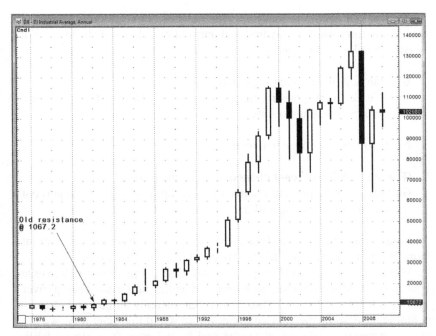

FIGURE 1.9 Yearly Cash Dow Jones Industrial Average Chart from 1982 Break of Old Highs to July 2010

Source: CQG, Inc. © 2010. All rights reserved worldwide.

If, on the other hand, the trade feels like easy money . . . run the other way. We are all human beings, experiencing greed and fear at the same moment; if it feels easy for us, it feels easy for everyone else and is almost guaranteed to be a losing proposition. If, by contrast, it feels almost impossible for us, then few others can take the trade, and by doing that which is psychologically uncomfortable—by taking the difficult trade—you make the money being lost by the other 90 percent of all speculators.

Although the reader now knows why 90 percent of all speculators fail, we can learn more about how to succeed and how to develop positive expectancy models as well as risk management by examining the psychological biases that lead to failure for the majority of speculators. In 1979, two social scientists, Daniel Kahneman and Amos Tversky, developed an alternative to the dominant efficient market hypothesis of market behavior. As opposed to assuming rationality of market participants and our preference for choices with the greatest risk-adjusted utility, Kahneman and Tversky posed various questions regarding risk and reward. The results of their research became known as Prospect Theory and the Reflection Effect. Their work proved that people were irrational and biased in their decision-making processes.

They asked people to make specific choices between various alternatives. Kahneman and Tversky first had participants choose between one of the two gambles, or prospects:

Gamble A: A 100 percent chance of losing $3,000.
Gamble B: An 80 percent chance of losing $4,000, and a 20 percent chance of losing nothing.

Next, you must choose between:

Gamble C: A 100 percent chance of receiving $3,000.
Gamble D: An 80 percent chance of receiving $4,000, and a 20 percent chance of receiving nothing.

Kahneman and Tversky found that of the first grouping, 92 percent chose B. Of the second grouping, 20 percent of people chose D.

What the reflection effect proved was that people were risk-averse regarding choices involving prospects of gains and risk-seeking over prospects involving losses.[3] This means that virtually all human beings—including successful speculative traders—are wired the same way: We are all programmed to take small profits and large losses (see Figure 1.10). What then separates successful traders from the rest of the speculative community? Successful traders have developed and employ rule-based, positive expectancy models that force them to overcome their innate bias toward small profits and large losses. They have learned to accept small losses quickly and to let large profits grow larger. Or, as I like to tell my students, "You need to continuously ask yourself, 'How can I reduce the risk? How can I increase the reward?'" The positive expectancy models

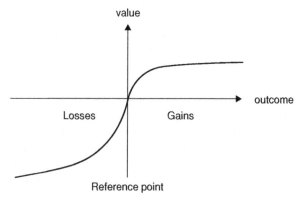

FIGURE 1.10   Prospect Theory

force us to do that which is psychologically unnatural and uncomfortable. They force us to succeed despite our biases and they do so by exploiting the irrationality and biases of other market participants.

"JUST MAKE THE MONEY"

Traders will often ask me why I think a particular market is going to go down, why I am long some other market when the inventory numbers just came out decidedly bearish, and so on. If I have the time, I might give them a reason or two, although I will more often simply respond with, "Do you want to understand all the intricate reasons behind the moves or do you want to make the money? Nobody can know all the reasons. Forget the reasons, just make the money."

The problem or limitation with fundamental analysis—as well as the problem with classical technical indicators such as a trendline—is its subjectivity. Development of positive expectancy models is much tougher with fundamental analysis because we are trying to develop models with disciplined rules to help us get away from our natural tendency to trade with a bias toward big losses and small profits. Remember, you can always find fundamental arguments for selling or buying at any given price, otherwise no one would be willing to buy or sell at that price. Also, these arguments can actually prevent you from acting on the high-probability move or—even worse—from managing the risk. In trading, we call this *paralysis from analysis*. Consequently, most positive expectancy models are based upon objective, mathematical technical indicators such as oscillators or moving averages. We can never know all the reasons why the market rose on bearish inventory numbers or why it fell despite a decrease in unemployment, but we can develop various rules for entry, exit, and risk management based upon objective, mathematically derived technical formulas.

Does this mean that fundamental analysis is useless for speculative traders? Not at all. Instead I am trying to establish a realistic understanding of its limitations before our examination of its utility. So how can we augment our positive expectancy models with fundamental analysis? The way I teach fundamental analysis to traders is through old Wall Street clichés. First cliché: "Buy the rumor, sell the news." If the rumor is that the unemployment report is going to show a decline in unemployment and therefore a strengthening economy, one might buy the stock market. Once the report comes out showing the anticipated improvement in jobs, sell the market. Why? Because the reason for the rally has come to fruition and there is therefore no longer any reason to own equities. However, there is one caveat to this cliché, and it is another Wall Street cliché: "The market hates surprises." This means that if the market was rallying before the release of the unemployment report based on the rumor of the jobless rate falling to 9.7 percent, and the rate actually falls to 9.1 percent, equities should probably still be bought because the news was a bullish surprise beyond the expectations of market participants.

Another valuable way of incorporating fundamental news into our positive expectancy trading models is to capitalize on times when the market reacts in the opposite manner from what would be expected based upon the release of a bearish or bullish fundamental news item. For example, on April 29, 2009, the U.S. Energy Information Administration released its weekly inventories report, which showed that crude oil stockpiles increased by twice the expected amount.[4] Despite this bearish news, the oil market rallied (see Figure 1.11). This rally on bearish news was the most bullish information the market could offer. It suggested buyers were waiting for bearish news to establish or add to their existing long positions; consequently, the market could not drop despite the release of negative fundamental news. Or as my friend Richard Hom likes to say, "If they can't sell off on this news, what'll they do when the bullish news hits?"

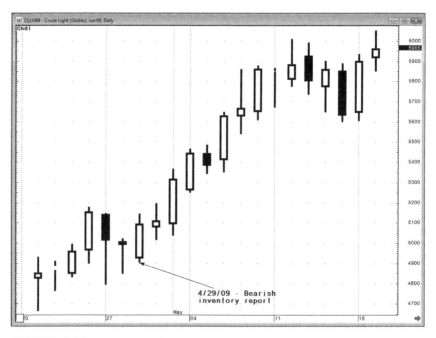

FIGURE 1.11   June 2009 Daily CME Group Crude Oil Futures Contract Rallies Despite Bearish Inventories Report

Source: CQG, Inc. © 2010. All rights reserved worldwide.

Perhaps the most invaluable way of incorporating fundamental analysis into our positive expectancy model is its ability to help us distinguish between price shock events and paradigm shifts. We have already defined a paradigm shift during our examination of the crude oil market and its shift of long-term value from below to above $40 a barrel. You may recall that this shift in the perception of value of crude oil occurred because of a combination of fundamental supply and demand factors. By contrast, a price shock is a headline-driven event that temporarily spikes the price of an asset beyond its value.

The easiest way to distinguish between the two is by looking at some historical examples. Figure 1.12 clearly illustrates a long-term shift in the perception of value for high-grade copper. Before 2005, the $1.60 area acted as resistance to higher prices throughout the contract's history. In 2005, the perception of value of copper underwent a paradigm shift and as of the writing of this book in 2011, the $1.60 area represents a long-term support level for the asset. One of my favorite examples of a price shock event was the capture of Saddam Hussein on Saturday, December 13, 2003, by coalition forces during the second Gulf War. Hussein's capture occurred over

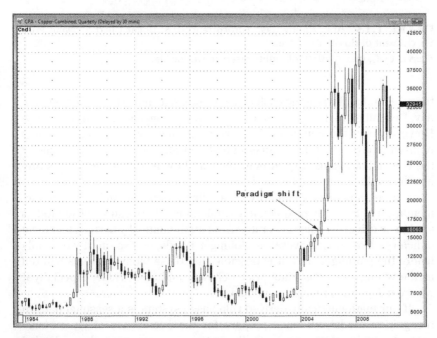

FIGURE 1.12 Quarterly Continuation Chart of CME Group Copper Futures Showing 2005 Paradigm Shift

Source: CQG, Inc. © 2010. All rights reserved worldwide.

FIGURE 1.13 2003 Hourly Cash Eurocurrency–U.S. Dollar Chart Showing Price Shock Event of Hussein's Capture
Source: CQG, Inc. © 2010. All rights reserved worldwide.

the weekend and when the cash foreign exchange markets opened on Sunday, December 14, the U.S. dollar rallied sharply against the eurocurrency. However, over the course of the next 24 trading hours, currency traders realized that the capture of Hussein had no lasting impact on the value of the U.S. dollar against the eurocurrency and the asset returned to its pre-headline value area (see Figure 1.13).

Why is the ability to identify a paradigm shift essential to our implementation of a positive expectancy trading model? Because these models tend to be driven by rules generated from mathematically derived technical indicators like moving averages, Bollinger Bands, and so on. If we blindly ignore the paradigm shift, it is possible that these technical tools will tell us the wrong story regarding price behavior and asset value, especially if we are using mean reversion models.

If our mathematically derived rule-based system is a seasonal pattern recognition model, we must prepare for the occurrence of an anomaly year. Anomaly years are well illustrated by examining the unleaded gasoline–heating oil spread. Historically, unleaded gasoline had always traded at a premium to heating oil during the spring, typically peaking

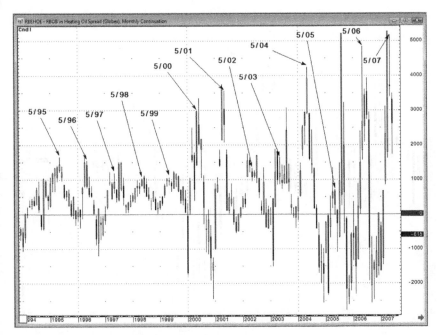

FIGURE 1.14 1995–2007 Monthly Continuation Chart of CME Group Unleaded Gasoline–Heating Oil Spread Showing Pattern of Seasonal Strength in May
Source: CQG, Inc. © 2010. All rights reserved worldwide.

against the winter fuel during the calendar month of May in anticipation of summer driving season (see Figure 1.14). However, in 2008, the market experienced an anomaly year in which petroleum product prices moved counter to this historical relationship. Increasing demand for middle distillates like heating oil from developing world nations drove the price up against unleaded gasoline because the latter was not used as the primary transportation fuel in those countries (see Figure 1.15). For those who blindly followed their technical models to the exclusion of fundamental news, it seemed like easy money to buy the undervalued unleaded gasoline and sell the overvalued heating oil. By contrast, those with one eye on the fundamentals tempered their technically driven models in light of this shift in the value of petroleum products.

Regarding price shock events, I have often heard traders dismiss such events as completely random and therefore a 50-50 chance. In other words, they do not concern themselves with price shock events and rationalize away their occurrence through the delusional belief that over the long run they will end up on the winning side of the shock 50 percent of the time. Having done the research, I can assure you that price shock events are

FIGURE 1.15 2005-2010 Monthly Continuation Chart of CME Group Unleaded Gasoline-Heating Oil Spread Showing 2008 Anomaly Year
Source: CQG, Inc. © 2010. All rights reserved worldwide.

not 50-50 propositions. Instead, you have a greater probability of being on the right side of the event if you are trading in the direction of the long-term—one to six months—trend, and a greater likelihood of being on the wrong side if you employ a mean reversion model (see Figure 1.16).

Now that we have examined the strengths of positive expectancy models derived from mathematical technical indicators as well as their weaknesses and tools to offset such weaknesses, we will briefly review turning these models into mechanical trading systems. I say, "Briefly review," because for those interested in an in-depth study of the topic, I refer you to my first book, *Mechanical Trading Systems: Pairing Trader Psychology with Technical Analysis.* Instead of rehashing materials presented in that book, I merely point out here that mechanical trading systems based on mathematical technical indicators help us determine the following:

- Does this model enjoy positive expectancy?
- What kinds of weaknesses—maximum consecutive losses, worst peak-to-valley equity drawdowns, percentage of winning trades, average trade duration, and so forth—did this model experience in the past?

FIGURE 1.16 September 2001 E-Mini S&P 500 Futures Contract Showing Close Below 40-Day Simple Moving Average Before 9/11/01
Source: CQG, Inc. © 2010. All rights reserved worldwide.

- Am I willing to endure these weaknesses in my real-time trading account or do I need a model better suited to my individual psychological profile as a trader?

FINAL THOUGHTS

Finally, let us examine the augmentation of rule-based, positive expectancy mechanical trading models with what speculators commonly call trader intuition. When people ask me whether my own trading is 100 percent mechanical, I hesitate, because it is, but it is not. It is 100 percent rule-based trading. It never violates rules of the positive expectancy model or of risk management. It does, however, augment rule-based trading with what is commonly referred to as trader intuition.

We need first to differentiate between what gamblers call intuition and authentic trader intuition. If by trader intuition we mean finding an excuse to abandon a rule-based positive expectancy model or rules of risk management, then such intuition must be avoided at all costs. By contrast, if we are speaking of a method of augmenting our mechanical rule-based models with what is commonly and incorrectly described as intuition, this is another matter entirely.

What is trader intuition? It is a method by which our unconscious augments purely mechanical rule-based trading models. In reality, it is not intuition at all. It is instead a subconscious memory that cannot express itself according to rational proofs because our memories do not typically work in this manner. For example, you look at a chart and your rule says, "Buy at 25." However, your intuition says, "I have seen this type of chart setup before. I know it is going to 12. I am buying at 12." Your decision was truly based on trader intuition or fuzzy memories of a similar setup—perhaps many similar setups—in which the market dropped below the rule-based entry level. Unfortunately, because of the way memory works, we do not say, "I remember that on March 13, 1976, the chart setup with a similar pattern and so there is a high probability of us printing 11 and that is why I am buying at 12 instead of 25." We say instead, "I have seen this setup before. I am buying at 12 instead of 25."

CHAPTER 2

Price Risk Management Methodologies

A ship in harbor is safe, but that is not what ships are built for.

—John A. Shedd

Nobody goes into an investment hoping its value will decline and it will one day be worth less than what was paid for it. This chapter examines the development of price risk management methodologies and shows why positive expectancy trading models as standalone solutions are insufficient for success as a trader. Specifically, the chapter explores the full array of methodologies, including stop loss placement, volumetric position sizing, Value-at-Risk, stress testing, and management discretion. Particular emphasis is placed on combining these various tools to generate robust price risk management solutions.

ONE SURE THING

In speculative trading, many are obsessed with pursuit of the elusive sure thing. Chapter 1 specifically addressed the development of positive expectancy models because they are the single most important ingredient for success as a trader. But even the most robust positive expectancy models cannot guarantee a profit on every single trade. In fact, the only sure thing—aside from the cyclical nature of volatility, which is examined in Chapter 4—in trading is that there is no sure thing. Since there is no such thing as a sure thing we must assume that each and every trade we take will be a loss. In this manner, we are always prepared for the worst and can never be surprised when the worst occurs.

Many traders find this expect-and-prepare-for-the-worst attitude toward trading pessimistic and discouraging. Some even feel that such an attitude invites bad luck and failure. This is part of what makes successful trading so challenging. Traders must have unwavering confidence in their positive expectancy models, while simultaneously expecting and preparing for failure on every single trade. Remember, our goal is to trade like a casino. Casinos never abandon their table limits. Not once. No exceptions, ever. Why? Because they always assume that any particular spin of the roulette wheel will result in a win for the player despite simultaneously knowing that probability is always skewed in their favor. It has nothing to do with luck or pessimism or displeasing the trading gods. As financial mathematicians like to say, "It's not magic; it's just math." Play the odds, manage the risk, and you succeed. Fight the odds or be lax in managing the risk and you will fail.

Some will overstate the importance of risk management by claiming it is the single most important ingredient for success in trading. This is not true. You can be the greatest risk manager in the world, but without a positive expectancy model, your superior risk management skills will only mean that you will eventually lose all of your money in a methodical and orderly fashion. That stated, the only thing that can dismantle adherence to a positive expectancy model is failure to manage the risk. This being the case, why would anyone possessing a positive expectancy model not manage the risk? Greed kills and speed kills. We abandon safe, prudent risk parameters because of impatience and lack of discipline. We cannot wait to safely grow rich from speculation and so we rationalize ourselves out of risk management. Once we have $100,000 or $500,000 or $1 million or $5 million, then we will adhere to strict rules of risk management. In the meantime, as long as we are diligent in playing the probabilities and as long as we are lucky, everything will work out for us.

I can assure you that over the long run there is no such thing as luck. If you are counting on luck saving you when risking too much on a single trade, then over the long run it is only a matter of time before your trading account blows out. As John Maynard Keynes wrote, "In the long run, we are all dead."[1] At least once every three months an aspiring trader will ask what she can do with one or two thousand dollars in a trading account. My answer is always exactly the same: "Absolutely nothing." For many, that ends our conversation, but some will ask for further clarification. "Are you saying there is absolutely no way to turn my $1,000 account successfully into a million from speculative trading?" "Yes, this is exactly what I am saying."

These are strong statements coming from someone who works with probabilities for a living. Certainly it must be possible to turn $1,000 into a million from successful speculative trading, even if the probability of such an occurrence is extremely remote. Perhaps it is possible. But, if possible, the odds of success at such a proposition are so remote that it would be extremely irresponsible for me to even hint at this remote possibility.

Why is it so unlikely? Let us assume that you have developed a positive expectancy trading system that experiences around 58 percent winning trades and whose average win is roughly 1.15 times larger than its average loss. You decide to open a $2,000 trading account, to trade only the mini cash foreign exchange contracts of 10,000 baseload currency, and to limit the risk on any particular trade to $360 ($350 plus $10 per round-turn for slippage[2] and commissions). Despite this being a positive expectancy trading model, when I ran a 10-year back test on 10,000 baseload currency of the British pound against the U.S. dollar from January 1, 2000, to December 31, 2009, the model[3] experienced a worst peak-to-valley drawdown[4] in account equity of $2,505. So a $2,000 account would have been totally wiped out by 2005, despite the fact that over the course of the entire 10-year back test this same model actually enjoyed an overall profit of $5,974 (see Figure 2.1).

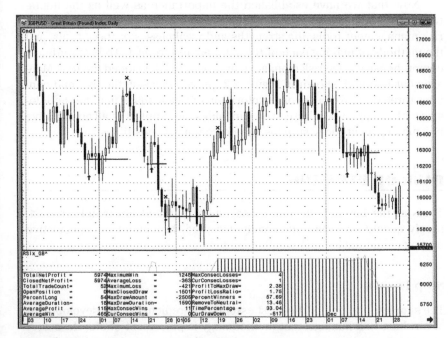

FIGURE 2.1 Daily Chart of Spot British Pound–U.S. Dollar with RSI Extremes Trading System

Note: Trade summary includes $10 round-turn deductions for slippage and commissions.

Source: CQG, Inc. © 2010. All rights reserved worldwide.

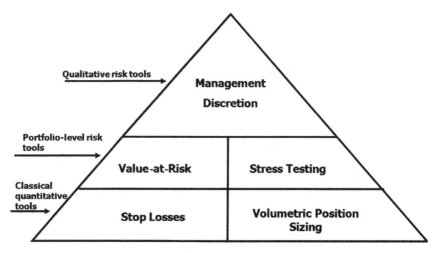

FIGURE 2.2   Weissman's Risk Management Pyramid

Now that we have established the importance as well as the limitations of risk management techniques in general, we can explore specific risk management tools, the strengths and weaknesses of these tools, and the methods of making each of these tools more robust. To best outline a comprehensive price risk management program, I developed the Risk Management Pyramid, shown in Figure 2.2. As you can see, the pyramid contains three tiers. We begin our exploration of risk management methodologies with the pyramid's base, which includes the simplest of all quantitative risk management tools, stop losses and volumetric position sizing.

BASE OF PYRAMID

Tools at the base of the risk management pyramid are simple, robust, purely quantitative, and universally accepted throughout the speculative trading community.

Stop Losses

The simplest and one of the most essential ingredients in the development of a robust risk management methodology is placement of stop losses. A stop loss is the cornerstone upon which all more complex risk tools are built. Why are stop losses so essential to successful risk management trading programs? Because a stop loss becomes a market order to exit once its price level has been triggered. Stops force traders to quantify risk before entry and therefore habituate us to their placement instantaneously following entry. Placing stops immediately after entry means that risk management maintains its objective, rule-based criteria as opposed to being placed after the onslaught of the greed and fear that typically characterize our emotional response to open positions in the markets. The stop order cannot rationalize or debate. It does not understand supply, demand, weather patterns, or geopolitical anomalies. It only knows that our predetermined criterion for trade exit has been triggered and therefore forces that exit despite any reason for abandonment of discipline.

Rookie traders become optimistic when studying price histories. They look at lows toward the chart's lower right-hand corner, then at highs toward the upper left-hand corner and imagine untold wealth in simply buying those lows and selling the highs. They tend to assume away all the price action in between. Unfortunately, as illustrated in Figure 2.3, it is not enough to have bought the 10-year U.S. Treasury note futures at 120-18 on May 25, 2010, even though they traded at 126-28 on August 25, 2010. Instead, after buying on May 25, 2010, at 120-18, we have to immediately manage the risk by placing a protective sell stop order. In other words, despite

FIGURE 2.3 Daily Chart of September 2010 CME Group 10-Year U.S. Treasury Note Futures

Source: CQG, Inc. © 2010. All rights reserved worldwide.

correctly assessing the market's overall bullish trend, it is quite possible that our risk management stop would have triggered a loss as the market dropped to its cycle low of 118-26 on June 3, 2010 (see Figure 2.3). Bottom line, it is not enough that our model makes money in general; it has to be robust enough to make money even when coupled with a stop loss order.

Before examining stop loss order placement in greater detail, I want to differentiate stop orders from stop-limit orders. For reasons stated earlier in this section, stop orders are the key to risk management methodologies and stop-limit orders are not. Stated simply, stop-limit orders are for offense and stop orders are for defense. Stop-limit orders are for position entry since they offer the ability to enter into breakouts from sideways markets or trend reversals without obligating us to enter at the next available price.

For example, on May 24, 2010, Microsoft closed at $26.27 per share. Placing a stop-limit order to short the stock at $26.27 was a prudent entry order that would have been filled at our limit price of $26.27 on May 26, 2010. By contrast, if we had sold the stock on a stop we would have been filled at the next available bid price on May 25, 2010, of $25.65, which is obviously an inferior sale price (see Figure 2.4). Examining the Microsoft

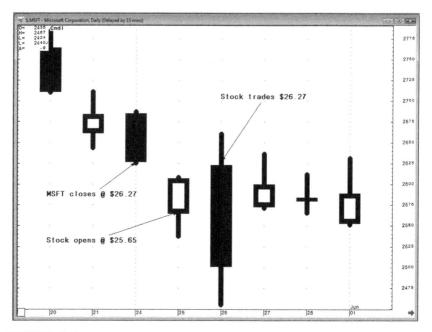

FIGURE 2.4 Daily Chart of Microsoft Showing Gap Lower Opening on May 25, 2010

Source: CQG, Inc. © 2010. All rights reserved worldwide.

chart we might infer that since it was better to initiate a short position on May 26, 2010, at $26.27, it is safe to assume that if we already owned Microsoft shares and were looking to manage risk on a losing position in the stock, it would have been better to have been stopped out of a losing position on May 26, 2010, at $26.27 with a stop-limit sell order than on May 25, 2010, at $25.26 with a stop order.

Admittedly, in the preceding example it was true that the stop-limit order proved the superior exit tool. That stated, in trading you only need to go broke once. In other words, it does not matter if 99 out of 100 times the superior-priced exit of the stop-limit order would have been filled if on the hundredth occasion we go bankrupt. This problem is well illustrated by an examination of a daily cash U.S. dollar–Mexican peso chart. Let's say that you sold the U.S. dollar-Mexican peso short on December 20, 1994, at 3.464 and placed a buy stop-limit order at 3.500. Unfortunately, the next day's low was 3.962 (see Figure 2.5). As of the writing of this book in 2011, that buy stop-limit order at 3.500 would still remain unfilled and the market is now trading at 12.7275 (see Figure 2.6).

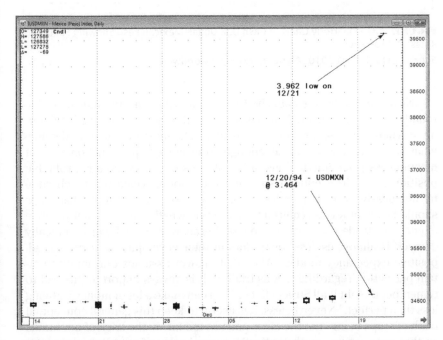

FIGURE 2.5 Daily Chart of Cash U.S. Dollar-Mexican Peso Showing U.S. Dollar Gapping Higher on December 21, 1994

Source: CQG, Inc. © 2010. All rights reserved worldwide.

FIGURE 2.6 Quarterly Chart of Cash U.S. Dollar-Mexican Peso Showing Failure to Retest 3.4500 Area

Source: CQG, Inc. © 2010. All rights reserved worldwide.

Now that we have established why stop orders are the indispensable foundation of all robust risk management methodologies, we need to determine where these stops should be placed. The most obvious—and somewhat wiseguy—answer is far enough from current price action so that meaningless price fluctuations fail to stop us out of eventually profitable positions, yet close enough so that we do not sacrifice too much capital needlessly on losing trades. Another way of stating this is that stops should be set at levels required to determine whether a particular positive expectancy trade will work. Of course this answer, while being technically correct, is almost useless for traders in their development of rule-based, positive expectancy models. Also, that answer assumes our ability to attain perfection regarding risk as traders. It is always important instead to remember the old Wall Street cliché, "You can make a lot of money by being less than perfect." Nevertheless, it is useful to keep this general conceptual truth of stops being "not too close and not too far" in the back of our minds so that once we put mathematically derived rules of stop loss placement into action we can measure how well such rules match this broad conceptual goal.

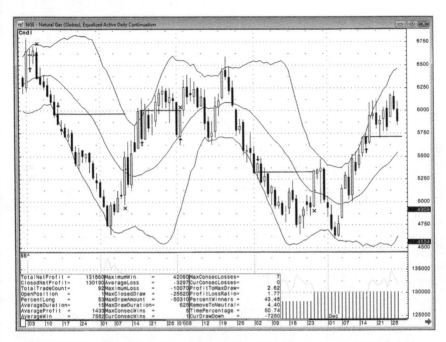

FIGURE 2.7 Equalized Active Daily Continuation Chart for CME Group Natural Gas Futures Contract with Bollinger Band Breakout System Where Stop Is Placed at Previous Day's 20-Day Simple Moving Average

Note: Trade summary includes data from January 1, 2000, to December 31, 2009, and includes $10 round-turn deductions for slippage and commissions.

Source: CQG, Inc. © 2010. All rights reserved worldwide.

Although the variety of tools for stop loss placement is only limited by the trader's imagination, the vast majority of stops can be broken down into one of three major categories: mathematically derived technical stop orders, stops based on support and resistance levels, and monetary or percentage-based stops. Among the more popular types of stop loss orders are those derived from mathematical technical indicators. Examples of mathematically derived stops are placing a stop loss order at the previous day's 20-day simple moving average (see Figure 2.7) or stops placed at the previous day's upper or lower Bollinger Band. One cautionary note regarding mathematically derived stops is that stops based upon exiting only after the termination of the trading day cannot offer a crisp, disciplined answer regarding risk management. For example, a 9- and 26-day moving average crossover system can be stopped out of a position only after the end of the trading day because we cannot be certain of the crossover on a closing basis until after the trading day has ended (see Figure 2.8). Consequently,

FIGURE 2.8   Daily Chart of Google with 9- and 26-Day Simple Moving Average Crossover System

Note: Trade summary includes data from January 1, 2000, to December 31, 2009, assumes position size of 100 shares, and includes $10 round-turn deductions for slippage and commissions.

Source: CQG, Inc. © 2010. All rights reserved worldwide.

traders using some of these types of indicator-derived stops cannot definitively state when the stop loss will be triggered beforehand and so have no crisp, predetermined stop loss exit order placement before trade entry.

Stops based on violation of support and resistance levels are especially attractive because they are attuned to "price having memory" as stated in Chapter 1. These stops are typically placed to trigger at violation of the highest high or lowest low of a particular number of previous trading days (see Figure 2.9).

Monetary or percentage stops are also quite popular because they force us to quantify risk in relationship to reward prior to trade entry, and in this way, ensure that we are consistently adhering to one of the cardinal rules of positive expectancy trend-following trading models: large profits and small losses. Figure 2.10 shows a countertrend system that enters when both Bollinger Bands and a relative strength index signal extreme overbought or oversold levels. Exit occurs with profit if the market returns

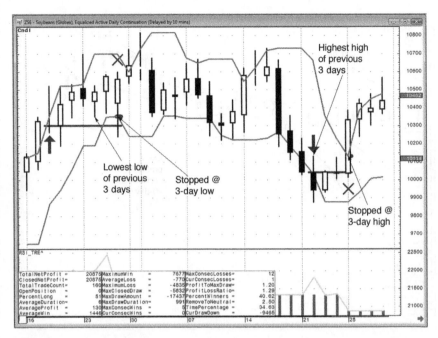

FIGURE 2.9 Equalized Active Daily Continuation Chart for CME Group Soybean Futures Contract with RSI Trend System Where Stop Is Placed at Lowest Low or Highest High of Previous Three Trading Days

Note: Trade summary includes data from January 1, 2000, to December 31, 2009, and includes $10 round-turn deductions for slippage and commissions.

Source: CQG, Inc. © 2010. All rights reserved worldwide.

to the previous day's 20-day simple moving average or a stop loss order is triggered when the asset violates a $1,000 monetary stop loss level (see Figure 2.10).

A word of caution on monetary or percentage stops: They should never be constrained solely by assets under management irrespective of an asset's volatility. In other words, if you cannot risk more than $1,000 without becoming overleveraged, the answer is not to blindly place $1,000 stop loss orders in all available markets, but instead to limit one's trading to lower volatility assets in which such stop orders can be placed without being triggered by meaningless market fluctuations (see Chapter 5 for a more comprehensive explanation).

Finally, an examination of stops would be incomplete without discussing time as a stop loss exit criterion tool. In fact, using the calendar—or even the clock—for stop placement was implied in some of tools already discussed, such as our price-driven stop (see Figure 2.9), in which trailing stops were set at the highest high or lowest low of the preceding three

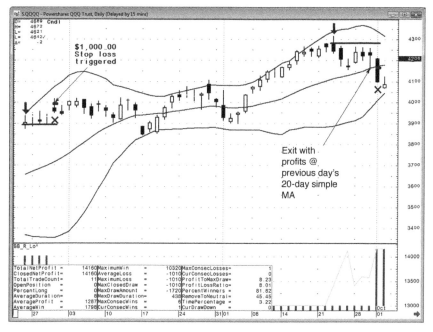

FIGURE 2.10 Daily Chart of Powershares QQQ Trust ETF with Bollinger Band Countertrend System Using $1,000 Monetary Stop Loss

Note: Trade summary includes data from January 1, 2000, to December 31, 2009, assumes position size of 1,000 shares, and includes $10 round-turn deductions for slippage and commissions.

Source: CQG, Inc. © 2010. All rights reserved worldwide.

trading days. Beyond price and indicator-derived stops, which were somehow time-dependent, the clock itself can also be the primary method of forcing trade exit.

A common example of this is a trading system that forces an exit if mark-to-market settlement on the position shows an unrealized loss after three trading days. My only caution on using time as a stop is to restrict the forcing of exits to trades that are showing unrealized losses. Exiting of trades showing unrealized profits because you have been in the profitable trade too many days is not only counterintuitive, but also extremely counterproductive, as will be shown in great detail throughout Chapter 5.

Volumetric Position Sizing

Although stop loss placement is the most rudimentary and indispensable form of price risk management, it is not robust enough as a standalone to ensure success as a trader, and must be combined with volumetric position sizing. Whereas stop loss orders answer the question "Where do I exit this position in order to preserve capital," volumetric position sizing answers the question "How many units of this asset can I trade without becoming overleveraged?" The most robust response to this question is the wise-guy answer: "small enough to ensure that a positive expectancy model will not blow up, while still producing returns in excess of the risk-free rate." Although technically accurate, this answer is too vague to be useful to risk managers or traders. We need instead to examine the per trade percentage risk of assets under management in relation to the worst peak-to-valley drawdown experienced by our positive expectancy trading system.

The general guideline regarding volumetric position sizing in relationship to assets under management is the 1 percent rule.[5] This rule states that traders should risk no more than 1 percent of assets under management on any single trade. The idea here is that the vast majority of positive expectancy trading models will be robust enough to survive peak-to-valley drawdowns in equity if we risk only 1 percent of assets under management on any single trade.

Returning to our back-tested trading results in Figure 2.1 for a 10,000 baseload currency of the British pound against the U.S. dollar from January 1, 2000, to December 31, 2009, the reader will recall that despite enjoying an overall profit of $5,974, the model experienced a worst peak-to-valley drawdown in account equity of $2,505. To better understand the significance of this drawdown in relation to the 1 percent rule, we need to look at our model's performance in relation to its expected worst per trade loss.

Our RSI extremes trading system for cash foreign exchange British pound–U.S. dollar used a $350 stop loss, and we assumed a $10 per round-turn cost for slippage and commissions. This means that according to the 1 percent rule, we need $36,000 to trade the system without being overleveraged. It also means that our worst peak-to-valley drawdown in account equity of $2,505 represented a very manageable worst peak-to-valley drawdown of 6.96 percent. The bad news is that our 10-year total net profit of $5,974 translated into an annualized average total net profit of $597.40, or a 1.66 percent annual rate of return.

If the 1.66 percent rate of return seems unattractive, the simplest solution is to risk 2 percent of assets under management on a per trade basis.[6] The good news is that by doing this, our annualized rate of return increases to 3.32 percent, but the bad news is that we now have to endure a worst peak-to-valley equity drawdown of 13.92 percent of assets under management. If a 3.32 percent annualized return on investment is still too anemic for us, we might be tempted to risk 10 percent of assets under management on every trade. In so doing we could enjoy a robust 16.6 percent annualized rate of return, but would have to risk enduring the near fatal worst peak-to-valley drawdown of 69.58 percent.

Why is a peak-to-valley drawdown in equity of 69.58 percent considered to be "near fatal"? Because if it occurs at the outset of our trading—which we always have to assume as a distinct possibility—we would need a return on investment in excess of 225 percent to regain our initial asset under management investment. Also, this extraordinary rate of return would have to be accomplished with a stake of less than one-third of our initial assets under management. While achieving such a rate of return with this diminished equity stake is not mathematically impossible, I would prefer betting against, as opposed to in favor of, such an occurrence.

Now that we have proven the robustness of the 1 percent rule for volumetric position sizing, how can we safely increase our position size without increasing risk as our account equity increases? Also, how do we determine when it is necessary to decrease our volumetric position size as our account equity decreases? Although there are numerous methods of handling the adjustment of volumetric position size as assets under management change, one of the best-known techniques is Ralph Vince's fixed fractional position sizing.[7]

The most conservative way of using fixed fractional position sizing is to look at the worst peak-to-valley drawdown over the back-tested period. Returning to a volumetrically modified version of our RSI extremes back test of cash British pound–U.S. dollar (see Figure 2.11), we can see that by trading 100,000 base currency, our worst drawdown was $23,160 and that this represented a worst peak-to-valley drawdown of 6.43 percent of assets under management if we adhered to the 1 percent rule. This being the case—based on our historical back-tested performance—if we started with $360,000 in assets under management, we could safely increase our position size from 100,000 base currency to 110,000 base currency without exceeding this 6.5 percent worst peak-to-valley equity drawdown when assets under management increased to around $395,000. By contrast, if assets under management decreased to around $325,000, we would need to decrease our volumetric position size to 90,000 base currency in order to maintain the fixed fractional worst peak-to-valley drawdown in equity of around 6.5 percent.

While the 1 percent rule is a robust solution for the vast majority of trading models, in rare instances it is sometimes a suboptimal solution for certain shorter-term trading models. Imagine a model that enjoys 95 percent winning trades, but the average win is around one-fifth the size of its average loss. For these models, adherence to the 1 percent rule is counterintuitive since after experiencing a loss, the odds of enduring a second consecutive loss are astronomically low. In such instances, since the average profit per trade is so small when compared to the average loss and

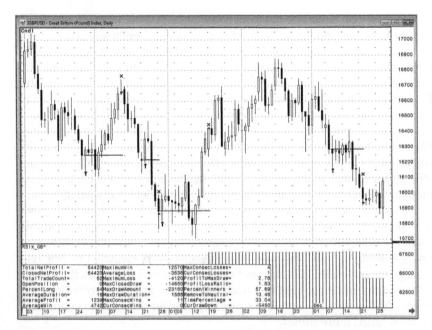

FIGURE 2.11　Daily Chart of Spot British Pound–U.S. Dollar Chart with RSI Extremes Trading System

Note: Trade summary includes data from January 1, 2000, to December 31, 2009, and assumes $10 round-turn deductions for slippage and commissions.

Source: CQG, Inc. © 2010. All rights reserved worldwide.

because the model's suffering of losses so rare, an argument can be made for using a stop loss of 6 or 7 percent of assets under management. This stated, until you can prove the robustness of these short-term model results, it is always safer to stick with the 1 percent rule.

MIDDLE OF PYRAMID

Quantitative tools in the middle level of the risk management pyramid offer robust solutions to issues, including correlations between assets held in a portfolio as well as the volatilities of those assets.

Value-at-Risk

A more robust answer regarding stop loss placement is that our stop levels should be attuned to the current volatility of the asset traded. In other words, in higher volatility environments, we will need to place our stops further from our entry price so we can avoid being needlessly stopped out of trades that would eventually result in profit, while in lower volatility markets we can place our stop levels much closer to entry without getting stopped out on false countermoves. This relationship between volatility and stop level placement is the reason we never look at stop losses in a vacuum but instead examine them in conjunction with volumetric position sizing. In other words, when the volatility of the asset is higher, we place our stop further from the entry price level but we could potentially trade fewer contracts, whereas when the volatility is lower, we place the stop closer to our entry price and could therefore potentially trade a larger number of contracts without violating rules of prudent risk management.

This relationship between stop loss placement level, volumetric position sizing, and the volatility of the asset—or assets—traded transitions us to the middle tier of our risk management pyramid and specifically to Value-at-Risk, or VaR. VaR adds two indispensable elements to our risk management models: volatility and correlations. VaR examines the historical volatility of assets held in a trading portfolio and the correlations between those assets so as to make our stop loss placement and volumetric position sizing more robust.

In addition to incorporation of historical volatility of assets traded giving us a more robust answer as to where to place our stops and what our position size in the market should be, volatility is a natural complement to stop placement and position sizing because it automatically attunes us to changes in asset risk due to shifts in the asset's value.

For example, in December 1991, Procter & Gamble traded at $10 per share; a $0.50 stop loss therefore represented a significant 5 percent move in the stock. By contrast, in March 1999, P&G was trading at $50 per share. If we continued to blindly set our stop at the static $0.50 level, we were now only risking 1 percent of the stock's value and could be stopped out by a minor fluctuation (see Figure 2.12). Switching from static dollar amount stop loss placements to stops attuned to shifts in asset value—and volatility—also has implications for position sizing. In 1991, when P&G traded at $10 per share, a $500 per trade risk ceiling translated into trading 1,000 shares with a $0.50 per share, or 5 percent stop loss. On the other hand, in 1999 when the company traded at $50 per share, traders needing to retain the stop loss of 5 percent of the stock's value as well as the $500 risk ceiling not only changed the per share stop loss level to $2.50, but were also forced to reduce their volumetric position size to 200 shares.

In addition to attuning us to historical volatility, Value-at-Risk makes position-sizing decisions more robust by analyzing historical correlations among assets held in our portfolio. This is an important consideration because, as a standalone, volumetric position sizing gives a static—and

FIGURE 2.12 Monthly Procter & Gamble Chart Showing Change in Stock's Value during 1990s

Source: CQG, Inc. © 2010. All rights reserved worldwide.

therefore suboptimal—answer regarding how many units of a particular asset we can trade without being overleveraged.

For example, a 10-year back test of a 9- and 26-day moving average crossover trading system for a CME Group front month-deferred month crude oil calendar spread experienced a worst peak-to-valley drawdown of $7,490 per contract. If we have $1 million in assets under management and are willing to endure a worst peak-to-valley drawdown of 7.49 percent, our volumetric position limit for the calendar spread would therefore be 10 contracts. If we then blindly applied this static volumetric position-sizing formula of 10 contracts to an outright position in CME Group crude oil, we would have endured a 31.15 percent peak-to-valley equity drawdown using the same mechanical trading system over the same back-tested period. This example illustrates how the strong positive correlation between the calendar months in the spread translated into lower risk than outright long or short positions in the commodity (see Figure 2.13).

Table 2.1 shows a first quarter of 2010 correlation study of various assets, including cash foreign exchange instruments like the eurocurrency against the U.S. dollar, the Australian dollar against the U.S. dollar, CME

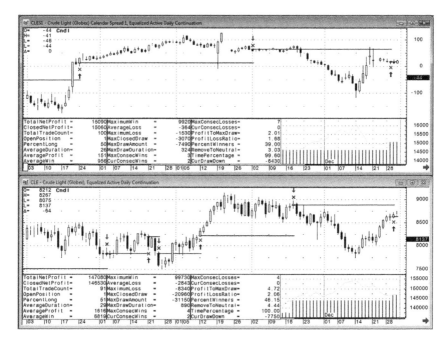

FIGURE 2.13 Equalized Active Daily Continuation Charts for CME Group Crude Oil Futures Contract and Crude Oil Calendar Spread with 9- and 26-day Moving Average Crossover System

Note: Trade summary includes data from January 1, 2000, to December 31, 2009, and includes $10 round-turn deductions for slippage and commissions.

Source: CQG, Inc. © 2010. All rights reserved worldwide.

TABLE 2.1 First-Quarter 2010 Correlation Studies

	AUDUSD	EURUSD	Corn	E-Mini S&P 500	US T-Notes	Crude Oil	Gold
AUDUSD	1.0	.32	.32	.86	−.36	.82	.73
EURUSD	.32	1.0	.73	−.08	−.67	.05	.39
Corn	.32	.73	1.0	.01	−.65	.34	.53
E-Mini S&P 500	.86	−.08	.01	1.0	−.16	.85	.51
US T-Notes	−.36	−.67	−.65	−.16	1.0	−.28	−.34
Crude Oil	.82	.05	.34	.85	−.28	1.0	.73
Gold	.73	.39	.53	.51	−.34	.73	1.0

All futures data are equalized active daily continuation. Data shown are from January 4, 2010, through March 31, 2010.

Source: CQG, Inc. © 2010. All rights reserved worldwide.

TABLE 2.2 Third-Quarter 2010 Correlation Studies

	AUDUSD	EURUSD	Corn	E-Mini S&P 500	U.S. T-Notes	Crude Oil	Gold
AUDUSD	1.0	.80	.86	.89	.49	.92	.74
EURUSD	.80	1.0	.51	.84	.33	.40	.41
Corn	.86	.51	1.0	.59	.59	−.34	.93
E-Mini S&P 500	.89	.84	.59	1.0	.17	.44	.41
U.S. T-Notes	.49	.33	.59	.17	1.0	−.33	.62
Crude Oil	.92	.40	−.34	.44	−.33	1.0	−.50
Gold	.74	.41	.93	.41	.62	−.50	1.0

All futures data are equalized active daily continuation. Data shown are from July 1, 2010, through September 30, 2010.
Source: CQG, Inc. © 2010. All rights reserved worldwide.

Group corn, E-Mini S&P 500 futures, U.S. 10-year Treasury note futures, CME Group crude oil, and CME Group gold futures (see Table 2.1). Notice how certain strong positive correlations like the +0.82 correlation between the Australian dollar and crude oil are exactly as expected, while others like the low correlation of 0.05 between the euro and crude oil differ dramatically from assumptions. This is why it is always safer to perform correlation studies instead of blindly assuming that historically strong, stable correlations will hold up indefinitely despite the ever-changing nature of markets.

Although correlation anomalies shown in Table 2.1 were somewhat surprising, a bigger problem is revealed by comparing Table 2.1 to Table 2.2 (which shows correlations of the same assets during the third quarter of 2010). In comparing the tables, although we find some correlations such as the Australian dollar and the E-Mini S&P 500 remained stable, many correlations changed dramatically from the first to the third quarter of 2010 (see Table 2.2). Such shifts in historical correlations are precisely why VaR should always be augmented by stress testing (which allows for correlation breakdowns).

Now that we have shown how VaR makes our stop loss placement and position sizing more robust, let us examine VaR as a risk metric and see how it incorporates historical volatilities and correlations in its attempt to measure future portfolio risk. Although an in-depth presentation of VaR is beyond the scope of this volume, my book *Mechanical Trading Systems* offers readers a good overview explanation of the topic:

Value-at-risk methodologies attempt to quantify the standard deviation (or historical volatility) of a trading asset or portfolio of *assets and the historical correlations between these assets in order to answer the question: "What is the likelihood of our losing X dollars or more over a specified time horizon under normal market conditions?" For example, a particular hedge fund might have a daily VaR of $30 million at the 95 percent confidence level. This would translate into there being a 95 percent probability of the portfolio not experiencing a loss in excess of $30 million over the next twenty-four hours.*[8]

So a basic question regarding historical volatility as well as historical correlations as inputs for our VaR models is "What is our lookback period?" Remember, "it's not magic; it's just math." In other words, there is no perfect lookback period. The advantage of shorter lookback periods—such as 90 trading days—is that it gives greater emphasis to recent readings of volatility and correlations. The problem with shorter lookbacks is they can give a view of correlations and volatilities that are distorted by short-term trends in the market. By contrast, longer lookback periods—such as 250 days—give a broader view of correlations and volatility but can dampen the current risk suggested by those inputs. Also remember that correlations and volatilities of many physical commodities shift because of seasonal factors each year; risk managers consequently should augment ordinary 90- and 250-day studies with three-to-five-year seasonal lookbacks (see Figure 2.14).

Risk managers attempt to address these problems of lookback periods in a wide variety of ways, including—but not limited to—the use of exponentially weighted moving averages so they can give greater weight to the most recent volatilities and correlations. But here again, there is no perfect answer as to how much weighting is too much and how much is too little. Instead of giving a suboptimal answer to these questions, my suggestion to risk managers and traders is to explore a multitude of lookback periods along with a multitude of data weightings so you can gain a robust and accurate feel for current as well as future trends of volatility and correlations.

Another problem regarding historical volatilities and correlations is that of throwing away data. There are two ways in which historical data can be discarded: intentional exclusion and scenario roll-off. Intentional exclusion is fairly straightforward and self-explanatory. It occurs when risk managers intentionally exclude segments of data by convincing themselves—and the organization they work for—of the prudence in deleting a segment of data history because it represents a historical anomaly. Some risk managers in the natural gas industry did this after the 2005 hurricane season, reasoning that data derived from that season—which included Hurricane Katrina—represented an outlier event and therefore should be omitted from volatility and correlation studies (see Figure 2.15).

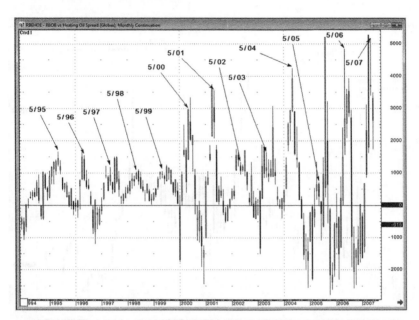

FIGURE 2.14 1995–2007 Monthly Continuation Chart of CME Group Unleaded Gasoline–Heating Oil Spread Showing Pattern of Seasonal Strength in May
Source: CQG, Inc. © 2010. All rights reserved worldwide.

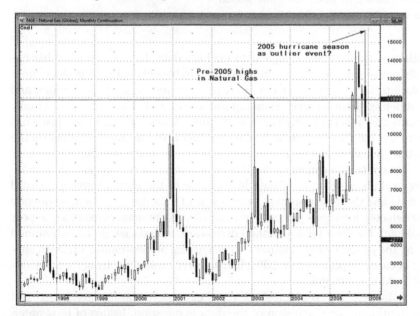

FIGURE 2.15 Monthly CME Group Natural Gas Futures Continuation Chart Showing 2005 Hurricane Season
Source: CQG, Inc. © 2010. All rights reserved worldwide.

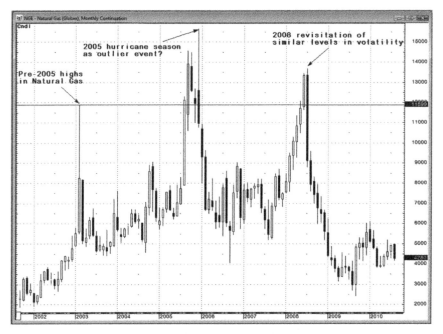

FIGURE 2.16 Monthly CME Group Natural Gas Futures Continuation Chart, Including Data after 2005 Hurricane Season

Source: CQG, Inc. © 2010. All rights reserved worldwide.

Although it might seem logical to exclude data that represents a historically unprecedented event, the practice is extremely dangerous since these volatilities and correlations are part of a real historical data segment, and in deleting them we are assuming away levels of risk that were actually endured by market participants in the past. Worse still, because price has memory, the fact that such data history occurred in the past suggests the distinct possibility of their reoccurrence in the future (see Figure 2.16).

By contrast, scenario roll-off occurs when risk managers unintentionally exclude a segment of data history due to the model moving forward in time and thereby assuming away levels of volatility experienced outside the selected lookback period. For example, risk managers using a one-year lookback for their volatility and correlation analysis would have assumed away the possibility of another 9/11 occurring on September 12, 2002, simply because September 11, 2001, had suddenly rolled off from their historical lookback window.

Solutions for problems of data exclusion—both intentional and unintentional—are inclusion of the data in question. Issues of how much or how little weighting to give to outlier events that would otherwise be excluded from our data history is part art and part science, and risk managers should augment any purely quantitative tools for data measurement of outliers and data otherwise subject to roll-off with their knowledge of assets held in the portfolio.

Stress Testing

As suggested in our discussion of VaR, it is the risk manager's attempt to gain a robust and accurate feel for current as well as future trends of volatility and correlations that represents his greatest challenge. The challenge is particularly acute because of two problems: first, the cyclical nature of volatility and second, correlation breakdowns. The cyclical nature of volatility suggests that even a robust measure of historical volatility necessarily falls short because periods of high volatility lead to low volatility and more dangerously, periods of low volatility resolve themselves in high volatility (see Figure 2.17). The risk manager should consequently always err on the side of caution in his estimation of future volatility trends.

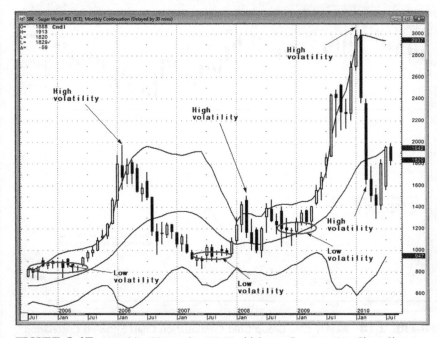

FIGURE 2.17 Monthly ICE Number 11 World Sugar Continuation Chart Showing Cyclical Nature of Volatility

Source: CQG, Inc. © 2010. All rights reserved worldwide.

Correlation breakdown is also a significant problem inherent in VaR model assumptions. Historical correlations among assets held in a portfolio are not only subject to breaking down in the future, but their breakdown tends to occur when we need them to hold up the most, when market volatility increases. This is exemplified by the correlation breakdown between gold and equity index futures during the credit crisis of 2008. In Figure 2.18, we see that for much of the first half of 2008, CME Group gold and stock index futures displayed a significant and stable negative correlation exceeding −0.8. By contrast, throughout the credit crisis of 2008, formerly stable negative correlations broke down precisely when traders needed those most to dampen portfolio risk in an environment of increasing market volatility (see Figure 2.18).

Problems of the cyclical nature of volatility as well as correlation breakdowns (along with seasonal volatility shifts and seasonal anomalies of physical commodities—see Figures 2.14 and 2.15) illustrate why VaR modeling is not robust as a standalone risk management metric and why

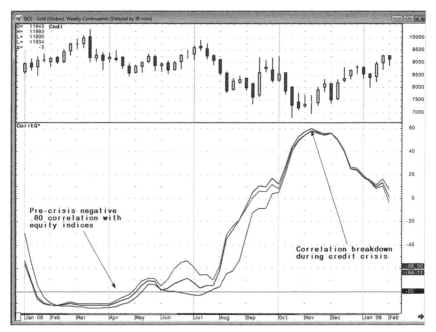

FIGURE 2.18 Weekly CME Group Gold Continuation Chart Showing Correlation Breakdown with Stock Index Futures during Credit Crisis of 2008

Note: Correlation study is a 20-week lookback period.

Source: CQG, Inc. © 2010. All rights reserved worldwide.

it should always be augmented by stress testing. VaR incorporates historical volatilities and correlations in an attempt to quantify the likelihood of a portfolio's breaching of a particular loss threshold over a specified time horizon, but says nothing regarding the severity of a particular loss. Stress testing attempts to determine how bad this low probability event could become. In addition, it allows for correlation breakdown as well as attempting to model for the cyclical nature of volatility.

Just as an in-depth examination of VaR is beyond the scope of this book, so too our presentation of stress testing is necessarily cursory and is limited to its overall value as one segment within our risk management pyramid. One of the most commonly employed types of stress tests is known as scenario analysis. In scenario analysis, the risk manager applies her current portfolio holdings to either a hypothetical scenario such as a 100 basis point rise in interest rates, or an actual historical scenario like the credit crisis of 2008. The purpose in running either of these types of scenarios is identification of excessive risk levels in our current portfolio holdings, and where appropriate, implementation of corrective risk reduction measures including exiting of positions, purchasing of options, and so forth.

APEX OF PYRAMID

When some traders first hear the term *management discretion* in relation to the risk management pyramid, a spark of hope reignites in their gambling hearts. Let me therefore extinguish that spark from the outset by reminding readers that this is a risk management pyramid, and therefore any managerial discretion could be used only to augment and strengthen purely quantitative tools at the pyramid's lower rungs and never to relinquish those tools in favor of discretionary risk-increasing behavior.

By definition, the term *discretion* suggests tools that defy purely quantitative mathematical modeling. It is consequently virtually impossible to provide an exhaustive list of all the possible ways in which management discretion can supplement a quantitative risk management model. Instead, let me outline a scenario in which management experience and discretion could be used to complement such quantitative risk models. On September 11, 2001, acts of terrorism are shifting markets to heightened levels of panic. A hedge fund's risk manager checks portfolio exposures against VaR limits, even runs a stress test to determine if the fund's trading book is enduring excessive levels of risk. Despite the fact that all her quantitative models suggest exposure is within normal tolerances, she calls the fund's head trader, suggesting a reduction of portfolio exposures.

Another example of management discretion is especially instructive as it simultaneously illustrates how manager experience can be used to augment quantitative risk tools of our pyramid's lower rungs while highlighting instances in which we might ignore entry signals generated by mechanical trading models. Regarding this second point, when people ask me if my own risk management is 100 percent mechanical, I answer that it is 99 percent mechanical and 1 percent discretionary. When they roll their eyes at the seemingly arbitrariness of this answer, I elaborate, explaining the discretionary element can only reduce and never increase the risk endured. Then I show them specific examples such as the September 2010 CME Group wheat futures contract (see Figure 2.19).

On August 5, 2010, wheat futures closed locked limit up. The following day, August 6, 2010, it traded up almost the 60-cent daily limit, only to turn around and settle locked limit down on the day. The following trading day, August 9, 2010, saw some good follow-through selling in the market, which resulted in the triggering of a sell signal for one of my countertrend trading models. Despite the fact that I could have sold September wheat futures without violating volumetric position-sizing limits (or any other

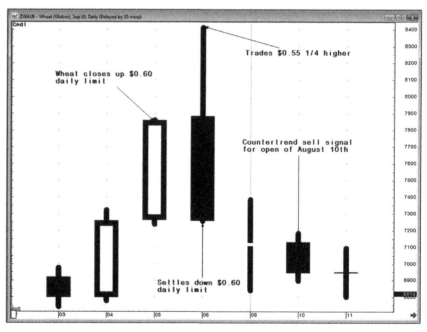

FIGURE 2.19 Daily Chart of September 2010 CME Group Wheat Showing Extraordinary Levels of Volatility

Source: CQG, Inc. © 2010. All rights reserved worldwide.

purely quantitative risk criteria), I used discretionary risk management as an overlay of those purely quantitative tools and chose to ignore the sell signal for wheat generated by my mechanical trading system.

PROS AND CONS OF THE RISK MANAGEMENT PYRAMID

The pyramid discussed in this chapter is a comprehensive model for traders and risk managers combining a diverse array of quantitative tools such as stop losses, volumetric position sizing, volatilities, and correlations—represented by its lower rungs—which are augmented by a discretionary overlay at its apex. Also, the weaknesses of each tier of the pyramid are offset by other tiers.

Despite the robustness of the pyramid as a risk management model, it is not the ultimate solution to price risk management, but instead should function as a solid foundation upon which leaders in the field can build. Although the model augments purely quantitative tools with managerial discretion, I intentionally avoided the temptation of formulating some suboptimal, quantitative—volatility-based—rules as to when this discretionary overlay should be introduced. I offered instead some obvious examples where the introduction of managerial discretion proved prudent in hopes of showcasing robust management discretion.

PUTTING IT ALL TOGETHER: A CASE STUDY

A speculative trader decides to fund a futures account with $100,000. He is comfortable with risking 2 percent of assets under management on any single trade and wants to simultaneously trade gold, corn, and the E-Mini S&P 500 futures. This means he can trade only when their strategy's initial stop loss levels are $2,000 per contract or less. If his back-tested correlation study of gold, corn, and the E-Mini S&P 500 suggests a low and stable correlation, he could potentially have as much as $2,000 at risk in each of the three assets traded. This would not account for the possibility, however, of correlation breakdown. He consequently decides that despite the historically low correlations between the assets, he will not commit more than $2,500, or 2.5 percent, of total assets under management in all the assets traded simultaneously.

In October 2010, his strategies have simultaneously generated two trading signals: a Fibonacci retracement buy signal in December 2010 corn

FIGURE 2.20 Daily Chart of December 2010 CME Group Corn Showing Limit Buy Level as Well as Initial Sell Stop Level
Source: CQG, Inc. © 2010. All rights reserved worldwide.

futures and a breakout signal in the E-Mini S&P 500 futures. The strategy in corn is to buy at the limit price of $4.5875. The initial sell stop loss order is at $4.445 and represents 14.25 cents, or $712.50 per contract, so he can buy two contracts without violating his 2 percent rule. His limit order to buy at $4.5875 was executed on October 4, 2010 (see Figure 2.20).

Simultaneously, he has been waiting for a breakout from a narrow trading range in the December E-Mini S&P 500 futures. He wants to place a buy stop at the resistance area of 1153.50 and a sell stop at the support area of 1127.25. His protective stop loss order would be the other side of the sideways channel, which represents a $1,312.50 per contract risk level, which means that he could buy one contract without violating his 2 percent rule. On October 4, 2010, however, when his order to buy two corn contracts is filled, it represents an initial risk of around $1,425, excluding commissions and slippage. He should therefore cancel resting orders in the E-Mini S&P 500 futures, otherwise he risks getting stopped out on both corn as well as the stock index futures and enduring a loss of $2,737.50, or 2.74 percent, of assets under management, which is beyond his stated risk tolerances (see Figure 2.21).

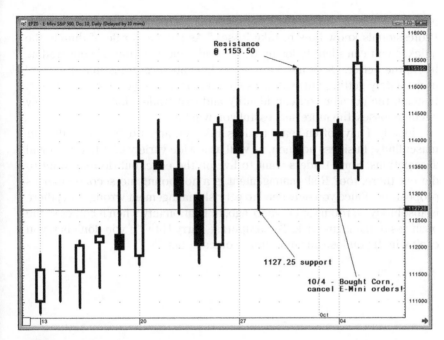

FIGURE 2.21 Daily Chart of December 2010 CME Group E-Mini S&P 500 Showing Buy and Sell Stop Orders
Source: CQG, Inc. © 2010. All rights reserved worldwide.

Despite its simplicity, this case study used clearly defined stop loss levels, volumetric position sizing, and correlations between assets traded. Also, although not explicitly stated in the example, since stop loss levels were based on support and resistance of the assets traded (as opposed to monetary stops irrespective of volatility—see Chapter 5 for more details), we *were* adjusting our position size based on historical volatility of the assets.

FINAL THOUGHTS

Before moving on from the topic of price risk management, I wanted to share some final thoughts based upon personal trading experiences and extensive research.

As stated earlier, successful speculative trading demands doing that which is uncomfortable and unnatural. For this chapter, that specifically means exiting losing trades quickly. As the cliché goes, "Big winners and small losers," or as I tell my students, "Any idiot can take a profit. Professionals know how to take losses." As a general rule of thumb, the quicker you can identify losing trades and kick them out of your trading book, the better. Of course I am not talking about putting on a trade and immediately getting out with a loss merely to prove you have discipline. Instead, the quicker you can identify and exit trades that will ultimately become losses, the more successful you will be.

Finally, I have often heard traders link their appetite for risk with their masculinity, business acumen, as well as a wide variety of other irrational associations. Sure, traders want to live on the edge, but do they want to die out there, too? Risk management is a no fooling, no second chances proposition. Since you only need to get risk management wrong once, there is absolutely no room for bravado, ego, or irrationality when it comes to the business of managing risk. To paraphrase Larry Hite, "If you don't bet, you can't win. If you lose all your chips, you can't bet."[9]

CHAPTER 3

Maintaining Unwavering Discipline

It's not the work that's hard, it's the discipline.
—Anonymous

Positive expectancy trading models fail because speculators abandon prudent risk management methodologies or they deviate from the models themselves. This chapter completes our introduction to the casino paradigm by exploring why traders abandon positive expectancy models or price risk management. Particular emphasis is on development and use of various psychological tools to aid in maintaining trader discipline.

DEFINING DISCIPLINE

What makes successful trading so challenging is that it is possible to develop a positive expectancy trading model and still lose overall even if you are properly capitalized and employ prudent rules of price risk management. The problem is best illustrated by the analogy of the opaque urn.[1] An opaque urn containing 100 marbles is placed in the center of the room. Fifty-seven of those marbles are green and 43 are red. Now I ask you to bet on the color of the marble you will pull from the urn, and you pick green. Out comes a red marble. I again ask you to pick the color of the marble, again you choose green, and again you pull a red marble. Third time: You choose green, and out comes a red marble. Fourth time, you again choose green and again pull out a red marble. After the fourth loss, you begin to doubt. Maybe there are more red marbles than green. And so you either stop betting altogether or worse still, you bet on the red marble.

Now look at Figure 3.1. I chose to reexamine this particular graph and back-tested model specifically because it was already shown to you twice in the previous chapter (see Figures 2.1 and 2.11). Here we look at it again in the context of trader discipline (see Figure 3.1). In particular, look at the number next to the heading marked "MaxConsecLosses," which stands for maximum number of consecutive losses. As you can see, this positive expectancy model experienced four consecutive losses, despite producing an overall profit of $64,420. This means that if you are either unable—because of overleveraging on any particular trade—or unwilling—because of a lack of confidence in the robustness of the model—to take the fifth trade after four consecutive losses, you do not enjoy the profit of $64,420. You lose the maximum drawdown amount of $23,160 instead. Worse yet, if after four consecutive losses and a drawdown of $23,160, you decided not only to abandon the model, but instead to fade[2] it (that is, bet on the red marble), your next trade would have resulted in a loss of $6,320 and total

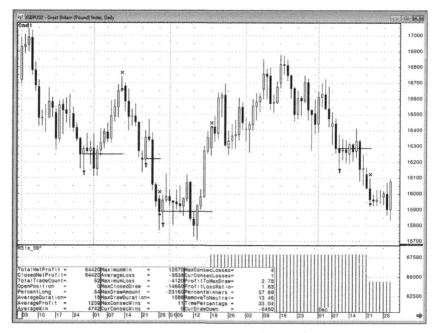

FIGURE 3.1 Daily Chart of Spot British Pound–U.S. Dollar Chart with RSI Extremes Trading System

Note: Trade summary includes data from January 1, 2000, to December 31, 2009, and assumes $10 round-turn deductions for slippage and commissions.

Source: CQG, Inc. © 2010. All rights reserved worldwide.

psychological demoralization. So it is not enough to have a positive expectancy model; it is not even enough to successfully manage the risk while employing that model; we must also have confidence in its robustness during those inevitable periods when it underperforms.

Returning to the casino paradigm, how does the casino handle inevitable periods of player success? Do they become despondent, close the casino, or start betting on the success of the players? Quite the contrary; when players win, the casino goes wild with lights and noises, all emphasizing the point that despite probability favoring the house, it is *possible* for players to win. The goal is to have the casino's attitude of unwavering discipline in the face of losses. As long as we truly have probability skewed in our favor while adhering to rules of risk management, there is no reason to abandon the positive expectancy model despite its endurance of losses. We need instead to train ourselves to trade like the casino, adhering to the probabilities and managing the risk 24 hours a day, seven days a week, 365 days a year. That is unwavering discipline, and that level of consistency is the prerequisite for successful speculation. This being the case, there is only one acceptable reason for abandoning a positive expectancy trading model, namely, its replacement with an even more robust model.

An investment professional once asked, "You already have a positive expectancy model. Why are you still doing research?" I answered, "Can you get from New York to Los Angeles by Greyhound bus? Is it a safe form of travel? Why bother taking a plane?" We continue searching for more robust models because it is the only way of finding more robust models. The only caveat is, never abandon a successful model until you have proven beyond all doubt that its replacement is more robust.

DISCIPLINE AND THE POSITIVE EXPECTANCY MODEL

Developing positive expectancy trading models takes time and research but it is probably the easiest aspect of successful speculation trading. In fact, throughout the course of this book I offer readers throwaway positive expectancy models as a starting point for their own research. A disclaimer regarding the models presented throughout this book: I do not call them throwaways for nothing. They are examples so basic that I offer them to the general public. The best analogy is someone who just bought a brand new Ford Mustang convertible and is selling his 20-year-old Ford Mustang convertible. The old Mustang still runs, but it obviously does not have all the bells and whistles of the newest model. The purpose of these throwaway models is not real-time trading, but instead to use as starting points for research that will lead to the development of even more robust positive expectancy models.

FIGURE 3.2 Equalized Active Daily Continuation Chart for ICE Brent Crude Oil
Futures with MACD Crossover Trading System

Note: Trade summary includes data from January 1, 2000, to December 31, 2009,
and assumes $10 round-turn deductions for slippage and commissions.

Source: CQG, Inc. © 2010. All rights reserved worldwide.

It is not enough, however, to develop a positive expectancy model. The
model must instead be able to be implemented in real time with real capital. In other words, even if I were to give you the most robust model ever
developed, it might not help because, in order for you to implement that
model, it has to match your trading personality.

For example, Figure 3.2 shows the 10-year back-tested results of a simple MACD crossover trend-following system on ICE Brent Crude Oil. The
model is a stop-and-reverse system that buys when the MACD line crosses
above the MACD's signal line and the MACD's signal line is greater than
zero. The system is stopped out of long positions and enters short positions
when the MACD line crosses below the MACD's signal line and the MACD's
signal line is less than zero. Notice that the column "AverageDuration" is
150 trading days. Although some traders are fine with an average hold time
of more than six months, I would argue that they are the exception.

Using CQG, the programming code for the MACD crossover system is
written this way:

Long Entry and Short Exit:

```
MACD(@,13.000,26.000)[-1] XABOVE MACDA(@,13.000,26.000,
9.000) [-1] AND MACDA(@,13.000,26.000,9.000) [-1] > 0
```

Long Exit and Short Entry:

```
MACD(@,13.000,26.000) [-1] XBELOW MACDA(@,13.000,26.000,
9.000) [-1] AND MACDA(@,13.000,26.000,9.000) [-1] < 0
```

We next compare the MACD crossover system with another extremely simple trend-following model that I call the Bollinger Band breakout. This system will enter long positions whenever the asset closes above the previous period's 20-bar upper Bollinger Band and will enter short positions whenever it closes below the previous period's 20-bar lower Bollinger Band. Exit occurs when the asset breaks the previous period's 20-bar simple moving average. Notice that the column "AverageDuration" is now only 14 trading days. Although this is much more palatable to most traders than the MACD crossover system's average trade duration, three weeks is still too long for many traders (see Figure 3.3).

Using CQG, the programming code for Bollinger Band breakout is written this way:

Long Entry:

```
Close(@)[-1] > BHI(@,Sim,20,2.00)[-1]
```

Short Entry:

```
Close(@)[-1]< BLO(@,Sim,20,2.00)[-1]
```

Long Exit and Short Exit:

```
MA(@,Sim,20)[-1]
```

Now compare both results to a third trend-following model that I call RSI Trend. The system is somewhat counterintuitive, as most traders think of Wilder's Relative Strength Index as a mean reversion indicator. Nevertheless, by entering long positions when the nine-bar RSI signals a slightly overbought reading of greater than 65 (or short positions when it gives a slightly oversold reading of less than 35) and combining it with a tight risk management criterion for exit (stops at previous three-bar low for long positions and previous three-bar high for short positions), it offers a somewhat respectable positive expectancy model. More importantly, for

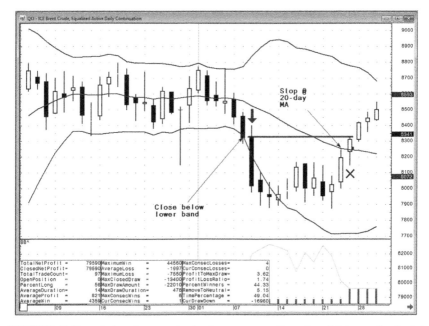

FIGURE 3.3 Equalized Active Daily Continuation Chart for ICE Brent Crude Oil Futures with Bollinger Band Breakout System

Note: Trade summary includes data from January 1, 2000, to December 31, 2009, and assumes $10 round-turn deductions for slippage and commissions.

Source: CQG, Inc. © 2010. All rights reserved worldwide.

our purposes, the tight risk management exit means that our average trade duration is now reduced to an even more attractive six trading days (see Figure 3.4).

Using CQG, the programming code for RSI Trend is written this way:

```
Long Entry:

RSI(@,9)[-1] > 65

Short Entry:

RSI(@,9)[-1] < 35

Long Exit:

LoLevel(@,3)[-1]

Short Exit:

HiLevel(@,3)[-1]
```

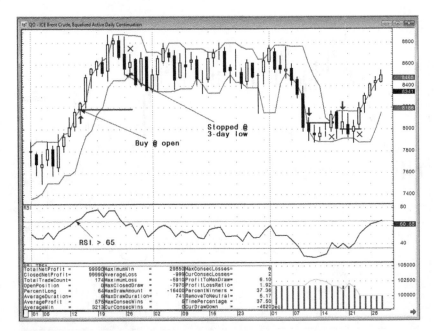

FIGURE 3.4 Equalized Active Daily Continuation Chart for ICE Brent Crude Oil Futures with RSI Trend System

Note: Trade summary includes data from January 1, 2000, to December 31, 2009, and assumes $10 round-turn deductions for slippage and commissions.

Source: CQG, Inc. © 2010. All rights reserved worldwide.

Finally, by using the same RSI Trend model and simply tightening the exit criterion from stops at the previous three-bar low (or high) to the previous bars' low (or high), our average trade duration is cut from six to three trading days (see Figure 3.5).

Using CQG, the programming code for short-term RSI trend is written this way:

```
Long Entry:

RSI(@,9)[-1] > 65

Short Entry:

RSI(@,9)[-1] < 35

Long Exit:

LoLevel(@,1)[-1]

Short Exit:

HiLevel(@,1)[-1]
```

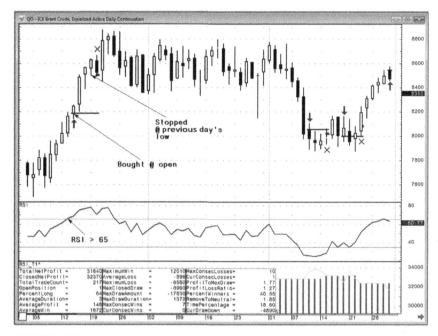

FIGURE 3.5 Equalized Active Daily Continuation Chart for ICE Brent Crude Oil Futures with Short-Term RSI Trend System

Note: Trade summary includes data from January 1, 2000, to December 31, 2009, and assumes $10 round-turn deductions for slippage and commissions.

Source: CQG, Inc. © 2010. All rights reserved worldwide.

In summary, based on a comparison of the models examined over the back-testing data history for Brent Crude Oil, if we were only interested in the best risk-adjusted rate of return, we would choose RSI Trend since it enjoyed the best total net profit to maximum drawdown ratio, which is shown in the graphs as "ProfitToMaxDraw" and in Table 3.1 as "P:MD." But disciplined trading requires recognition of which type of positive expectancy model our personality can actually adhere to, or, as I like to say, "You choose your poison in trading." If we blindly ignore our inability to take a large number of consecutive losses, then after the sixth consecutive loss, we will abandon the hypothetically superior RSI Trend and lose $16,400, instead of maintaining discipline, adhering to the system, and enjoying a total net profit of $99,990. Acknowledging our need for more winners and fewer consecutive losses, we would instead implement the Bollinger Band breakout system since it had both the best winning percentage as well enduring the lowest number of consecutive losses. If, on the other hand, we are interested in exiting losing positions

TABLE 3.1 Comparison of Trend-Following Models

Model	P:MD	% Win	Max # Loss	Avg Loss	Avg Days
MACD	1.07	41.18%	5	(9269)	150
BB Breakout	3.62	44.33%	4	(1997)	14
RSI Trend	6.10	37.36%	6	(999)	6
Shorter RSI	1.77	40.55%	10	(896)	3

Daily equalized continuation contract results for ICE Brent Crude Oil from January 1, 2000, to December 31, 2009.
Source: CQG, Inc. © 2010. All rights reserved worldwide.

quickest, enduring the lowest average loss size and enjoying the shortest trade duration, then the Shorter RSI system is the superior performer (see Table 3.1). Bottom line: There is no single answer as to what is the most robust model. The essential point instead is discovering which is the most robust for us.

TYPES OF TRADERS

Although positive expectancy models are as varied as the individuals tailoring them to match their trading personalities, in general, these models can be divided into the following categories (see Table 3.2): Long-term trend followers, swing traders, day traders, and scalpers.

Long-Term Trend Followers

Long-term trend followers typically only take trades in the direction of the longer-term trend. Here we define the long-term trend as the trend over the previous six months, which includes both MACD and the Bollinger Band breakout systems. Long-term trend followers tend to hold trades for more than 10 trading days and so must adhere to the Wall Street cliché of "being right and sitting tight." Because markets trend around only 30 percent of the time, asset class diversification and being well capitalized are indispensable prerequisites for success. They enjoy superior average size profit to average size loss ratios, but must be willing to endure more losses and poor win-loss ratios to ensure participation in every major trend. Consequently, the other cliché commonly associated with adherence to these types of systems is "Death by a thousand paper cuts." If you are uncomfortable sitting on your hands as big unrealized gains get stopped out for smaller realized gains, if you need to experience more winning trades than losers, if taking a large number of losses is problematic, then long-term trend trading is probably not for you. Key tools to aid in adherence to these models are:

- Asset class diversification to ensure participation in any and all trending markets
- Taking partial profits—typically one-third to one-half of total position —at logical technical support and resistance levels (these techniques are examined throughout Chapter 6)
- Using oscillators, retracements (see Chapter 8), or timeframe divergence (see Chapter 7) to find low-risk entry levels

Swing Traders

Swing traders can trade either in the direction of the longer-term trend or participate in countertrend moves. They tend to hold trades for 2 to 10 trading days. We therefore categorize both RSI Trend as well as the shorter-term RSI models as swing systems. Although they typically enjoy superior winning percentages and smaller average loss sizes, swing traders must be willing to reestablish positions after multiple small losses and their average win to average loss ratio is inferior to long-term trend followers.

Key tools to aid in adherence to these models are:

- Asset class diversification to ensure participation in any and all swing moves
- Taking partial profits—typically one-half to three-fourths of the total position—at logical technical support and resistance levels (these techniques are examined throughout Chapter 6).

Day Traders

Day traders can trade in the direction of the short- or long-term trend or participate in countertrend moves. Since by definition they exit trades within 24 hours, they are not subject to price shock event risk occurring when markets are closed. Because they exit at or before the close each day, they take smaller profits and losses, and as a result, they must develop models with higher winning percentages. Although their flat-by-day's-close rule means restful sleep each night, they typically make more intraday trades and therefore more intraday trading decisions. More intraday trades and trading decisions generally translates into more stress and being married to the screen, since it is more difficult to program for all the intraday fundamental market-moving events that they want to avoid or capitalize on (this also makes back testing of a model's robustness more challenging). Though diversification is possible, they typically focus on a few extremely liquid assets.

Key tools to aid in adherence to these models are:

- Using the clock—specifically the close—as a secondary risk management tool
- Capitalizing on short-term news events such as government reports in conjunction with technical support and resistance levels to initiate or liquidate positions

Scalpers

Scalpers experience typical hold times of anywhere from seconds to a few hours. Although they can trade in the direction of the short- or long-term trend or participate in countertrend moves, they tend to use models that are counter to the shorter-term, intraday trend. Because of this and because they tend to exit at the mean as opposed to letting profits run, the cliché often associated with their trading style is "Picking up pennies in front of a steam roller." Since the duration of their trades is so short and the number of transactions per day so large, they typically focus on trading one or two extremely liquid assets. Like day traders, they exit quickly and are not subject to price shock event risk occurring when markets are closed. In contrast to day traders, because they focus on capturing small profits quickly, scalpers typically avoid taking positions before the release of potential high-risk events such as government reports. Because their typical trade duration is shortest, they take the most trades on a per day basis, typically enjoying the highest win-loss ratios and worst average profit to average loss ratios. More trades per day means more stress and being even more married to the screen than day traders.

TABLE 3.2 Summary of Trader Types

Trader Type	Duration	Pros	Cons	Key Point
Long-Term	>10 days	P:L Ratio	1,000 paper cuts	Diversification
Swing	2–10 days	Flexible: trend or countertrend	Re-entry after multiple losses	Taking partial profits
Day	<1 day	No overnight risk	Married to screen	Capitalizing on news releases
Scalper	Minutes	W:L Ratio	Pennies/Steam Roller	Using clock as risk tool

Key tools to aid in adherence to these models are:

- Using the clock—typically represented by two-, three-, or five-minute bar charts—as the primary risk management tool in conjunction with a catastrophic stop based on longer-term—hourly or daily—technical support and resistance levels
- Taking both profits and losses quickly
- Avoidance of short-term news events such as government reports, which unfavorably skew the risk and reward of these systems

In summary, developing positive expectancy trading models is not about finding the best risk-adjusted rate of return; it is instead about discovering the best risk-adjusted rate of return for our trading personality.

DISCIPLINE AND PRICE RISK MANAGEMENT

The most common manifestations of failure in trader discipline occur in risk management. As shown in Chapter 1, according to Tversky and Kahneman, this is because all humans have a psychological bias against taking losses. Nearly all social conditioning reinforces this innate bias. Until embarking on the career of trading, you were constantly taught not to lose and to associate losing with being a loser. Paradoxically, in trading, the winners are those who have learned that they are not their trades and can disassociate self-image from their trades by taking losses as quickly and efficiently as possible. I am not suggesting putting on a trade, watching it go a tick against you, and then exiting simply to prove you have the discipline to take small losses. I am talking instead about the discipline to exit with a loss as soon as you can identify the trade as a probable loser.

On first entering the futures industry in 1987, I interviewed various clearing firms. One particularly memorable interview was with a clerk at SLK Futures (SLK Futures is now part of Goldman Sachs). He asked, "You a college kid?" Replying in the affirmative, he shook his head gravely, advising, "It'll never work." I was naturally confused and asked him to elaborate. He continued, "Yeah, we tried hiring college kids. Hired 20 of 'em, all top in their classes from Ivy League MBA programs. Gave 'em each a hundred grand and within six months, they all blew up. Every one of 'em." Of course they blew up. Ironically, the rigidity and unwillingness to admit they were wrong, which had led to success in the academic world, proved fatal in speculative trading.

Unwavering discipline is challenging because it requires that we quickly admit when we are wrong while simultaneously continuing to trust in our ability to execute a positive expectancy model. Any idiot can take a profit; professionals know how to take losses. Professional traders consistently embody a disciplined mindset toward losing that enables them to disassociate the outcome of a single trade or even multiple consecutive losing trades from their self-image as traders. They have reprogrammed themselves away from the self-destructive delusional belief that they are their trades. There are many tools to aid in promoting this psychological shift in self-image; those specifically associated with discipline as it relates to risk management are discussed here, the remainder in the final chapter. For now, the point is development of unwavering discipline regarding risk management.

Returning to our casino analogy, the casino never abandons its rules of risk management regardless of winning streaks, losing streaks, the types of players entering, the time of day, and so on. More importantly, they remain emotionally unaffected irrespective of winning or losing streaks. When players win, the casino does not consider itself bad or think that it does not understand its business. It is precisely because they *do* understand the business that they are psychologically okay with taking losses and continuing their disciplined adherence to rules of risk management.

Starting out as a local on the floor of a futures exchange, I used to watch various traders in hopes of learning the business. Most of the posturing, gesturing, and screaming proved useless to my education as an aspiring speculator, but there was one exception. I noticed one local who would consistently buy the market at 20 and sell at 10. Then he would sell at 30 and buy at 35. Next, he would buy at 90 and sell at 80. It was almost painful to watch, loss after loss after loss. Until he bought for 50, and suddenly the market was 70 bid. Then he would fold his arms. I never knew him personally, but my guess is someone taught him when you get a profitable trade, fold your arms so you are not tempted to exit prematurely. I would say he folded his arms 3 out of every 10 trades and yet there he was, day after day, week after week, month after month, year after year. Why? Because he trained himself to exit losses as quickly as possible and let the winners run. Now review Table 3.1. Notice that despite enjoying positive expectancy, every model shown experienced more losing trades than winning trades and that they all endured at least four consecutive losses.

We abandon discipline in risk management because we do not want to admit that we are wrong. Somehow we have deluded ourselves into believing that if we do not exit the losing trade we have not *really* lost. The beauty of twenty-first century electronic trading is that our screen acts as the ultimate dispeller of this delusion. Our current significant negative unrealized loss proves that we are already—at least temporarily—wrong irrespective of whether we close out the position or not. The only question remaining is how large of a loss we are going to accept. Hopeful amateurs may respond, "Yes, we are temporarily experiencing an unrealized loss, but it could come back. Then we could exit at breakeven or perhaps a small gain." Such a response embodies the precise psychology of failure that Tversky and Kahneman outlined in their article "Prospect Theory." Rereading the sentence closely, we see it is programmed for small profits and big losses. The willingness to endure the possibility of allowing a small manageable loss to escalate into a large catastrophic one in hopes of achieving, ". . . breakeven or perhaps a small gain . . ." is ultimately a recipe for disaster. Such speculators are not psychologically trading to win; they are instead trading not to lose.

When training rookie traders, the psychological predisposition to entry as well as exiting with profit is overwhelming. All the focus is on the elusive perfect entry price, the myth being that if their entry price is good enough, they need not think about losses. Consequently, immediately after they determine entry price, I force them to place a stop loss order. Inevitably, they hesitate. They refuse to consider the emotionally painful possibility of loss. The dialogue typically goes something like this:

RW: "Where is your stop?"

Student: "I'll tell you later . . . once the market moves in my favor."

RW: "Okay, fine. But at least put in a catastrophic stop. Just in case the president is assassinated or there's a terrorist attack in Times Square. Put a sell stop at 10,000."

Student: "I can't put a stop there."

RW: "Why not?"

Student: "They could stop me out."

RW: "The fact that you *can't* put it there is exactly why you *must* put it there."

Closely related to the unwillingness to place stop loss orders is the placement of the order only to cancel it as the market approaches the stop price because we refuse to accept the painful reality of loss and being wrong. Whether we fail to place stops or place and then cancel them, the long-term outcome is inevitably the same: termination of our career as traders. Beginning traders will sometimes pose the question "How far can the market move against me?" Of course, no one knows the answer. Nevertheless, we do absolutely know it could move far enough to end our career. When we trade without a stop loss order over the short term, two things can happen, though both of them will ultimately lead to the same disastrous results. The first possibility is that the market moves against us until we blow up. The other possibility is that it comes back in our favor and we close out the position for a profit. This second possibility is ultimately just as disastrous as the first because we have learned the exact wrong lesson regarding market behavior, namely that if you deny the possibility of loss, the market will allow you to exit with profits. Unfortunately, the market can reinforce this delusional belief over and over again, giving traders a false sense of security regarding a disciplined approach to risk until that one time when the market fails to come back, ending our trading career. If you cannot take small losses quickly, one day the mother of all losses will take you, slowly, imperceptibly at first, then violently and relentlessly until your career is swallowed completely by it. Just ask those who bought and held Enron, WorldCom, or Lehman.

PATIENCE AND DISCIPLINE

Another reason trader discipline breaks down is impatience. Although impatience can stem from a virtually infinite number of causes, the four most common reasons for impatience among traders are boredom, lack of confidence in the positive expectancy model, fear of not getting enough signals, and what is commonly called the Protestant work ethic.

Boredom

Many traders become impatient when their model is not generating signals and they tire of waiting for probabilities to become skewed in their favor. These emotions play perfectly into the myth of trading as an exciting career. If we are properly managing the risk and adhering to a positive expectancy model, the act of trading a position *should* be boring. I like to call successful speculators glorified actuarial accountants, and few enter the field of actuarial accounting for excitement. The only good news is speculation offers the potential for a higher income than accounting. If you want excitement, take up skydiving or bungee jumping. Casinos do not operate for thrills or entertainment; they do it for profits. By contrast, it is the players—who have probabilities skewed against them—that go to casinos for entertainment.

Positive expectancy models are generally divided into two categories: trend following and mean reversion, because markets exhibit only mean reverting and trending behavior. Regardless of how robust a model is, there are times when the odds do not favor its use. Standing aside during such periods requires patience and discipline, specifically the discipline not to trade until the market displays the kind of behavior in which the odds are in our favor. As I like to say, "When there is nothing to do, do nothing." If, for example, you are implementing a mean reverting model and the market is trending—and therefore not exhibiting the type of action in which you have an edge—the correct action is to patiently stand aside until it once again displays the type of behavior in which probability is skewed in your favor. The market knows only two songs: trending and mean reverting. When it is playing its trending song, mean reversion traders should sit patiently waiting for the song's end. While waiting there will be lots of noise and excitement coming from the trend-following casino, but mean reversion traders should not walk in and try to make money. That is the trend-follower's casino, so only they have positive expectancy there. As a mean reversion trader, your job is to patiently wait until the market stops playing its trend-following song and again plays the mean reversion song. When it does, your casino again fills with players, proving it is your time to trade.

The key to maintaining discipline during times when the market's environment does not favor implementation of our model is remembering the cyclical nature of volatility. Markets move much faster than we imagine. While flat and waiting, we think we will never get a position. Once in a position, we think it will take forever to reach our profitable exit target. This is because present price action distorts our view of future price possibilities—especially during a low volatility cycle—and this leads to impatience and a breakdown of discipline. The psychological antidote to this problem is reminding ourselves of volatility's cyclical nature and how periods of low volatility resolve themselves in high volatility and vice versa (see Chapter 4). While this is true of all market environments, it is especially true for bear markets, which are typically faster and more violent than bull markets.

Another analogy I developed to explain the concept of patience when faced with markets exhibiting behavior contraindicated for your model is that of eating your own lunch. You hungrily peruse the menu at your favorite restaurant. You want every entrée listed, but simultaneously realize that irrespective of how hungry you are, you can eat only your own lunch. As traders, we want to capitalize on every single market wiggle but eventually learn we can participate only in specific types of behavior that constitute our edge. Of course, there is one exception to the eating-your-own-lunch rule. As will be shown in Chapter 8, as long as the trader is sufficiently capitalized, he can simultaneously execute both trend-following and mean reversion models. Nevertheless, even in such instances, both of these models are still only executing trades when their standalone probability edge arises.

Lack of Confidence in the Model

One of the most common reasons for impatience leading to a breakdown in discipline is a lack of confidence in the model. We have already outlined many manifestations of these issues earlier in the chapter by showing how models can simultaneously exhibit positive expectancy while being antithetical to our particular trading personality. Other reasons for abandonment of the model stem from a lack of confidence in its robustness irrespective of performance issues like percentage of winning trades and maximum number of consecutive losses. These issues are not performance related per se but are instead linked to lack of confidence in general and typically manifest as trading the money (which we cover in Chapter 5), anticipating the signal (which is discussed throughout Chapter 9), and second-guessing the model by abandoning entry levels, exit points, or risk management criteria. The antidote for lack of confidence in the model is exhaustive researching and back testing before real-time implementation (these issues are examined in detail throughout Chapter 8).

Fear of Not Getting Enough Signals

The *irrational* fear of not getting enough signals must be distinguished from our earlier discussion of executing a model that is contraindicated for our trading personality. Instead, here we are dealing with a robust model that *is* well suited to our personality, but becoming impatient because of an irrational fear of the model's inability to generate an adequate number of trading signals. These issues most commonly stem from thinking about the money—specifically, how much we need to earn so we can pay our bills—instead of market dynamics. Also, it is about needing to win instead of knowing that the positive expectancy model is robust and will therefore generate a competitive rate of return. Casinos never let their overhead or lack of opportunities at 2 A.M. on a Wednesday lead to closure of the casino, changing of the odds on their games, or abandonment of table limits. Similar to the problem of impatience as it relates to a lack of confidence in the model, here, too, the solution to an irrational fear of not getting enough signals is exhaustive research and back testing.

Protestant Work Ethic

Whenever traders talk about monetary goals on a per day or even a per month basis, I e-mail them the link to Huey Lewis and the News' song, "Workin' for a Livin'." Then I specifically point out the line, "I'm taking what they givin' 'cause I'm working for a livin'." You are not laying bricks at a construction site; you are trading the markets, and are therefore able to take only the money that the markets are currently giving. If they are giving $10,000 today, then that is what you are taking. If they are giving $50, then that is what you are taking. If today they are giving nothing, then you cannot force the market to give more than what is being offered. Consequently, applying the Protestant work ethic of actively laboring in the markets every day irrespective of the opportunities available on that particular day is a recipe for disaster.

By trying to force a specific amount of money out of the markets every day, you are thinking about the money, not about probabilities and risk management. Every day is different, and some days the market skews the odds against us. On such days the hard work is having the discipline not to trade. When temptations to trade arise from feeling you need to earn money, remind yourself that being flat *is* a position in the market. It is the position of actively refraining from putting capital at risk on low-probability or high-risk situations. If feelings of guilt arise from equating being flat with laziness, put these feelings where they can be constructively and—more importantly—safely applied, into researching and back testing of positive expectancy models.

FINAL THOUGHTS

Discipline in speculation exhibited by master traders is inexorably linked to even-mindedness, which is examined throughout Chapter 12. Most seek simple, one-dimensional answers to challenging endeavors such as trading. Unfortunately, speculative trading defies simplistic solutions. Development of positive expectancy trading models is a prerequisite for success in trading, but these models must be coupled with stringent rules of risk management. Furthermore, disciplined adherence to the casino paradigm despite periods of suboptimal performance is also an undisputed prerequisite for success in trading, but master traders do not allow unwavering discipline to devolve into complacency, laziness, or rigidity. The key to transcending self-imposed performance ceilings and the antidote to rigidity is tempering discipline with open-mindedness and flexibility. Although terms like *flexibility* and *discipline* sound contradictory, successful speculators simultaneously maintain disciplined adherence to the casino paradigm while embodying open-mindedness through their commitment to ongoing research regarding model development and tools for risk management.

PART II

Trading Tools and Techniques

CHAPTER 4

Capitalizing on the Cyclical Nature of Volatility

Baccarat is a game whereby the croupier gathers in money with a flexible sculling oar, then rakes it home. If I could have borrowed his oar I would have stayed.

—Mark Twain

T he single most important tool in developing positive expectancy trading models is the cyclical nature of volatility. Particular emphasis will be on incorporating volatility indicators so as to make both trend-following and countertrend models more robust.

THE ONLY CONSTANT

I'm sure you've heard it said that the trend is your friend. And it is true; the trend is your friend... until it ends. Unfortunately, its end is never announced on the front page of financial media publications, so we can never count on a trend's continuation. Another commonly repeated phrase regarding market behavior is that assets trade in a range around 70 percent of the time. While this is also true, it too is not nearly as helpful as traders would hope because breakouts from trading ranges are unpredictable and violent. In summary, traders can never count on a bear trend, bull trend, or even a trendless market. Instead the only constant in every market, at all times, is change. At first glance, this truth of the ever-changing nature of market behavior might seem to be a worthless fact. Instead, I have found it to be the core concept behind many robust positive expectancy trading models. No, we cannot count on a trend, or on trendless action, but we always know that sideways markets will eventually resolve themselves into trending markets and vice versa. I call this truth of market behavior the cyclical nature of volatility, and other than uncertainty itself (which was covered in Chapter 2), it is the only constant in the markets.[1]

Admittedly, we never know ahead of time when trendless, low-volatility environments will resolve themselves into trending market action, nor can we know when trending, high-volatility markets will cycle to low volatility, but we absolutely know that the longer they display either low or high volatility, the greater the odds of them shifting to the opposite end of the volatility spectrum.

A final introductory word on the cyclical nature of volatility: All volatility environments are not created equal. As we will see throughout the chapter, trading countertrend models to better capitalize on a market cycling from high to low volatility is much riskier than trading a trend-following model in which traders try to participate in breakouts from a low-volatility environment.

To understand why trading breakouts from low-volatility environments are, in general, less risky, let us consider what a low-volatility environment signifies. Low volatility is a period of consensus regarding the fair value of an asset. Consequently, when a new piece of information leads to a shift in perception of that asset's value and the market cycles out of low volatility, there is a greater-than-normal probability of a sustainable trend in the direction of that breakout.

Another way of understanding why trading breakouts from low-volatility environments are—in general—less risky is illustrated by looking at September 2010 high-grade copper futures (see Figure 4.1). This market was indisputably experiencing a period of low volatility. When it broke above the horizontal resistance at $3.0705, there were two possibilities: a false breakout and a real breakout. If the breakout turned out to be a false breakout, it would have been a false breakout in the context of a low-volatility—and therefore low-risk—environment (see Figure 4.2). The other possibility was a real breakout, in which we experienced a shift from low to high volatility and enjoyed large profits.

By contrast, taking countertrend trades in high-volatility environments after the asset signals a peak in volatility is a riskier proposition. Although just as in our low-volatility breakout example, there are still two possibilities: a false mean reversion signal and a valid one, now the false signal occurs in the context of a high-volatility—and therefore high-risk—environment. Although our 10-period average true range volatility indicator signaled a peak in September 2010 CME Group wheat futures

FIGURE 4.1 September 2010 Daily CME Group High-Grade Copper Futures Showing Breakout from Low Volatility

Source: CQG, Inc. © 2010. All rights reserved worldwide.

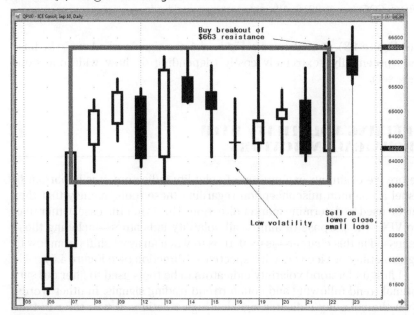

FIGURE 4.2 September 2010 Daily ICE Gas and Oil Futures Showing False Breakout from Low Volatility

Source: CQG, Inc. © 2010. All rights reserved worldwide.

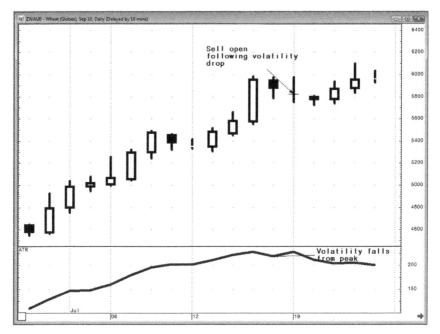

FIGURE 4.3 September 2010 CME Group Daily Wheat Futures Showing Fall from Peak in 10-Day Average True Range
Source: CQG, Inc. © 2010. All rights reserved worldwide.

(see Figure 4.3), as evidenced in Figure 4.4, the signal turned out to be false and—potentially—extremely costly (depending on how wide our stops were set).

DEFINING VOLATILITY WITH TECHNICAL INDICATORS

Before we begin our exploration of volatility indicators, it is important to dispel a common misconception regarding these tools, namely that they can be used to determine market direction. This is not the case. Other than the VIX,[2] the purpose of almost all volatility indicators—including those discussed in this chapter—is to alert us to when an asset shifts from low to high volatility or vice versa, irrespective of direction (see Figure 4.5).

I first understood volatility indicators to be tools used to filter out suboptimal trend-following and countertrend trading signals. In other words, when the volatility indicator signaled high volatility, it was safer to take trend-following signals, and when it signaled low volatility, mean reversion signals had a greater probability of success. By contrast, I have found that

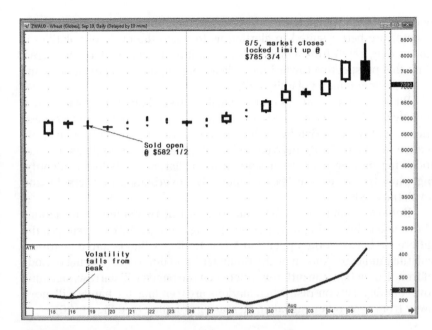

FIGURE 4.4 September 2010 CME Group Daily Wheat Futures Showing Huge Potential for Risk in Selling of False High-Volatility Signal
Source: CQG, Inc. © 2010. All rights reserved worldwide.

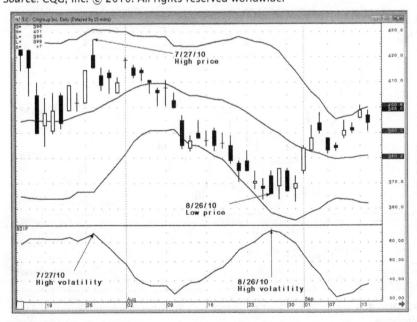

FIGURE 4.5 Daily 2010 Chart of Citigroup Showing Lack of Correlation between Volatility and Price Direction
Source: CQG, Inc. © 2010. All rights reserved worldwide.

because of the cyclical nature of volatility, the indicators examined in this chapter are better suited to alerting us to when the cycle of volatility is undergoing a shift from a high- to low-volatility environment, or vice versa. With this perspective toward the indicators in mind, let us examine some of the most common volatility indicators.

While teaching courses on technical analysis, I am often asked which technical indicator is my personal favorite and my answer has always been the same, Bollinger Bands. Bollinger Bands are an extremely robust, objective, mathematically derived technical indicator that contains a trend-following moving average, a statistical oscillator that helps in identifying when trends are—at least temporarily—overbought or oversold, and a volatility indicator.

Bollinger Bands are most commonly set at two standard deviations above and below a simple 20-period moving average. We can then turn the difference between the upper and lower Bollinger Bands into a historical volatility indicator known as the Bollinger Band difference. During periods of trendless action, the difference between the bands will narrow, signaling low volatility. By contrast, when markets are trending, the bands will move away from each other, signaling increasing volatility (see Figure 4.6).

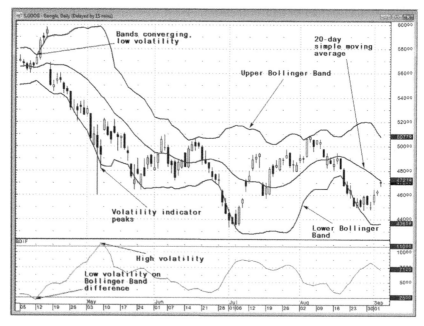

FIGURE 4.6 Daily 2010 Chart of Google with Bollinger Bands and Bollinger Band Difference

Source: CQG, Inc. © 2010. All rights reserved worldwide.

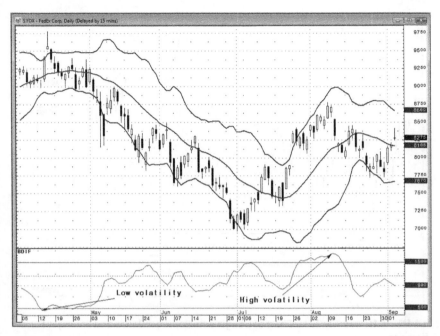

FIGURE 4.7   Daily 2010 Chart of FedEx with Bollinger Bands and Bollinger Band Difference

Source: CQG, Inc. © 2010. All rights reserved worldwide.

The advantage of using Bollinger Band difference as a volatility indicator is that it offers an objective—as opposed to subjective, nonmathematically derived—statistical measure of the asset's historical volatility. Its limitations are that since it is the difference of two standard deviations of the 20-period simple moving average for a particular asset, the numbers generated by the indicator have little or no significance to other assets, nor do they have significance for the same asset for a longer or short timeframe, nor even for the same asset over different periods of a 24-hour trading day. In other words, looking more closely at Figure 4.5, we would conclude that $25 is low volatility for a daily chart of Google and $110 is high volatility. By contrast, if we look at a daily chart of FedEx over the same lookback period, we now define $15 as high volatility and $5 as low volatility (see Figure 4.7). Then, if we return to Google but change our timeframe so that every bar represents one week, low volatility increases to $100 and high volatility becomes $300 (see Figure 4.8). Also, when using Bollinger Band difference as a volatility indicator, even over a particular 24-hour lookback period, our definition of high and low volatility will change depending on whether we are examining an asset at 1 A.M. or 1 P.M. (see Figures 4.9 and 4.10). Finally, because of the

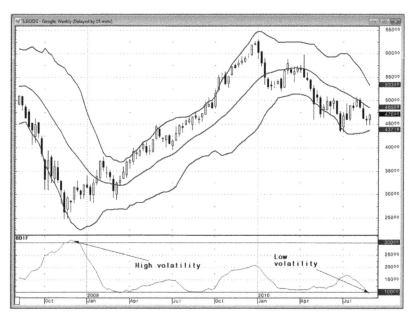

FIGURE 4.8 Weekly 2010 Chart of Google with Bollinger Bands and Bollinger Band Difference

Source: CQG, Inc. © 2010. All rights reserved worldwide.

FIGURE 4.9 Five-Minute Chart of September 2010 CME Group E-Mini S&P 500 with Bollinger Band Difference Showing 1.00 as Low Volatility and 3.75 as High Volatility from 1:00 A.M. EST to 6:00 A.M. EST on September 3, 2010

Source: CQG, Inc. © 2010. All rights reserved worldwide.

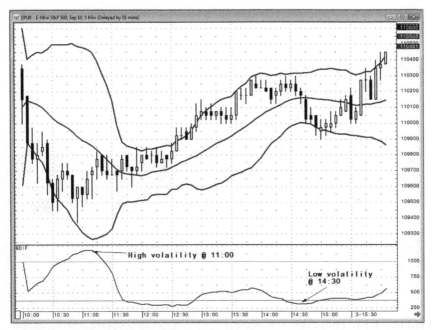

FIGURE 4.10   Five-Minute Chart of September 2010 CME Group E-Mini S&P 500 with Bollinger Band Difference Showing 3.75 as Low Volatility and 10.00 as High Volatility from 9:00 A.M. EST to 4:00 P.M. EST on September 3, 2010

Source: CQG, Inc. © 2010. All rights reserved worldwide.

cyclical nature of volatility, what is high volatility during a particular six-month lookback period will be low volatility during a different six-month lookback period (see Figures 4.11 and 4.12).

The next two mathematically derived historical volatility indicators were both developed by J. Welles Wilder Jr. in the 1970s and both require calculation of an asset's true range.[3] Wilder defined *true range* as the true high minus the true low, whereby:

True High = The greater of the current bar's high or the close of the previous bar

True Low = The lesser of the current bar's low or the close of the previous bar

By measuring the asset's true range as opposed to measuring from daily high to low—or vice versa—the data account for price gaps and are therefore a more accurate measure of an asset's historical volatility (see Figure 4.13).

FIGURE 4.11 Daily Chart of November 2008 CME Group Soybeans with Bollinger Band Difference Showing $4.00 as High Volatility and $1.20 as Low Volatility
Source: CQG, Inc. © 2010. All rights reserved worldwide.

FIGURE 4.12 Daily Chart of May 2006 CME Group Soybeans with Bollinger Band Difference Showing $0.90 as High Volatility and $0.27 as Low Volatility
Source: CQG, Inc. © 2010. All rights reserved worldwide.

FIGURE 4.13 Daily Chart of October 2010 Pit-Traded CME Group Live Cattle Futures Showing True Range

Source: CQG, Inc. © 2010. All rights reserved worldwide.

Now that we have defined the asset's true range, we can examine Wilder's volatility indicators. We will start with the simpler volatility calculation, average true range. The average true range takes the moving average of the asset's true range over a specified period. Typically, the average true range, or ATR, is calculated on a 14-period simple moving average. That stated, I have commonly seen it calculated on a 10-period simple moving average as well as a 14-period exponentially weighted moving average. As noted earlier, it's not magic; it's just math. Different periods and weightings of the moving averages tell slightly different stories regarding the historical volatility of an asset (see Figure 4.14).

The main limitations mentioned earlier regarding Bollinger Band difference also apply to average true range. To recap, the problem with both of these mathematically derived volatility indicators is that the numbers generated by the indicator have little or no significance to other assets, nor do they have significance for the same asset for either a longer or shorter timeframe, or even for the same asset over different periods of a 24-hour trading day. Wilder's other historical volatility indicator, average

FIGURE 4.14 Daily 2010 Chart of Apple Computer Comparing 10-Day Exponentially Weighted ATR with 14-Day Simple Weighted ATR

Source: CQG, Inc. © 2010. All rights reserved worldwide.

directional movement index, or ADX, solves these problems by giving us an indicator that is bounded, meaning that it is a percentage oscillator that cannot go below zero or above 100. Consequently, its volatility readings are applicable to all assets and on any timeframe. This is illustrated by Figure 4.15, in which high and low volatility in cash eurocurrency is objectively identified with 4-day ADX readings above 75 and below 25.

The average directional movement index is a moving average—commonly set to 10 periods—of directional movement index, or DMI. DMI is a momentum indicator that compares the current price with the previous price range. Specifically, DMI measures positive net directional movement or +DI vis-à-vis negative net directional movement or −DI over a specified lookback period (commonly set to 10 or 14 periods). Wilder defines positive net directional movement as an interval of time in which the majority of directional movement is higher than the previous time period. By contrast, negative net directional movement is an interval of time in which the majority of directional movement is lower than the previous time period.

FIGURE 4.15 Daily 2010 Cash Eurocurrency–U.S. Dollar Chart with 4-Day ATR, Bollinger Band Difference, and ADX
Source: CQG, Inc. © 2010. All rights reserved worldwide.

For positive price intervals, the formula is:

$$+DI = (+DI \div TR) \times 100$$

where $+DI$ = positive Directional Movement and TR = True Range
For negative price intervals, the formula is:

$$-DI = (-DI \div TR) \times 100$$

where $-DI$ = negative Directional Movement and TR = True Range
We can then calculate DIdiff and DIsum as follows:

$$DIdiff = |((+DI) - (-DI))|$$

and

$$DIsum = ((+DI) + (-DI))$$

Directional Movement Index, or DX, is calculated as:

$$DX = (DIdiff \div DIsum) \times 100$$

Finally, we calculate ADX as follows:

$$ADX = SUM[(+DI - (-DI)) \div (+DI + (-DI)), N] \div N$$

where N = the number of periods used in the calculation.

Although these objective, mathematically derived volatility indicators are extremely valuable in providing us with indicators that can augment both trend-following and countertrend systems, classical technical analysis is also useful in giving us a sense of where we are in the volatility cycle. For example, Figure 4.16 shows a prolonged, multi-month period of low volatility in CME wheat futures with a classical rectangular formation of sideways, horizontal support, and resistance, which ultimately resolves itself in a breakout to the upside and high volatility. By contrast, Figure 4.17 offers a shorter-term view of the cyclical nature of volatility in which a two-day vertical flagpole—of high volatility—leads to a 14-day,

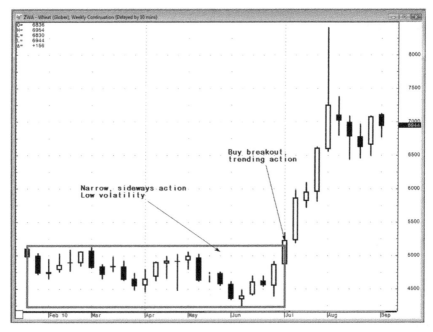

FIGURE 4.16 Weekly 2010 Front-Month Continuation Chart of CME Group Wheat Futures Showing Breakout from Low Volatility
Source: CQG, Inc. © 2010. All rights reserved worldwide.

FIGURE 4.17 August 2008 Daily Chart of CME Group Crude Oil Futures Showing Cyclical Nature of Volatility

Source: CQG, Inc. © 2010. All rights reserved worldwide.

low-volatility consolidation period in August 2008 CME Group crude oil futures.

Among the more popular of the objective, mathematically derived volatility indicators are historical and implied volatility of the traded asset. Regarding historical volatility, it is important to remember that Bollinger Band difference, ATR, and ADX are in fact all calculations of historical volatility of the asset. In addition to these aforementioned indicators, I also use a statistical measurement of historical volatility calculated as the standard deviation from the mean of the most recent 20 bars. The main limitation to all measures of historical volatility is that they are lagging indicators. In other words, because they are derived from historical data, they are always telling us more about the volatility of the asset in the past as opposed to its current volatility. Implied volatility addresses this problem by calculating volatility of asset based on current option premiums. It consequently tends to respond to changes in the volatility of the asset more quickly. Although there are numerous formulas for calculating implied volatility, the inputs I use are premiums of both puts and calls struck at-the-money as well as three strikes above and below the at-the-money

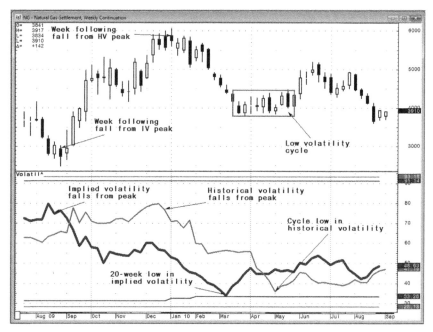

FIGURE 4.18 Weekly CME Group Natural Gas Futures Showing Implied and Historical Volatility
Source: CQG, Inc. © 2010. All rights reserved worldwide.

options for the three series of months closest to expiration.[4] Figure 4.18 is particularly useful because it not only gives us a chart of historical volatility, but perhaps more importantly, it charts the history of—and therefore the trend of—implied volatility.

A final, cautionary note regarding the cyclical nature of volatility as it relates to implied as opposed to historical volatility indicators: When markets anticipate the release of major fundamental reports (for example, quarterly earnings, central bank policy statements, crop reports, and so on), implied and historical volatility indicators tend to diverge. Historical volatility tends to decrease ahead of such reports as cash and futures traders stand aside because of market uncertainty. By contrast, options traders will purchase calls and puts—thereby increasing implied volatility—as protection against post-report spikes in volatility irrespective of market direction.

After the news event's release, market participants assimilate new information regarding the asset's value, and historical volatility tends to increase. On the other hand, the behavior of implied volatility is much less predictable after the release of market-moving news. If the news diverged

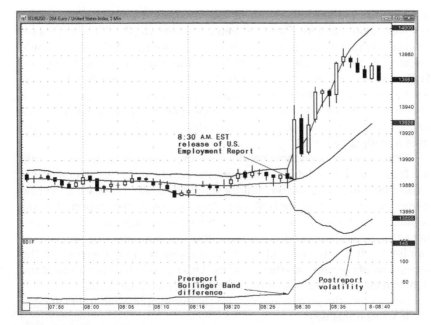

FIGURE 4.19 One-Minute Cash Euro–U.S. Dollar Chart Showing Increase in Historical Volatility after 8:30 A.M. Release of Monthly U.S. Employment Report on October 8, 2010
Source: CQG, Inc. © 2010. All rights reserved worldwide.

dramatically from pre-release consensus opinion, implied volatility will increase as options traders seek to participate in the embryonic phases of the fat tail event. On the other hand, if the news was within the range of market expectations, option premiums—as well as implied volatility—will decrease despite increases in historical volatility (see Figure 4.19).

BUILDING POSITIVE EXPECTANCY MODELS WITH VOLATILITY INDICATORS

As stated earlier, we can use volatility indicators in two ways: first, to identify periods of low volatility and employ trend-following indicators to take advantage of when the market breaks out of its low-volatility cycle; and second, to identify periods of high volatility and use countertrend tools to participate in the asset's reversion to the mean.

Although there is a vast multitude of ways in which to combine trend-following tools with volatility indicators so as to participate in instances in which the market breaks out of low volatility, I introduce the reader to a basic example here. First we need a mathematically objective tool for determining that we are in a low-volatility environment. Although we could use any of the tools mentioned earlier in this chapter, we will focus on ADX since its definition of low volatility is universally applicable to any asset and all trading timeframes. While there is nothing magical about a 10-period ADX, we will stick with it simply because of its popularity. We will also define *low volatility* as times during which the 10-period ADX gives a reading below 20.

Next, we need a mathematically objective criterion to define a breakout from this low-volatility environment. Again, there are innumerable ways of defining this breakout, but for simplicity's sake I define it as a close above the 20-period upper Bollinger Band or below the 20-period lower Bollinger Band. Finally, we need a mathematically objective risk management rule along with a criterion for exiting with profits. For the sake of simplicity, after entry we will set a trailing stop for long positions at the lowest low of the previous three trading days and for short positions at the highest high of the previous three trading days (see Figure 4.20).

Using CQG, the programming code for this simple trend-following system is written this way:

```
Long Entry:

Close(@)[-1] > BHI(@,Sim,20,2.00)[-1] AND ADX(@,10)[-2] <20

Long Exit, set "Price" field to:

LoLevel(@,3)[-1]

Short Entry:

Close(@)[-1]< BLO(@,Sim,20,2.00)[-1] AND ADX(@,10)[-2] < 20

Short Exit, set "Price" field to:

HiLevel(@,3)[-1]
```

For countertrend systems that use volatility indicators to help identify setups with a high probability of success, we need evidence of trend exhaustion. Although this does not guarantee protection against a false trend reversal signal, at least it decreases the odds of such an occurrence. In other words, despite the 10-period ADX signaling high volatility by giving a reading greater than 50, the asset could generate such readings day after day as we continue to fight a persistently trending market. By adding a

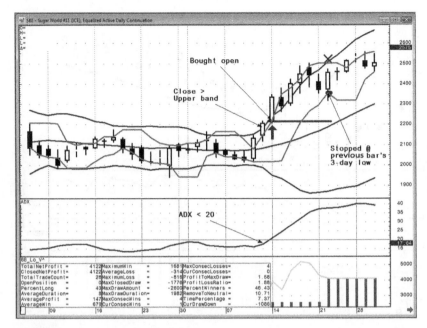

FIGURE 4.20 Equalized Active Daily Continuation Chart for ICE Sugar Futures Contract with ADX Low-Volatility Breakout System. Data Show Results from January 1, 2000, to December 31, 2009

Note: Trade summary includes $10 round-turn trade deduction for slippage and commissions.

Source: CQG, Inc. © 2010. All rights reserved worldwide.

criterion that a high-volatility market that is trending lower needs to violate the previous day's highs before signaling a buy (or violating the previous day's lows before signaling a sell), it reduces this risk. We will revisit the dangers of anticipating the signal in great detail throughout Chapter 9, but for now it is essential to avoid developing high-volatility trading models that try to pick tops and bottoms merely because the volatility indicator signals a high volatility reading. In addition to requiring that ADX signals a high volatility reading, I added a percentage oscillator (Relative Strength Index) to ensure that the asset has in fact become overbought or oversold.

Since we are fighting the trend, our stop loss exit is set to the previous bar's low for long positions and previous bar's high for short positions. This is a tighter risk management criterion than the three-bar high or low used in our low-volatility breakout model because countertrend signals are generated in a high-volatility—and therefore high-risk—environment. Finally, if the asset reverts to the mean, our model exits with profits at the previous bar's 20-period simple moving average (see Figure 4.21).

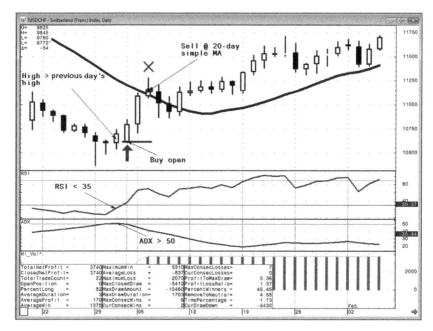

FIGURE 4.21 Cash Daily U.S. Dollar–Swiss Franc Chart with ADX High-Volatility Countertrend System. Data Show Results from January 1, 2000, to December 31, 2009

Note: Trade summary includes $10 round-turn trade deduction for slippage and commissions.

Source: CQG, Inc. © 2010. All rights reserved worldwide.

Using CQG, the programming code for this high-volatility countertrend system is written this way:

```
Long Entry:

ADX(@,10)[-1] > 50 AND High(@)[-1] > High(@)[-2] AND RSI
(@,9)[-1] < 35

Long Exit:

LoLevel(@,1)[-1] OR MA(@,Sim,20)[-1]

Short Entry:

ADX(@,10)[-1] > 50 AND Low(@)[-1] < Low(@)[-2] AND RSI
(@,9)[-1] > 65

Short Exit:

HiLevel(@,1)[-1] OR MA(@,Sim,20)[-1]
```

A final word of caution regarding the incorporation of volatility indicators into countertrend trading models: Be careful. Despite the protective fail-safe criteria that were built into the high-volatility mean reversion system, because these are countertrend systems, they are by definition subject to fat tail event risk. In other words, when a market shifts—without warning—from a normal trending environment to a parabolic trending environment, these systems are subject to risks, which could potentially overshadow rewards, sometimes dramatically. For example, on January 8, 1980, March 1980 Comex Silver traded below the previous day's low, the 9-day RSI reading was a dramatically overbought 92.82, and the 10-day ADX was at 82.27. The criteria required to sell the market were met so our countertrend system would have sold the January 9 open at $33.50. Although our protective buy stop for January 10 would have been set at the January 9th high of $33.50, silver, unfortunately, opened locked limit up that day. Worse still, the market traded locked limit up through January 21. Finally, on January 22, our sell stop would have been elected at $40.50, for a loss of $35,000 per contract (see Figure 4.22).

Admittedly, it is possible for trend-following traders to endure a fat tail event risk scenario, but it is much less likely than for those consistently

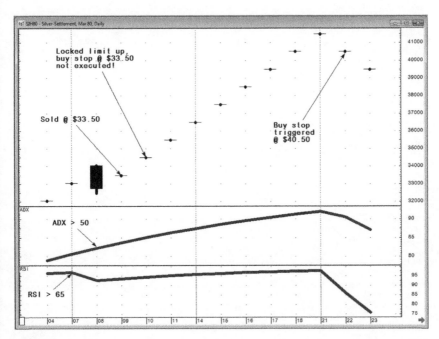

FIGURE 4.22 March 1980 Daily Chart of Comex Silver Futures Showing Fat Tail Event Risk

Source: CQG, Inc. © 2010. All rights reserved worldwide.

using countertrend trading models. Despite the fact that by definition option premiums will be most expensive when markets signal high volatility, buying options remains the safest antidote to problems of fat tail event risk for countertrend traders. Or as I like to say, everyone wants to surf the wave, but no one wants to surf during a Category 5 hurricane.

FINAL THOUGHTS

Volatility studies are indispensable in defining current risk and reward as well as helping to model future risk and reward through analysis of where the asset is in regard to its historical volatility cycle. Also, although it is possible to develop robust positive expectancy trend-following and countertrend trading models without the volatility indicators showcased throughout this chapter, whenever asked how to make a model more robust, I always begin by examining these tools.

CHAPTER 5

Trading the Markets and Not the Money

What does a man do when he sets out to make the stock market pay for a sudden need? Why, he merely hopes. He gambles. He therefore runs much greater risks than he would if he were speculating intelligently.

—Edwin Lefèvre

Why do speculators end up trading the money instead of the market's dynamics? This chapter explores various ways speculators trade the money, including superimposing artificial monetary profit targets onto the market irrespective of conditions, exiting profitable trades because of monetary—as opposed to market-derived—targets, and placing stops too close to entry price because of fear of loss irrespective of market volatility.

TEN THOUSAND DOLLARS IS A LOT OF MONEY!

Bernard Baruch once stated, "Nobody ever lost money taking a profit." To which I respond, "No, they lost all their money on the next three trades." If all we do is take small profits, then we have nothing to offset the inevitable losses. Although many books advise traders to cut losses and let profits run, the problem is we always think about the money instead of market dynamics, and so when we have significant unrealized profits we translate them into monetary terms and end up exiting trades prematurely. Chapter 6 outlines specific methods for enabling traders to simultaneously take money off the table while letting part of our position run. By contrast, the goal of this chapter is showing the pitfalls for intermediate to long-term trend traders in not allowing profits to run.

It is only natural for speculators to translate unrealized profits into monetary terms since we all entered the business of trading to make money. But that which is psychologically natural and comfortable leads to failure. That which is unnatural and uncomfortable leads to success. Stated more simply, thinking about the money is poison. Trade the market, not the money. The markets offer examples every year of large trends morphing into monster trends, yet year after year inexperienced traders continue to think about the money and settle for small gains despite huge profit opportunities.

One of my favorite examples of large unrealized profits turning into obscenely large realized profits is the 2008–2009 CME Group natural gas futures market. On July 8, 2008, the market broke significant support and many technical traders sold at the $12.628 level. Within a week, the market broke the $11.53 level, which represented an unrealized profit of $10,980 per contract. Ten thousand nine hundred and eighty dollars is a lot of money to many of us, especially when generated over five trading days (see Figure 5.1). But the market does not know what "a lot of money" means; it only knows that it is going from $12.628 down to $3.155 over the next nine months and it is going to offer long-term trend-following traders well over $80,000 per contract. The question is, are you going to take what the market is offering by allowing its own internal dynamics to determine when you will exit with profits, or are you going to superimpose an artificial ceiling on profits based on an irrational internal psychological bias regarding how much money over what period of time is too much, too fast (see Figure 5.2)?

Why do traders cut unrealized profits short instead of letting them run? Fear of leaving money on the table, or worse, fear of allowing a significant unrealized profit to turn into a significant realized loss. Fear of leaving money on the table is quite debilitating to the psyche of traders because you had the opportunity to capture larger profit levels and failed to capitalize on it. Many times as the market falls from its highs, traders will place their exit orders at these old highs. At this point, one of two things can happen: First, the market can plow through those previous highs, enabling us to minimize our regret by selling the highs. This typically happens because the market is destined for significantly higher levels and we soon regret our premature exit. The other possibility is that the market fails to retest its old highs and our rigid focus on exiting at the old high prevents us from protecting significant unrealized profits by moving stops to logical

FIGURE 5.1 August 2008 Daily CME Group Natural Gas Futures Move Over $10,000 in Five Trading Days

Source: CQG, Inc. © 2010. All rights reserved worldwide.

technical support levels. It is this second scenario, in which our focus on exiting at a specific profit level blinds us to risk of reversals that can result in allowing significant unrealized profits to turn into significant realized losses. In either case, we are focusing on the asset's price irrespective of value.

The solution is to realize from the outset that we will almost never sell the highs or buy the lows and instead of focusing on the elusive perfect entry or exit price, shift our focus onto trading based on the market's dynamics (as defined by support, resistance, and volatility). Or as I like to say, "Always trade value; never trade price." Since fear of leaving money on the table leads to our premature exit of profitable positions, our positive expectancy model should include exit rules based on the dynamics of market action instead of artificial monetary price targets. If fear of allowing a significant unrealized profit to turn into a significant realized loss forces us to exit profitable positions prematurely, then incorporating rules for moving stops to breakeven as soon as the market moves significantly in our favor should be built into our positive expectancy models.

FIGURE 5.2 Rolling Front-Month Weekly CME Group Natural Gas Futures Move Over $80,000 before Achieving a Significant Technical Reversal
Source: CQG, Inc. © 2010. All rights reserved worldwide.

Another argument often stated in relation to trading the money is that "There must be some price at which you would be willing to exit your position." If I am short the asset and using an intermediate- to long-term trend-following model, then yes, the price I would be willing to exit would be zero. Otherwise, no, there is absolutely no arbitrarily derived monetary profit level at which I would be willing to sacrifice my profitable trend-following positions. This is because I have trained myself to be absolutely flexible regarding market prices. Our natural bias as traders is set by recent or current prices. Instead of biases related to current, recent, or even historical prices, I have trained myself to imagine the market trading at any and every price. It is because I unequivocally accept that any price is possible that I never hesitate in placing stop loss orders after entering a position, because I acknowledge that certain possible prices would result in my trading account blowing up. If we admit that any price is possible and that certain prices would result in the termination of our careers as traders, it is illogical for us to simultaneously dismiss the possibility of prices that could catapult our trading careers to new levels of success. Of course, just as our account would blow up long before the market reached its ultimate high or low, by the same token we will never capture the ultimate high or low when exiting on profitable positions, but as they say, "You can make a heck of a lot of money by being less than perfect."

BABY NEEDS A NEW PAIR OF SHOES

The phrase "Baby needs a new pair of shoes" originated in the casinos; specifically, it is the mantra of dice-tossing craps players. The fact that this phrase is attributed to those with the odds skewed against them is especially instructive to speculators wanting to trade like a casino. Focusing on a specific monetary goal, whether it is generic, like a thousand dollars a day, or specific, like a $3,500 mortgage payment, is equally poisonous to successful speculation because we are superimposing an artificial goal upon market activity. The market does not know or care whether we need to make $300 or $3 million, and our thinking about the market in these artificial terms blinds us from what the market is likely to offer based upon its internal dynamics (volatility, support, and resistance). To trade like a casino, we need to think about profits in terms of probabilities instead of personal monetary needs.

I am extremely familiar with the "baby needs a new pair of shoes" approach to speculative trading because when I first bought a seat on the New York Futures Exchange in 1987, the stated goal of our fledging corporation was to generate $2,500 per week from trading. We were thinking about the money, not the markets. Needless to say, that monetary goal acted as an albatross around my neck, blinding me to market dynamics and opportunities. It seemed like a logical approach for a business model, but trading is not a logical enterprise where X number of hours of hard work translates into Y salary. It is instead a business of attuning oneself to the emotions of other market participants and flowing seamlessly with their waves of greed, fear, and boredom. Sometimes the market offers $2,500 a week; sometimes it offers $500, sometimes $5 million. We are habituated to think in terms of steady monthly flows of income because our expenses come in steady increments . . . but the market does not care about us, our bills, or if our babies need new pairs of shoes. Forget about monetary goals; just take what the market is giving.

Of course, now more than 20 years later, I know from painful experience this truth of trading the markets and not the money. Now, whenever I start a month with gangbuster profits, friends that do not understand the nature of markets will say, "Wow, it's May 6 and you are already up 9 percent for the month? You should stop trading so you don't give it all back." This, too, is trading the money and not the markets. The markets do not know that you are already up 9 percent, have had five winners in a row, are overdue for a losing trade, and so on, nor do they care. They are offering you the opportunity to participate in their game of probabilities 24 hours a day, every week, every month. Whether you personally superimpose some artificial limitation upon these probabilities is entirely up to you. It has absolutely nothing to do with the markets and what they are offering.

At the other end of the irrational psychological spectrum is the cliché that you can be more aggressive or reckless after significant trading profits because you are now playing with the house's money. This, too, is trading the money instead of the markets. Since the probabilities of our positive expectancy trading models do not miraculously improve after profitable trades, we should not abandon our adherence to rules of risk management. As soon as you place the trade, even before exiting with realized profits, those unrealized gains are *your* money and need to be treated in the same casino paradigm manner as all monies in your trading account.

It is probably even more common to trade the money after a loss or series of losses. We suddenly abandon market dynamics and probabilities in hopes of regaining the breakeven level in account equity. This particular irrational attitude toward trading is especially dangerous to speculators because we now not only trade the money, but also abandon the goal of winning in favor of trading not to lose. Instead, after a string of losses, we should ask the following questions: "Are we adhering to a robust positive expectancy model?" and "Are we continuing to obey stringent rules of risk management?" If the answer to these questions is yes, then we should continue trading the markets in exactly the same manner as we would after a profit or even a string of profitable trades.

TRADING WITH SCARED MONEY

Whenever we place stops based upon monetary considerations instead of the dynamics of market volatility, we are also trading the money and not the market. There is a caveat to this rule of monetary stop loss placement, namely that we should not risk more than 1 to 2 percent of assets under management on any particular trading idea. At first glance, the 1 percent rule looks a lot like trading the money. The distinction is that we need to overlay the 1 percent rule on top of our market analysis so that we only execute trades in which market-derived stop levels are less than 1 percent of assets under management. In this way, we adhere to prudent risk management parameters while simultaneously allowing the market and not the money to determine where stops should be placed. If this means trading 200 shares of Microsoft at $25 a share instead of 200 shares of Google at

TABLE 5.1 Volatility-Derived Position-Sizing Limits

Asset	10-Day ATR	Max. Position Size
E-Mini S&P 500	$775.00	2
Corn	$1,137.50	1
Gold	$2,920.00	0
Crude Oil	$2,010.00	0
US T-Notes	$968.75	2
GOOG	$10.18	100
MSFT	$0.48	4,000
EURUSD	$1,840.00	100,000
AUDUSD	$1,300.00	100,000

Ten-day ATR calculated on November 18, 2010, for a $100,000 account, using 2 percent of assets under management rule.

Note: Position sizing shown does not account for correlations between assets.

Source: CQG, Inc. © 2010. All rights reserved worldwide.

$600 a share, then so be it. It is better to allow the probabilities of your positive expectancy model to play out in your favor than to superimpose an artificial monetary stop loss level onto a higher-volatility asset simply because it is more "exciting" (see Table 5.1).

Placement of stop loss orders at monetary thresholds irrespective of the asset's volatility is known in trading vernacular as "trading with scared money." Because they are afraid of large losses, traders place stop loss orders too close to entry prices, therefore virtually guaranteeing their endurance of numerous unnecessary small losses. We must instead be willing to accept the possibility of losses in order to enjoy the profitability of positive expectancy models. This not only means initial stop loss placement based upon market-derived volatility levels, but also moving of stops only after market-derived indicators justify their adjustment.

TIME IS MONEY

If you artificially superimpose a time-based exit criterion onto your trading model, you are by definition no longer exiting exclusively based upon the dynamics of the asset. To me, this is eerily similar to trading the money instead of the market. Although I freely admit that shorter-term traders want to avoid overnight or weekend event risk, it must simultaneously be acknowledged that it is counterintuitive and a wholly artificially imposed constraint to exit trades with unrealized profits simply because a clock has ticked one second beyond 4 P.M. Eastern Standard Time. Exiting profitable trades because of this artificially derived time constraint flies in the face of cutting losses and letting profits run.

That stated, I, too, have exited short-term mean reversion system trades because of various time-related issues such as lack of overnight liquidity, weekend event risk, and so on. Therefore, I have no problem with exiting short-term mean reversion trades because the clock has ticked forward beyond a predesignated cutoff point. But I do recognize that using the clock in this fashion is a form of trading the money instead of the markets. I consequently must ensure these time-based exit models enjoy higher winning percentages than models that allow profits to run in order to compensate for typically inferior average profit to average loss ratios.

Figure 5.3 shows a short-term trend-following system in which an exit is triggered when the market breaks the highest high or lowest low of the previous three trading days. Now look at Figure 5.4, which is a comparison of our original short-term trend-following system to a modified version whereby a time-derived exit criterion has been added

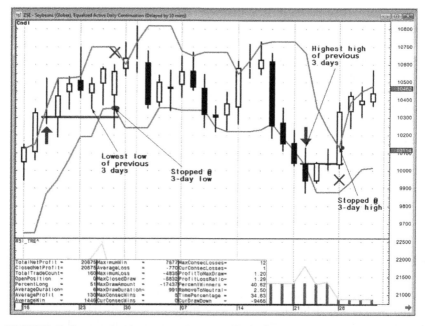

FIGURE 5.3 Equalized Active Daily Continuation Chart for CME Group Soybean Futures Contract with RSI Trend System Where Stop Is Placed at Lowest Low or Highest High of Previous Three Trading Days

Note: Trade summary includes data from January 1, 2000, to December 31, 2009, and includes $10 round-turn deductions for slippage and commissions.

Source: CQG, Inc. © 2010. All rights reserved worldwide.

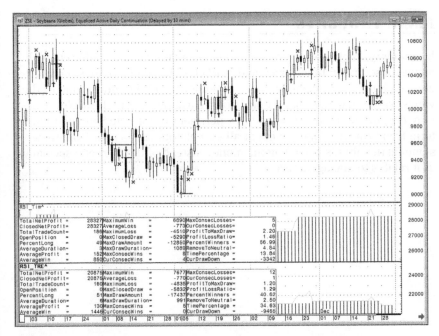

FIGURE 5.4 Equalized Active Daily Continuation Chart for CME Group Soybean Futures Contract Comparing Original RSI Trend System with Modified Version with Time-Based Exit Criterion

Note: Trade summary includes data from January 1, 2000, to December 31, 2009, and includes $10 round-turn deductions for slippage and commissions.

Source: CQG, Inc. © 2010. All rights reserved worldwide.

that forces an exit after the position has been held for more than one trading day.

Using CQG, the programming code for this time-based exit criterion is written this way:

```
Long Exit: BarsSinceEntry(@,0,All,ThisTradeOnly)
> 1 OR Price field set to: "LoLevel(@,3)[-1]"

Short Exit: BarsSinceEntry(@,0,All,ThisTradeOnly)
> 1 OR Price field set to: "HiLevel(@,3)[-1]"
```

Looking at the "PercentWinners" row, notice how the time-based exit improved our winning trade percentage from 40.62 to 56.99 percent. On the other hand, looking at the "AverageWin" and "AverageLoss" columns, we see the time-derived exit criterion simultaneously eroding the average profit to average loss ratio from 1.88:1 to 1.10:1 (see Figure 5.4).

FINAL THOUGHTS

In summary, I acknowledge that various speculators employ different techniques based upon timeframes and market action they are most comfortable exploiting (for example, mean reversion), and therefore some of the views espoused in this chapter may not seem applicable to them. Nevertheless, despite the material being most pertinent to intermediate- and long-term trend traders, I am confident all speculators can benefit from understanding the pitfalls in trading the money instead of the market, especially as it relates to managing risk.

CHAPTER 6

Minimizing Trader Regret

I see it all perfectly; there are two possible situations
—one can either do this or that. My honest opinion
and friendly advice is this: Do it or do not do it—you
will regret both.

—Soren Kierkegaard

C an anything be done to make adherence to disciplined, rule-based trading easier? Since the most common reason for abandonment of discipline is regret over losses or missed opportunities, this chapter offers various techniques to counteract these self-destructive tendencies. Particular emphasis is placed on specific techniques to minimize regret for both trend-following as well as countertrend traders.

THE SOFTER SIDE OF DISCIPLINE

Chapter 3 examined unwavering discipline as a prerequisite for our adherence to positive expectancy models and robust risk management methodologies. Here we will augment that work with what I like to call the softer side of discipline. These are techniques that make adherence to positive expectancy models and risk management more palatable. These techniques are consequently not necessarily intended to make positive expectancy models more robust, but merely to make sticking with them easier instead. Because each of these tools tries to minimize the emotion of regret that inevitably accompanies any and all trading decisions, my umbrella term for all these techniques is *regret minimization*. To explain the technique, let us return to the opaque urn introduced in Chapter 3. Remember that the urn contained 57 green marbles and 43 red marbles, and therefore the probability favored our betting on the green marble. The problem in consistently betting on the green marble was that occasionally we would pull out a number of red marbles consecutively. But what if we could cut the green marbles in half? No, it would not increase the probability of drawing out a whole red marble, nor even the number of whole green marbles. It would instead increase the number of times we pulled out a green piece as opposed to a red piece. This is what all the regret minimization techniques try to accomplish and what was alluded to earlier.

The other common denominator linking the techniques explored throughout this chapter is the assumption that traders are sufficiently capitalized so that the trading of multiple contracts will not result in their risking more than 1 to 2 percent of assets under management. This assumption of adequate capitalization introduces the question of how much is adequate—defined here by using the 1 to 2 percent rule—as well as the advantages and disadvantages in respect to levels of capitalization.[1] Another disclaimer is that none of these techniques is suggested as the only way of handling regret minimization issues. They are offered instead as jumping off points from which readers are encouraged to do further research. My final disclaimer applies only to trend followers, namely that the ability of trend followers to use regret minimization techniques is predicated on the market moving in our favor after entry. In instances in which we enter a trade and the market immediately moves against us, we will be stopped out with a loss and will not have an opportunity to use the techniques described further on.

ISSUES FOR TREND FOLLOWERS

Feelings of regret can arise for trend-following traders in a multitude of ways such as allowing significant unrealized profits to turn into significant realized losses, exiting trades with statistically significant profits only to watch from the sidelines as the market moves relentlessly in the direction of our prematurely exited position, as well as letting small manageable losses turn into large catastrophic ones. Although there is no single magic bullet to resolve all of these issues, I hope to offer some robust methodologies to aid in minimizing the regret surrounding these issues.

Trade: ICE Brent Crude Oil

Traditional trend-following rules remind us that the trend is your friend and simultaneously warn that we should cut losses and let winners run.

How can we reconcile these two seemingly antithetical ideas? Looking at Figure 6.1, we see that ICE July 2010 Brent Crude Oil is in a historically low-volatility environment as defined by its 10-day average true range. As discussed in Chapter 4, this favors implementing a trend-following breakout model, so we place buy and sell stops at classical technical horizontal support and resistance levels in hopes of participating in a breakout from this low-volatility environment. As shown in Figure 6.1, we placed a buy stop at $88.50 and a sell stop at $84.98. On April 29, 2010, the market broke through its resistance and we bought two contracts for $88.51. Our initial sell stop loss order could be placed at various levels—depending on our trading personality and timeframe as described in Chapter 3—including the previous day's low, the three-day low, or even the support level of $84.98. The April 30, 2010, close at $88.46 was so close to our entry level that no protective (risk-reducing) action could be taken. By contrast, on May 3, 2010, when the market settled at $89.87, this significant unrealized profit of $1,360 per contract enabled us to take profits on 50 percent of our position at the next open as well as raise our sell stop to the breakeven level of $88.51. Although there are numerous ways of defining a significant unrealized profit level, here we use 50 percent of the market's 10-day average true range. Since the previous day's average true range was $1.64, our unrealized mark-to-market profit of $1.36 exceeded our criteria for exiting 50 percent of the position and raising the stop on the remainder to breakeven.

At this point we have realized a partial profit of $1,360; we are allowing profits on the second contract to run (thereby trading the market and not the money, as described throughout Chapter 5) while simultaneously preventing a significant unrealized profit—as defined by the average true range—to turn into a significant realized loss. Two things could happen: If the market experiences a powerful breakout, then it will not be weak enough to trigger our breakeven stop on the other contract, allowing us to let the winner run. If it is a moderate breakout, it will trigger our stop loss, but at least we minimized feelings of regret by booking a notable profit on half of the position. This second possibility is what actually occurred. A moderate breakout ensued. Nevertheless, by being proactive and opportunistic, we booked a decent profit on half our position instead of allowing a significant unrealized profit to turn into a significant realized loss.

But after our breakeven stop triggered on May 4, 2010, we still remained in a low-volatility environment (as defined by the market's average true range). Consequently, on May 5, 2010, when our sell stop triggered, we sold two contracts at $84.97. The settlement price that day was $83.27, so we exited one contract on the next open at $83.75 for a profit of $1,220 and lowered the buy stop for May 6, 2010, on our other contract to the breakeven price of $84.97. Because this *was* a significant breakout, our buy stop was not triggered that day, allowing us to trail the stop based on our psychological temperament as defined in Chapter 3.

Returning to Figure 6.1, notice that I have shown multiple potential trailing stop styles based on various trader personalities. For example, if one feels the greatest regret watching significant unrealized profits evaporate before being stopped out, you could trail with a buy stop set to the previous day's high. If you chose this tight stop strategy, you exited the second contract on May 10, 2010, at $81.70 for a profit of $3,270. If your personality is more comfortable with letting unrealized profits evaporate in exchange for occasionally capturing bigger profits, you would keep your buy stop at the breakeven level until the highest high of the previous three days was below your short entry price. If you chose to use this three-day trailing stop, it would have been stopped out on May 12, 2010, at $82.83, for a profit $2,140. Finally, if your temperament is even more acclimated to sacrificing unrealized gains so as to enjoy an occasional home run win, you could use a five-day trailing stop. In this particular example, the five-day trailing stop proved well suited to the market action and would have exited this second contract on May 27, 2010, at $74.23, for a profit of $10,740. The key point here is not whether trailing the market with a three-day stop is inferior or superior to various alternatives; it is instead that irrespective of how we chose to trail the market, this regret minimization strategy

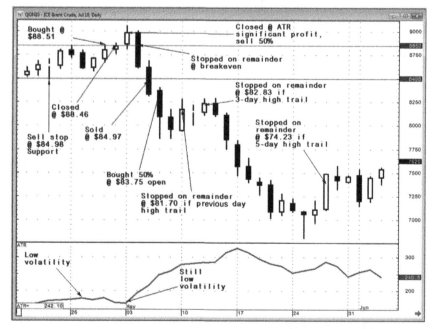

FIGURE 6.1 July 2010 Daily ICE Brent Crude Oil Futures Contract
Source: CQG, Inc. © 2010. All rights reserved worldwide.

TABLE 6.1 Sold 2 July Brent Crude Oil @ $84.97

Trailing Stop	Profit on 50%	Profit on Remainder
1-day	$1,220.00	$3,270.00
3-day	$1,220.00	$2,140.00
5-day	$1,220.00	$10,740.00

Note: Performance results shown excluding commissions and slippage.
Source: CQG, Inc. © 2010. All rights reserved worldwide.

prevented a significant unrealized profit from turning into a significant realized loss while simultaneously allowing profits on at least part of the position to run (see Figure 6.1).

Trade: Cash U.S. Dollar–Canadian Dollar

Our next trade is a false breakout signal in cash U.S. dollar–Canadian dollar (USD/CAD). All of the criteria for entry are the same, namely our 10-day average true range signaled low volatility; we placed a buy stop at the horizontal resistance level above the September 13, 2010, high of 1.0372 and below the September 17, 2010, low at 1.0215. On September 22, 2010, our sell stop order at 1.0214 triggered a short position of 200,000 base currency. Unfortunately, the breakout turned out to be false and we were either stopped out when the market violated the previous day's high at 1.0334 for a loss of $2,400 or when it violated its three-day high at 1.0353 for a loss of $2,760 or when it broke its longer-term resistance on September 23, 2010, at 1.0373 for a loss of $3,180. Although in this particular instance the tightest risk criterion represented the best decision, the main point is that our disciplined placement of the stop loss order prevented a manageable loss from needlessly turning into a catastrophic one (see Figure 6.2).

Our July 2010 ICE Brent Crude Oil led to a continuation of the low-volatility environment and enabled us to participate in the real breakout in the opposite direction. By contrast, the September 2010 cash USD–CAD *false* bearish breakdown led to a continuation of the low volatility reading in average true range, but offered a potentially tradable downside breakout. I say "potentially" tradable because this all depended on how tightly we managed risk. By setting our stop to the previous day's high, we endured the smallest loss on the false downside breakout. However, when we sold 200,000 USD–CAD on October 1, 2010, at 1.0190, if we set our buy stop at the previous day's high, we were stopped out for a second time on

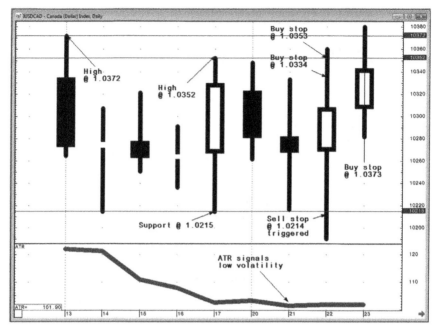

FIGURE 6.2 Daily Cash USD–CAD Chart
Source: CQG, Inc. © 2010. All rights reserved worldwide.

October 5, 2010, at 1.0246, for a loss of $1,120. By contrast, those willing to take more risk by setting their stops at either the three- or five-day highs were not stopped out for a loss on October 5, 2010, and so on October 6, 2010, when the market settled at 1.0111, they enjoyed a statistically significant unrealized gain as defined by exceeding 50 percent of the 10-day average true range. They consequently exited half their position on the open of

TABLE 6.2 Sold 200,000 Cash USD–CAD @ 1.0214	
Trailing Stop	**Loss**
1-day	($2,400.00)
3-day	($2,760.00)
5-day	($3,180.00)

Note: Performance results excluding slippage.
Source: CQG, Inc. © 2010. All rights reserved worldwide.

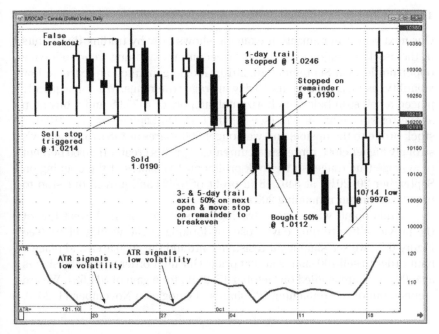

FIGURE 6.3 Daily Cash USD–CAD Chart

Source: CQG, Inc. © 2010. All rights reserved worldwide.

October 7, 2010, at 1.0112, for a profit of $780 and were able to lower their buy stop on the remainder to the breakeven entry price level of 1.0190, where they were stopped out later that day. As an aside, because we were unwilling to allow a significant unrealized profit to turn into a significant realized loss, we were stopped out at breakeven on the remainder of our position and so did not participate in the move to cycle lows on October 14, 2010, at the 0.9976 area (see Figure 6.3).

TABLE 6.3 Sold 200,000 Cash USD–CAD @ 1.0190

Trailing Stop	Profit or Loss on 50%	Profit on Remainder
1-day	($1,120.00)	Not Applicable
3-day	$780.00	$0.00
5-day	$780.00	$0.00

Note: Performance results excluding slippage.

Source: CQG, Inc. © 2010. All rights reserved worldwide.

Trade: Google

Our next regret minimization example shows how by trading three units of the asset, we enjoy even greater freedom in exploiting trend-following opportunities. On September 16, 2010, Google generated an extreme low volatility, as measured by its 10-day average true range. We consequently placed a sell stop below its horizontal support of $475.08 and a buy stop above resistance at $484.75 (see Figure 6.4). On September 17, 2010, the stock broke to the upside, and we bought 300 shares at $484.76. That day's strongly higher close represented unrealized profits greater than 50 percent of average true range, so we took profits on 100 shares at the opening on September 20, 2010, at $492.18 (a profit of $742) and moved our stop to breakeven on our remaining 200 shares.

At this point, we continue trailing our sell stop at the lowest low of the previous five trading days. Also, by looking at the weekly chart (see Figure 6.5), we see significant resistance around the $600 area and place a limit order to sell 100 shares at that price. Our limit order to sell 100 shares at $600 per share is filled on October 15, 2010, for a gain of $11,524. We are stopped out of our remaining 100 shares of Google on November 11, 2010,

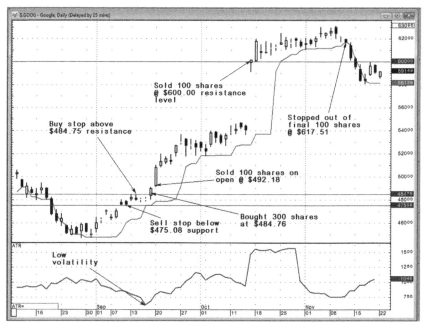

FIGURE 6.4 Daily Chart of Google Inc.
Source: CQG, Inc. © 2010. All rights reserved worldwide.

FIGURE 6.5 Weekly Chart of Google Inc.
Source: CQG, Inc. © 2010. All rights reserved worldwide.

when the stock takes out its five-day low at $617.51, generating a profit of $13,275.

ISSUES FOR MEAN REVERSION TRADERS

There are many reasons for mean reversion traders to feel regret. Some are easily resolved by techniques introduced in this chapter, whereas others are quite challenging. By definition, mean reversion traders tend to exit when the asset reverts to the mean, so there is a natural tendency for these methodologies to experience regret whenever positions they exit extend into significant trending opportunities. For example, Figure 6.6 shows a typical mean reversion set-up in which the nine-day relative strength index of cash euro–U.S. dollar (EUR–USD) crosses below overbought levels on November 5, 2010. Our mean reversion trader then sells the November 8, 2010, open at 1.4060, placing a protective buy stop at the previous day's high of 1.4248 and a limit order to exit with profits at the previous day's

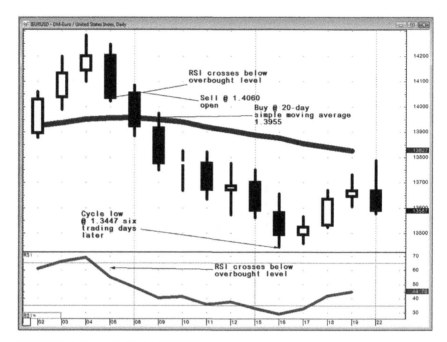

FIGURE 6.6 Daily Cash EUR–USD chart
Source: CQG, Inc. © 2010. All rights reserved worldwide.

20-day simple moving average at 1.3955 (see Figure 6.6). Despite our mean reversion trader realizing this high-probability profit of $1,050 per 100,000 base currency that same trading day, over the following six trading days the market continued trending down to its cycle low of 1.3447, which represented the potential for significantly greater additional profits.

Although it is possible to modify traditional mean reversion models so they minimize regret over trending market action, in doing so we typically shift away from the shorter trade duration and higher winning percentage type of market behavior that these traders were trying to capitalize on in the first place. Consequently, my answer for traders experiencing these types of regret was introduced in Chapter 3, where we discussed eating your own lunch.

Another disclaimer regarding mean reversion regret minimization techniques is that they should not be confused with adding to a losing position, averaging down, or dollar-cost averaging, which are antithetical to sound risk management techniques. When adding to a losing position, we are trying to extricate ourselves from a loss by lowering our average entry level. For example, let us assume in July 2007 we bought 1,000 shares of Citigroup Inc. at $50 per share. By October 2007, the stock had dropped to $40,

but instead of realizing a manageable—though admittedly painful—loss of
$10,000, we decide to buy 2,000 shares at $40 per share, thereby lowering our breakeven price on all 3,000 shares to $43.33. In November 2007,
Citigroup dropped to $30, representing an unrealized loss of nearly $40,000.
Because we were unwilling to accept such a large loss, we bought 4,000
shares at $30 per share, thereby lowering our breakeven price on all 7,000
shares to $35.71. In March 2008, the stock dropped to $20 per share, an unrealized loss of $109,970. Instead of accepting the loss, we decide to buy
8,000 shares at $20, lowering our average per share price to $27.33 on all
15,000 shares. By November 12, 2008, Citigroup was obviously insolvent
and would require a bailout by the U.S. government to survive (that bailout
was officially approved on November 23, 2008). Its drop to $10 per share
meant an unrealized loss of almost $260,000. Assuming we continued this
catastrophic averaging down game, we would have bought 16,000 shares
at $10, lowering our average share price to $18.39 on all 31,000 shares. By
March 2009, the stock dropped to $1 per share, for an unrealized loss of
$539,090 (see Figure 6.7).

The position-sizing method commonly known as *pyramiding* also differs from both averaging down, or adding to a losing position, as well as

FIGURE 6.7 Weekly Chart of Citigroup Inc.
Source: CQG, Inc. © 2010. All rights reserved worldwide.

TABLE 6.4 Averaging Down with Citigroup Inc.

Share Price	Shares Purchased	Avg Share Price	Unrealized Loss
$50.00	1,000	$50.00	$0.00
$40.00	2,000	$43.33	($10,000.00)
$30.00	4,000	$35.71	($39,990.00)
$20.00	8,000	$27.33	($109,970.00)
$10.00	16,000	$18.39	($259,950.00)
$1.00	Not Applicable	$18.39	($539,090.00)

Note: Performance results excluding commissions and slippage.
Source: CQG, Inc. © 2010. All rights reserved worldwide.

mean reversion regret minimization techniques. First, unlike both adding to losing positions and regret minimization for mean reversion traders, pyramiding should only be used in conjunction with trend-following trading models. Successful pyramiding is in many ways the polar opposite to averaging down in that pyramiding begins the trade with the largest number of contracts, and adds fewer contracts as the trade generates larger amounts of unrealized gains. By contrast, averaging down begins each trade with its smallest position size and adds larger numbers of contracts as unrealized losses rise in an exponential fashion (see Table 6.4). Consequently, many successful long trend-following traders adhere to pyramiding and argue in favor of it as a prudent position-sizing strategy.

It is obviously true that averaging down is not a prudent position-sizing technique whereas pyramiding could be. The problem is that most professional traders agree that markets only trend around 30 percent of the time, which is fine for trend-following traders because during those less frequent periods when they are in this trending mode, they offer larger profits than losses endured during the 70 percent of the time when reverting to the mean. For pyramiding to be successful, however, markets not only have to be trending, but trending in a near-parabolic manner. When they instead stair-step higher or lower, pyramiding is psychologically debilitating because it forces us to allow significant unrealized profits to turn into significant realized losses.

The summer 2010 rally in December 2010 CME Group wheat futures was a near-parabolic bull trend that was particularly well suited to pyramiding. In determining appropriate position-sizing limits and levels for our pyramiding strategy, we must ensure that our risk never exceeds 1 to 2 percent of total assets under management. Assuming a trading account with $650,000 and a risk appetite of 2 percent of total assets under management, we could place a buy stop at the resistance level of $5.20 per bushel on seven contracts. This allows us to place our stop loss order to sell at the cycle low of $4.83 per bushel, representing a $0.37 cent, or $1,850, risk per contract times seven contracts for a total position risk of $12,950, which is just under 2 percent of total assets under management for our $650,000 account.

On July 6, 2010, when the market rallies to $5.40 per bushel, we can buy four more contracts and raise our sell stop on all 11 contracts to our initial entry price of $5.20 per bushel. Notice that although we are adding to our existing position, our significant unrealized gains enable us to add to the position without violating our 2 percent risk rule. In fact, the addition of these four contracts along with the raising of our stop loss to $5.20 represents a $4,000 risk on the 11 contracts. This is because our average price per bushel is now around $5.2725 on all 11 contracts, which is well under 1 percent of total assets under management. As long as we are stopped out, there is little or no liquidity risk (for example, a locked limit down move that might prevent our sell stop from being elected at or near the $5.20 level).

On July 8, 2010, when the market rallies to $5.60 per bushel, we buy two more contracts and raise our stop on all 13 contracts to $5.40 per bushel. Now, if our $5.40 sell stop were triggered, we would be stopped out at a total profit of $9,000 on all 13 contracts because our average price per bushel was $5.3233 cents per bushel. Finally on July 13, 2010, the market has rallied to $5.80 per bushel, when we buy our final contract while raising our stop on all 14 contracts to $5.60 per bushel. If our sell stop at $5.60 per bushel were triggered, it would translate into a profit of $17,000, since our average price per bushel on all 14 contracts is now $5.3575. The wheat market rises instead in a near-parabolic fashion, achieving our long-term price target of $7.50 per bushel on August 4, 2010, when we sell out our position, realizing a profit of $150,000 (see Figure 6.8).

But remember that the 2010 wheat market was a near-parabolic trending market. Now let us apply this pyramiding strategy in an ordinary bull market like December 2010 U.S. 10-year Treasury note futures. During September 2010, the 10-year note futures displayed strong overhead resistance at 126'02.5,[2] and recent cycle lows were established at 125'05. This represented an initial risk of $937.50 per contract. Traders with $1 million in assets under management who were willing to use a 2 percent risk ceiling could place an order to buy 20 contracts at 126'03 on a stop and would be risking $18,750 if after entry they were stopped out at 125'05.

The good news was that the break of the resistance level of 126'02.5 was a real breakout in the context of a long-term bull market. Consequently, when on October 6, 2010, the market rallied to 127'00, our trader bought another 10 contracts and raised stops to his initial entry price level of 126'03 on all 30 contracts. Unfortunately, although the Treasuries were trending higher, they were not trending higher in a near-parabolic fashion,

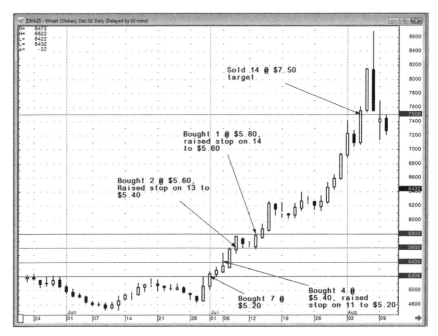

FIGURE 6.8 December 2010 Daily CME Group Wheat Futures
Source: CQG, Inc. © 2010. All rights reserved worldwide.

so on October 15, 2010, he was stopped out of all 30 contracts at 126'03, for a loss of $4,531.25 (see Figure 6.9).

Although this loss was well within acceptable risk tolerance levels, it may not have been psychologically palatable for our trader to watch a significant unrealized profit of $9,062.50 turn into a significant realized loss of $4,531.25. Unless your trading personality is well suited for enduring

TABLE 6.5 Pyramiding December 2010 Wheat Futures

Entry Price	Contracts	Avg Price	Market Price	Unrealized P/L
$5.20	7	$5.20	$5.20	$0.00
$5.40	4	$5.2725	$5.40	$7,000.00
$5.60	2	$5.3233	$5.60	$18,000.00
$5.80	1	$5.3575	$5.80	$31,000.00
		$5.3575	$7.50	$150,000.00

Note: Performance results shown exclude commissions and slippage.
Source: CQG, Inc. © 2010. All rights reserved worldwide.

FIGURE 6.9 December 2010 Daily CME Group 10-Year Treasury Note Futures
Source: CQG, Inc. © 2010. All rights reserved worldwide.

this kind of regret, pyramiding is probably not the best strategy. If you feel watching such unrealized gains turn into significant losses debilitating, then the portion of this chapter on regret minimization for trend followers is offered as an attractive alternative.

Now that we have clearly defined position sizing as it relates to both averaging down as well as pyramiding, we can distinguish both of these from mean reversion and countertrend regret minimization techniques. Some of the major problems with most mean reversion and countertrend

TABLE 6.6 Pyramiding with December 2010 Ten-Year T-Note Futures

Entry Price	Contracts	Avg Price	Market Price	Profit/Loss
126'03	20	126'03	126'03	$0.00
127'00	10	126'13	127'00	$9,062.50
		126'13	126'03	($4,531.25)

Note: Performance results shown excluding commissions and slippage.
Source: CQG, Inc. © 2010. All rights reserved worldwide.

models include missing our limit entry price target or enduring large draw-downs to better ensure trade participation. The techniques introduced here minimize trader regret through the staggering of limit entry orders at various support or resistance levels.

At first glance, staggering of entry orders looks somewhat similar to averaging down, which is why I clearly defined the latter earlier. The main distinction between averaging down and staggering is that averaging down involves an increasing of position size as unrealized losses mount so as to improve our average position price. Also, averaging down is, generally speaking, a reactive—as opposed to premeditated—volumetric position-sizing tool introduced in hopes of avoiding the pain of exiting with losses. By contrast, the staggering of limit entry orders is used by mean reversion traders who plan to achieve specific, predefined position sizes, but are willing to accept smaller positions to help them minimize the regret of missing a positive expectancy trading opportunity.

Trade: IBM

In October 2007, IBM shares began pulling back from cycle highs at $121.46 per share. Measuring from July 2006 cycle lows of $72.73, mean reversion traders noticed a wide array Fibonacci retracement levels to place buy orders at 38.2 percent, or $102.85 per share, 50 percent, or $97.09 and 61.8 percent, or $91.34. One possible solution according to regret minimization theory is not choosing at all. I like to say, "Don't anticipate, just participate." Instead of guessing which of these support levels would be tested, we place buy orders at each level along with a sell stop below the final 61.8 percent Fibonacci support area. Assuming a trading account has $2 million in assets under management and we are comfortable risking 2 percent of assets under management, or $40,000, on a per trade basis, we could safely place limit orders to buy 500 shares at each of the aforementioned Fibonacci retracement levels along with a sell stop order on all 1,500 shares at the cycle low level of $88.76 per share. Looking at Figure 6.10, we see that IBM pulled back 50 percent by January 2008 before the retesting of its previous cycle high at $121.46 per share in April 2008 (see Figure 6.10).

Table 6.7 shows how the staggering of buy orders enabled our participation in this trade setup instead of missing the opportunity by placing a single limit order at $91.34 per share. Also notice that staggering buy orders at $102.85 and $97.09 offered superior performance—and less regret—than placing a single buy order at the $102.85 price level. Admittedly, buying all shares at $97.09 would have proved even more successful, but again, our goal is minimizing regret of missed opportunities as opposed to capturing the elusive "perfect trade" (see Table 6.7).

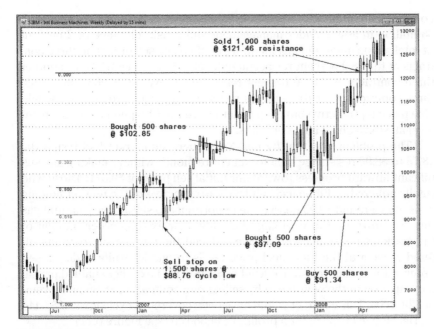

FIGURE 6.10   Weekly Chart of IBM Inc.
Source: CQG, Inc. © 2010. All rights reserved worldwide.

Trade: Natural Gas Futures

This trade illustrates an essential aspect of successful speculative trading, namely, not being rigid with entry—as opposed to risk management—order placement levels. On April 20, 2006, the natural gas market made its cycle high at $12.489 basis January futures. By September 29, 2007, it put in its cycle low at $7.444. At this point, traders started examining various Fibonacci retracement levels for establishing short positions into the

TABLE 6.7   Regret Minimization with IBM Inc.

Share Price	Shares Purchased	Avg Share Price	Market Price	Mark-to-Market	Profits at $121.46
$102.85	500	$102.85	$102.85	$0.00	$9,305.00
$97.09	500	$99.97	$97.09	($2,880.00)	$12,185.00
$91.34	None	$97.09	N/A	N/A	N/A
Actual Totals:	1,000	$99.97	$121.46	$21,490.00	$21,490.00

Note: Performance results shown exclude commissions.
Source: CQG, Inc. © 2010. All rights reserved worldwide.

countertrend pullback. Accordingly, assuming a trading account with $3 million in assets under management and a risk tolerance of 2 percent of total assets under management, we could place sell orders on three contracts at the 38.2 percent retracement level of $9.371 per MMBTU, another three contracts at the 50 percent retracement level of $9.966, and a final three contracts at the 61.8 percent retracement level of $10.562. We would also place a protective buy stop order above the 61.8 percent retracement level at $10.73 on all nine contracts.

The problem was that by mid-November, the market had tested the $8.75 to $8.90 resistance area for an entire month without making any significant upward progress toward our initial sell price of $9.371. Those who rigidly adhered to Fibonacci sell levels irrespective of the market holding resistance around $8.90 missed the opportunity to sell January natural gas futures. However, those willing to modify their existing orders in light of the market's resistance could have reduced the number of contracts offered at each of the Fibonacci price levels to one lot while adding a sell order at the recent resistance level of $8.88. This flexibility enabled partial participation in the bear move by selling one contract at $8.88 on November 29, 2006. This contract would have been covered at cycle lows of $7.444 on December 11, 2006, for a profit of $14,360.00 (see Figure 6.11).

FIGURE 6.11 January 2007 Daily CME Group Natural Gas Futures
Source: CQG, Inc. © 2010. All rights reserved worldwide.

TABLE 6.8 Regret Minimization with January 2007 Natural Gas Futures

Entry Price	Contracts Sold	Sale Price	Market Price	Mark-to-Market	Profits at $7.444
$10.562	0	N/A	N/A	N/A	N/A
$9.966	0	N/A	N/A	N/A	N/A
$9.371	0	N/A	N/A	N/A	N/A
$8.880	1	$8.88	$8.880	$0.00	$14,360.00
Actual Totals:	1	$8.88	$7.444	$14,360.00	$14,360.00

Note: Performance results excluding commissions.
Source: CQG, Inc. © 2010. All rights reserved worldwide.

FINAL THOUGHTS

Regret minimization techniques like taking partial profits and then moving stops to breakeven on the remainder are invaluable in reprogramming the trader away from irrational cycles of euphoria and fear in favor of even-mindedness. (The final chapter of this book examines even-mindedness in trading, which is our ability to embody an objective, emotionally tempered attitude toward trading opportunities.) In addition, regret minimization techniques are an antidote to the perfect trader syndrome. The perfect trader syndrome occurs when traders seek perfect entry and exit prices by buying the low tick and selling the high. Irrational attachment to buying the low and selling the high becomes obstacle impeding our ability to successfully enter and exit trades. Because regret minimization techniques train us to exit at a variety of profitable price levels, they aid in deactivating the perfect trader syndrome. In summary, through regret minimization, many of the Wall Street adages that formerly seemed like a pipe dream become emotional realities, including being right and sitting tight as well as the classic: cutting losses and letting winners run.

CHAPTER 7

Timeframe Analysis

A cloud is made of billows upon billows upon billows that look like clouds. As you come closer to a cloud you don't get something smooth, but irregularities at a smaller scale.

— Dr. Benoit Mandelbrot

One of the most robust tools for generating positive expectancy models is timeframe analysis. This chapter explores both traditional timeframe analysis and timeframe divergence. Particular emphasis is placed on using various mathematical technical indicators to understand likely market behavior in various timeframes.

TRADITIONAL TIMEFRAME ANALYSIS

I began studying market behavior in 1987 in the hope of developing positive expectancy trading models, and gravitated to the simplicity—when compared to fundamental analysis—of technical indicators. I began to understand the importance of market trends and that various technical indicators could help in trend identification. When struggling to determine the trend, I quickly realized that not all indicators were created equal, and that technical indicators derived from mathematical formulas offered an objective answer to the question "What is the trend?" As I continued studying price history, applying different mathematical technical indicators to determine the trend, I eventually learned that there was no single answer to the question. The only satisfactory answer to the question is another question: "What is your timeframe?"

In other words, according to objective mathematical technical indicators like moving averages or Wilder's relative strength index (RSI),[1] an asset could be in a bull trend (nine-period RSI above 50) on its monthly and weekly charts, a bear market (nine-period RSI below 50) according to its daily chart, and a bull market (nine-period RSI above 50) based on its hourly chart (see Figure 7.1).

Traditional timeframe analysis consequently always begins with determining the asset's trend, support, and resistance according to its longest timeframe. Once we have a clear picture of this macro perspective of market behavior, we can safely zoom in and examine the trend, support, and resistance based on shorter-term timeframes. This is illustrated by Figure 7.2, which shows a chart of 30-minute bars in ICE March 2011 sugar futures. Based on this chart, we would conclude that sugar was in a bear market and look to sell rallies near the overhead resistance level of $0.2893 per pound (see Figure 7.2). Now compare Figure 7.3 to Figure 7.2. Notice that by lengthening our timeframe from 30- to 60-minute bars, we define overhead resistance not at $0.2893, but at $0.2930 per pound instead (see Figure 7.3).

Next, contrast both the 30- and 60-minute charts to the daily chart and our definition of the asset's trend changes from bearish to bullish while our view of technical support levels shifts from $0.2703/lb. on the 30-minute timeframe (or $0.2545/lb. on the 60-minute timeframe) to $0.2530/lb. on the daily timeframe (see Figure 7.4). Finally, by examining Figure 7.5, we gain a macro understanding of sugar's trend—which is decidedly bullish—as well as a clear picture of multiple long- and intermediate-term support and resistance levels (see Figure 7.5). It is also important to realize that by switching from the daily to weekly timeframe in exchange-traded futures, we shift from a specific contract month—in our example, the March 2011 ICE sugar futures contract—to a rolling front-month continuation chart, and therefore older data points on the weekly chart (such as the long-term support level of $0.1300 established during May 2010) reflect support and resistance levels of front-month sugar contracts at that time in the asset's history.

The most robust and commonly employed solution to timeframe analysis issues is maintaining a single screen that instantaneously shows multiple timeframes for the traded asset (see Figure 7.6). The timeframes should provide a clear picture of the trend, support, and resistance according to the timeframe that you are trading, as well as longer timeframes. In other words, Figure 7.6 would be preferable to those making trade decisions based on 30-minute bars. By contrast, shorter-term traders might use 5-minute bars for their primary market analysis, while looking at 30- and

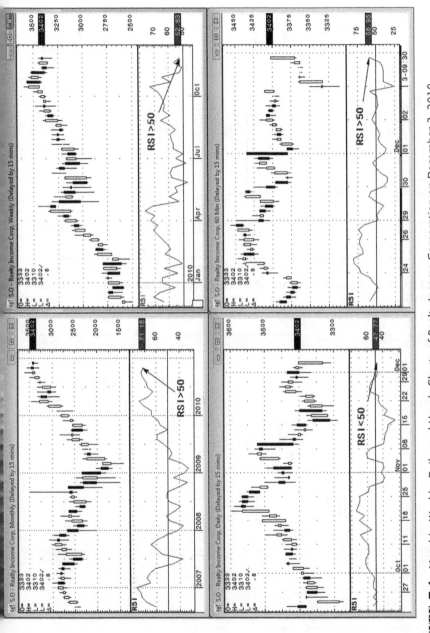

FIGURE 7.1 Monthly, Weekly, Daily, and Hourly Charts of Realty Income Corporation on December 3, 2010

Source: CQG, Inc. © 2010. All rights reserved worldwide.

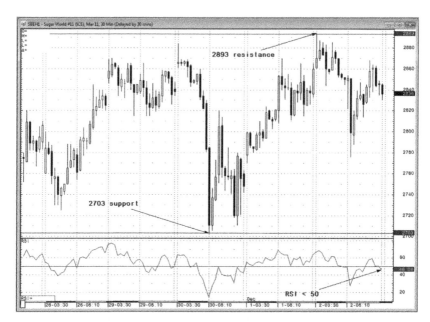

FIGURE 7.2 Thirty-Minute Chart of ICE March 2011 Sugar Futures on December 3, 2010

Source: CQG, Inc. © 2010. All rights reserved worldwide.

FIGURE 7.3 Sixty-Minute Chart of ICE March 2011 Sugar Futures on December 3, 2010

Source: CQG, Inc. © 2010. All rights reserved worldwide.

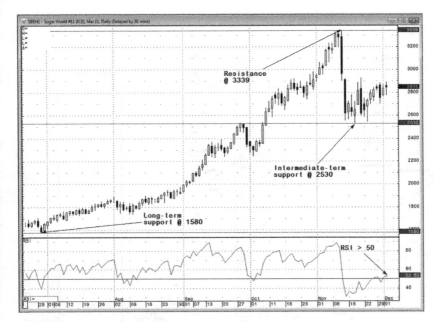

FIGURE 7.4 Daily Chart of ICE March 2011 Sugar Futures
Source: CQG, Inc. © 2010. All rights reserved worldwide.

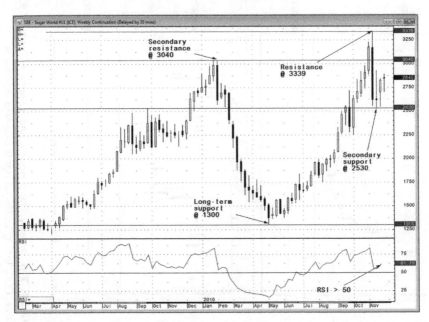

FIGURE 7.5 Rolling Front-Month Weekly Continuation Chart of ICE Sugar Futures
Source: CQG, Inc. © 2010. All rights reserved worldwide.

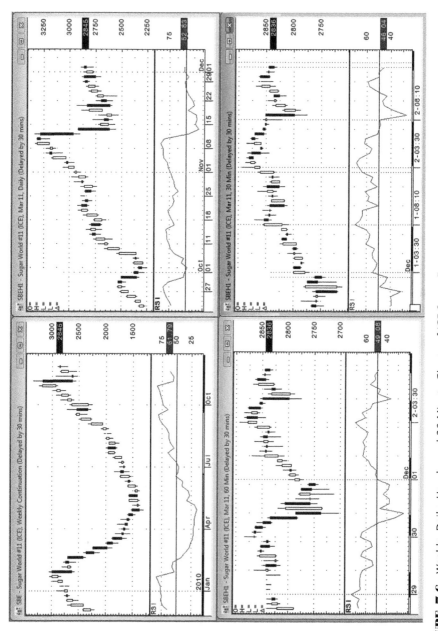

FIGURE 7.6 Weekly, Daily, Hourly, and 30-Minute Charts of ICE Sugar Futures

130

60-minute charts for the intermediate-term perspective, and daily charts for their long-term market view (see Figure 7.7).

TIMEFRAME CONFIRMATION TRADING

Traditional timeframe trading suggests buying when all timeframes analyzed are bullish or selling when all indicators are bearish according to mathematical technical indicators such as moving averages or percentage oscillators like Wilder's relative strength index (RSI). There are two commonly employed versions of generating timeframe confirmation trading signals; the first, suboptimal version blindly buys or sells anytime all timeframes are bullish or bearish regardless of how long ago the timeframes confirmed buy or sell signals (see Figure 7.8).

By contrast, the second, more robust version of timeframe confirmation allows trade execution only when longer timeframes show trend confirmation and the shortest timeframe shifts from divergence to confirmation. This is illustrated by examining Figure 7.10, which shows the purchase price for GE of $16.65 per share when RSI crossed 50 at 2:40 P.M. with buying at the close for $16.75 per share (see Figures 7.9 and 7.10).

Trade: International Paper Company

Figure 7.11 shows daily, hourly, and 30-minute charts confirming a bullish trend in International Paper. In addition, the 5-minute chart of International Paper shifts from divergence to confirmation of this bull trend at 12:00 noon EST on December 3, 2010, triggering our buy signal at $26.03 per share. Although there are many ways to manage risk on this trade, one of the most popular is by placing a protective sell stop at the previous cycle low of the longer, 30-minute timeframe chart at $25.89 per share (see Figure 7.11). There are also a wide variety of tools for exiting with profits, including the regret minimization techniques covered in Chapter 6. Here we offer a different mechanism from those previously shown, namely, exiting when the relative strength index of International Paper's 5-minute chart crosses above 75. This occurred at 2:20 P.M. EST and we sold the stock at $26.26 per share (see Figure 7.12).

TIMEFRAME DIVERGENCE TRADING

Although I believe that trading in the direction of the long-term trend is almost always a good idea, one of the most valuable tools I have

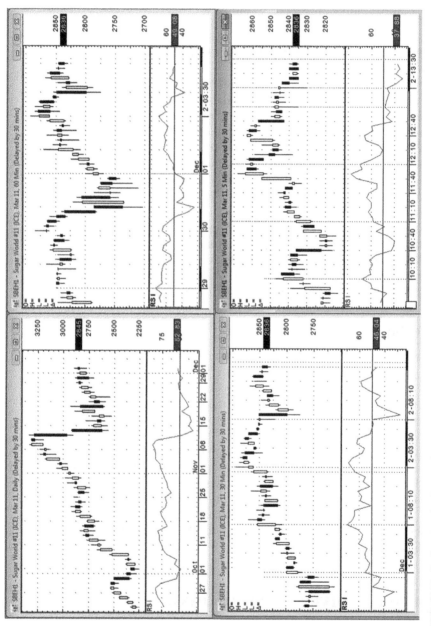

FIGURE 7.7 Daily, Hourly, 30-, and 5-Minute Charts of March 2011 ICE Sugar Futures

Source: CQG, Inc. © 2010. All rights reserved worldwide.

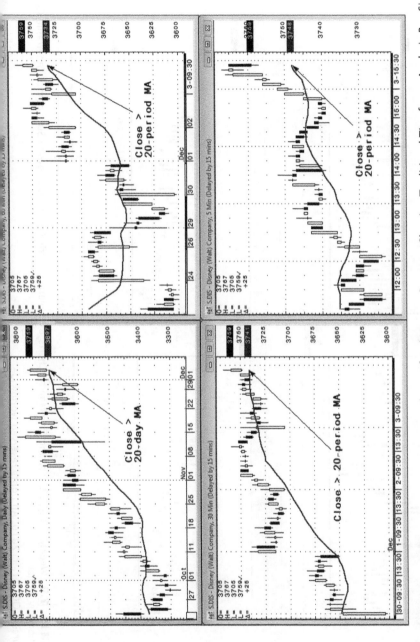

FIGURE 7.8 Daily, Hourly, 30-, and 5-Minute Charts of Walt Disney Company Showing Traditional Timeframe Analysis Buy Signal Based on 20-Period Simple Moving Average

Source: CQG, Inc. © 2010. All rights reserved worldwide.

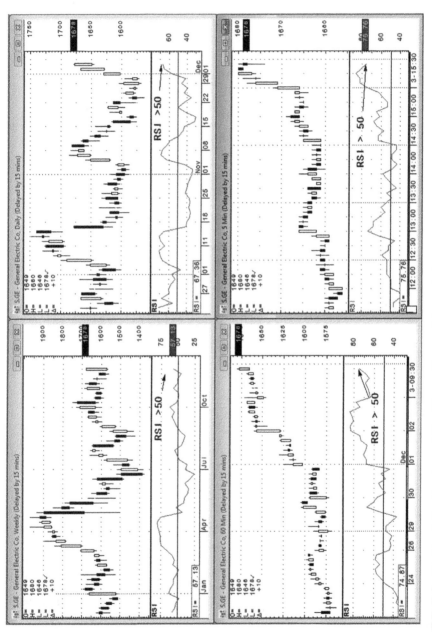

FIGURE 7.9 Weekly, Daily, Hourly, and Five-Minute Charts of General Electric Company Showing Suboptimal Timeframe Confirmation Buy Signal

Source: CQG, Inc. © 2010. All rights reserved worldwide.

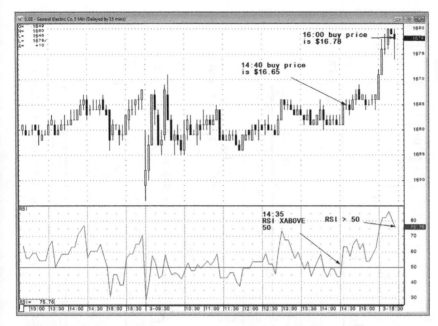

FIGURE 7.10 Five-Minute Chart of General Electric Company Comparing Buy Price at 4:00 P.M. EST on December 3, 2010, with Buy Price at 2:40 P.M. EST when RSI Crossed 50 Level

Source: CQG, Inc. © 2010. All rights reserved worldwide.

discovered in developing low-risk/high-reward trading models is what I call timeframe divergence. Timeframe divergence is the simultaneous examination of multiple timeframes so as to find assets in which the shortest timeframe diverges from longer ones. For example, let us assume that you execute trades on two-minute bars. Traditional timeframe analysis suggests that you only buy the market once all the timeframes analyzed generate bullish trend readings. By definition, this means higher risk and lower reward. By contrast, using timeframe divergence, we would wait for the two-minute bar chart to give a bearish or oversold relative strength index reading, which diverged from the still bullish readings offered by the asset's longer 30-minute, 60-minute, and daily charts. Because this is a mean reversion strategy, we will need to avoid suboptimal, high-risk environments such as trading before the release of news events like government reports. Also, because of the cyclical nature of volatility (see Chapter 4), we want to avoid entering trades in periods of low volatility since such environments offer low reward and could potentially entail high risk (if after entering the trade volatility increased).

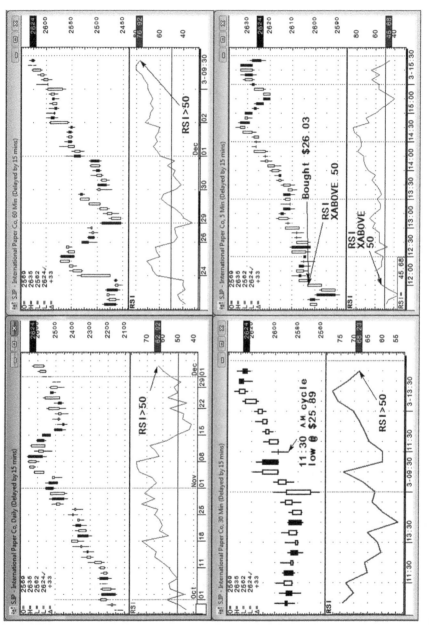

FIGURE 7.11 Daily, Hourly, 30-, and 5-Minute Charts of International Paper Company Inc. Showing Timeframe Confirmation Buy Signal on December 3, 2010

Source: CQG, Inc. © 2010. All rights reserved worldwide.

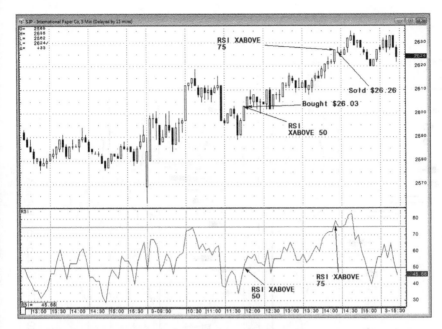

FIGURE 7.12 Five-Minute Chart of International Paper Company Inc. Showing Timeframe Confirmation Trade on December 3, 2010
Source: CQG, Inc. © 2010. All rights reserved worldwide.

Other considerations are stop loss order placement. These decisions will be determined by a multitude of factors such as expected hold time, win/loss ratios, probable profit target, and the current volatility of the traded asset (as measured by some objective technical tool such as the asset's 10-period average true range). These disclaimers aside, we can safely state that our stop loss should be derived from either the 30- or 60-minute timeframe's support and resistance levels. Exiting with profit could be based on the relative strength index crossing above 50, the violation of support or resistance levels on the two-minute bar, and so on.

Short-Term Trade: CME Group Gold

Figure 7.13 exemplifies a timeframe divergence trade for short-term traders. Notice how the nine-period relative strength index is bullish for all timeframes except the two-minute chart that signals a temporarily oversold reading of less than 35, according to its nine-period relative strength index. This oversold reading also occurs in a somewhat high-volatility environment as defined by its 10-period ADX being above 20. In this way,

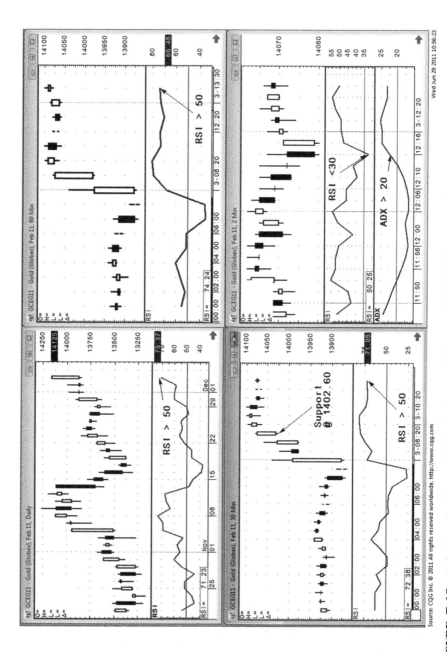

FIGURE 7.13 Daily, Hourly, 30-, and 2-Minute Charts of February 2011 CME Group Gold Futures

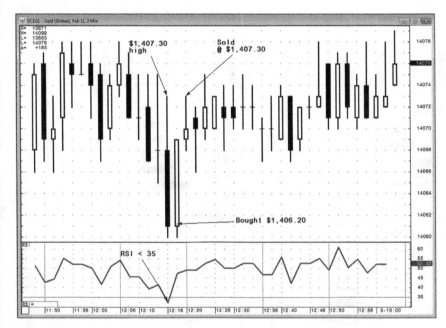

FIGURE 7.14 Two-Minute Chart of February 2011 CME Group Gold Futures Detailing Timeframe Divergence Trade
Source: CQG, Inc. © 2010. All rights reserved worldwide.

all of our criteria for trade entry were met, so we bought at the opening price of the following two-minute bar at $1,406.10. For risk management, we look at support levels of gold's longer timeframes. According to our 30-minute bar chart, this support was the swing low price of $1,402.60. Since traders using two-minute bars tend to look for quick profits and higher winning percentages, I placed our limit order to exit with profits at the highs of the bar before the relative strength index gave its oversold reading. This limit order to exit at $1,407.30 was triggered around four minutes later (see Figures 7.13 and 7.14).

Longer-Term Trade: CME Group Crude Oil

Figure 7.15 shows a timeframe divergence opportunity in January 2011 CME Group crude oil futures for longer-term traders. Because our trading timeframe is longer, we use the daily chart as the timeframe for identifying the temporary divergence with longer—weekly and monthly—timeframes. Nevertheless, many of the same basic principles apply, including the weekly and monthly charts signaling a bull trend according to their

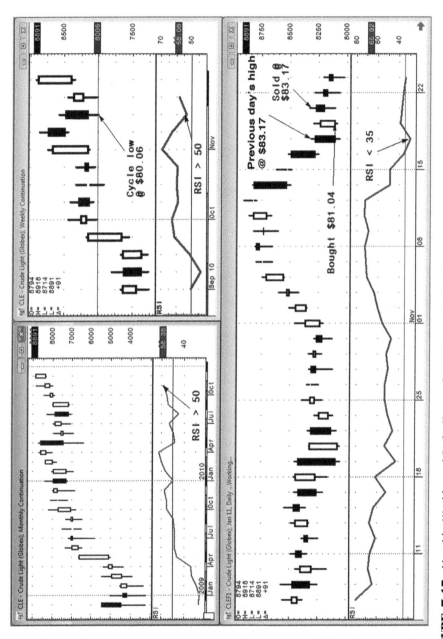

FIGURE 7.15 Monthly, Weekly, and Daily Charts of CME Group Crude Oil Futures

Source: CQG, Inc. © 2010. All rights reserved worldwide.

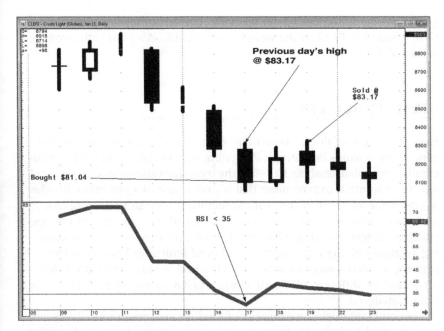

FIGURE 7.16 January 2011 Daily Chart of CME Group Crude Oil Futures Detailing Timeframe Divergence Trade

Source: CQG, Inc. © 2010. All rights reserved worldwide.

nine-period relative strength index readings, entering a long position after the daily chart drops below 35 on its nine-period relative strength index, placing a sell stop below recent cycle lows according to the longer (weekly) timeframe, and exiting with profits at the highs of the daily bar before the bar that triggered the oversold relative strength index reading (see Figures 7.15 and 7.16).

Although there are some obvious similarities between our short-term gold trade and this longer-term trade in crude oil, there are also important differences. The shorter-term gold trade was susceptible to many dangers that are not applicable to our longer-term crude oil trade such as event risk from news items like unemployment reports, FOMC meetings, and so on. Also, our short-term trade needed to avoid trading signals that were generated during periods of low volatility since such environments could result in low-reward/high-risk trades trades. None of these factors disqualify signals for timeframe divergence trades generated on daily charts. The reason we are willing to take timeframe divergence trades before market-moving news or in a low-volatility environment is that the longer-term trend as defined by the weekly and monthly charts acts as a powerful underlying factor supporting our trade. These factors were not present for the shorter-term gold trade since it is possible for the daily chart to be bullish and the longer-term trend as defined by the weekly and monthly charts to be bearish (as shown in Figure 7.15).

FINAL THOUGHTS

Despite their usefulness, timeframe confirmation and timeframe divergence have obvious limitations. First, although we can use objective mathematical technical analysis to define the trend for various timeframes studied, it is important to remember that it's not magic, it's just math. In other words, none of these mathematical technical indicators are universally accepted answers for defining an asset's trend, nor are any of the specific parameters—such as a 50-period moving average or a 26-period moving average—of any mathematical technical indicator. Various numerical periods, instead—such as a 9- and 14-period relative strength index—offer traders different views of market behavior on each of the timeframes analyzed.

Second, although timeframe confirmation and timeframe divergence are powerful techniques, they are not easily adaptable to back testing and optimization of programmable mechanical trading systems. It's consequently harder to gather valuable information such as maximum number of consecutive losses, percentage of winning trades, average profit to average loss ratio, maximum drawdown amount, profit to maximum drawdown ratio, and so on. Without such data, our continued adherence to these techniques might become problematic during inevitable periods of underperformance.

Finally, although timeframe divergence is extremely valuable in helping determine an asset's long-term trend, support, and resistance, we should not allow this strength to degenerate into complacency. Although the technique attunes us to the market's longer-term trend, it is important to remember that when this trend inevitably reverses, this shift from bear to bull market—or vice versa—will first be detected on our shortest time interval, and will only be confirmed by the longest timeframe after the new trend is somewhat mature. This final point is mentioned not as an excuse to avoid or dismiss timeframe analysis, but instead to reiterate the importance of diligence in respect to risk management as well as providing readers with the proper casino paradigm perspective on timeframe divergence. In other words, despite being robust, no tool—including timeframe divergence—works every time. This reality of every tool's imperfection must instead be accepted and embraced as the price to pay in order to exploit a positive expectancy trading model.

CHAPTER 8

How to Use Trading Models

The harder I work, the luckier I get.

—Anonymous

This chapter examines a wide array of positive expectancy trend-following and mean reversion trading models in hopes of expanding how readers view market behavior as well as ways of capitalizing on such idiosyncrasies. Particular emphasis is placed on models that enjoy low risk and high reward and are in the direction of the longer-term trend.

MECHANICAL TRADING SYSTEMS

Mechanical trading systems are rule-based models automated to execute trades without the discretionary input of speculators regarding entry or exit. These systems tend to focus on mathematical technical indicators—such as moving averages or oscillators—to develop objective rules of entry, risk management, and exiting with profits.

The first challenge for system developers is determining a starting point for their research. My rule of thumb for model development is that less is more. The goal is creating positive expectancy models containing the fewest parameters possible without sacrificing performance. In general, work with mathematical technical indicators that complement each other instead of those identifying the same type of market behavior. Specifically, start by building models with one trend-following indicator (like a moving average), one oscillator (such as relative strength index), one volatility

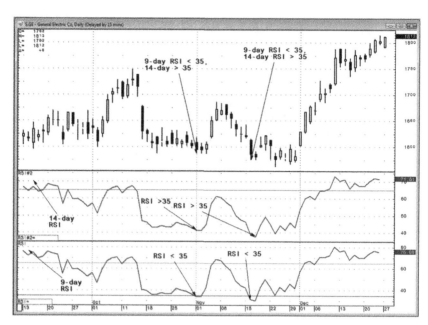

FIGURE 8.1 Daily Chart of General Electric Company Comparing 9- and 14-Day Versions of Relative Strength Index

Source: CQG, Inc. © 2010. All rights reserved worldwide.

indicator (like average true range), and volume. Next, traders developing models with mathematically derived technical indicators should ask, "Do I want more trading signals and more false positives or fewer, higher quality signals with fewer false positives?" Obviously, there is no single answer to this question and it is the task of each trader to tailor the answer to this question according to the individual desired hold time, risk appetite, and reward criteria (see Figure 8.1).

Although mechanical trading systems can be quite robust, they tend, in general, to underperform the best discretionary traders because the latter are highly adaptive to unique, unpredictable opportunities arising in the market. This disclaimer aside, mechanical trading systems remain among the safest, most reliable ways of transitioning speculators from negative to positive expectancy because the models train us to consistently temper emotionalism (see Chapter 3), play the probabilities (as discussed in Chapter 1), and adhere to rules of prudent risk management (see Chapter 2). Irrespective of a methodology's robustness, drawdowns in account equity and multiple consecutive losing trades are a fact of life for all speculators. Consequently, the ability to back test and forward test these systems before the commitment of capital are extremely valuable in development, nurturing, and maturation of the casino mentality in traders.

Throughout the book up to this point some mechanical trading systems were introduced so as to explain risk management (Chapter 2), trader discipline (Chapter 3), and the cyclical nature of volatility (Chapter 4). By contrast, mathematically derived mechanical trading systems are examined here to help traders develop positive expectancy trading models. Instead of attempting an exhaustive presentation of the full spectrum of mechanical trading systems, this chapter offers a sampling of some basic methods. At the risk of repetition, as stated in Chapter 3: "The purpose of these throwaway models is not real-time trading, but instead to use as starting points for research that will lead to the development of even more robust positive expectancy models."[1]

Explanation of Portfolio Tables

All data shown in this chapter come from equalized active daily continuation charts of exchange-traded futures contracts. Combined portfolio results are based upon trade entry date of each asset. Unless otherwise specified, all performance results use one lot of the futures contracts shown in Table 8.1.

Performance tables in this chapter will evaluate robustness of the models based on the following eight fields:

1. *Total net profit (Profit)* examines profitability irrespective of risk taken to achieve these results. Because of this limitation, other measures included in our back-tested results are superior analytical tools. This number is useful, however, because it allows us to quickly add and compare various portfolio component results for numerous systems without additional calculations.

2. *Number of trades (# Trades)* shows the total number of trades taken during the back-tested period. For long-term trend-following

TABLE 8.1   Composition of Back-Tested Portfolio

Asset Class	Asset	Asset Symbol
Equity Indices	CME Group E-Mini SP 500	ES
Interest Rates	CME Group 10-Yr Treasuries	ZN
Currencies	CME Group Eurocurrency	EU6
Currencies	CME Group Japanese Yen	JY6
Energy	CME Group Crude Oil	CL
Energy	CME Group Natural Gas	NG
Grains	CME Group Soybeans	ZS
Foods	ICE #11 World Sugar	SB
Metals	CME Group Gold	GC

Source: CQG, Inc. © 2010. All rights reserved worldwide.

systems, we want this number to be as low as possible without sacrificing performance.

3. *Number of days (# Days)* shows the average duration of a trade. As with number of trades, all else being equal, the lower the number of days in a trade while still generating superior results, the better.

   The only caveat here is whether the system is long-term trend following or mean reverting. If it is long-term trend following, then the higher number of days in the trade will usually result in larger profits.

4. *Maximum drawdown amount (Max Draw)* tells us the maximum peak-to-valley equity drawdown during the back-tested period.

5. *Maximum consecutive losses (MCL)* is the maximum number of consecutive losses endured throughout the back-tested period.

6. *Profit to maximum drawdown ratio (P:MD)* refers to the total net profit to maximum drawdown ratio. The higher this ratio is, the better. This is probably the most important field listed because it allows us to examine profit in relation to risk endured to achieve that profitability.

7. *Percent winners (%W)* is the percentage of winning trades. As stated, trend systems generally will have low %Ws, and mean reversion systems typically display high %Ws.

8. *Profit loss ratio (P:L)* refers to the average profit to average loss ratio. As with P:MD, the higher these numbers are, the better. Trend-following systems should have very good P:L ratios because they generally display a low winning percentage of trades. This means that large profits and small losses are key in generating a good P:MD ratio. These ratios will drop for mean reversion systems, but winning percentage of trades should compensate for this.

Trend-Following Systems

Trend-following systems are among the most popular of all mechanical trading systems because they tend to enjoy the highest average profit to average loss ratios and typically entail longer average holding periods (therefore requiring less monitoring or adjusting). Since Chapter 3 already discussed the psychological traits of various types of traders in detail, this chapter instead focuses on some throwaway mechanical trading systems along with simple techniques to make these systems more robust.

RSI Trend System   RSI Trend, like many of the other trend-following systems featured in this section, is based on one of my favorite trading concepts, turning the indicator on its head. The idea is that oscillators like relative strength index (RSI) are traditionally used to capitalize on the market's propensity to mean reversion, so, when the market trends, systems

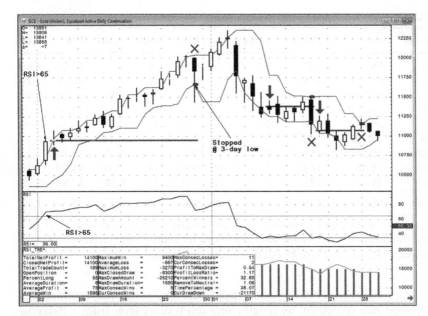

FIGURE 8.2 Equalized Active Daily Continuation Chart for CME Group Gold Futures with RSI Trend System

Note: Trade summary includes data from January 1, 2000, to December 31, 2009, and assumes $10 round-turn deductions for slippage and commissions.

Source: CQG, Inc. © 2010. All rights reserved worldwide.

like RSI Trend profit from losses suffered by those hoping for mean reversion (see Figure 8.2).

Using CQG, the programming code for RSI Trend system with a three-day high and low trailing stop is written this way:

```
Long Entry:

RSI(@,9)[-1] > 65

Long Exit:

LoLevel(@,3)[-1]

Short Entry:

RSI(@,9)[-1] < 35

Short Exit:

HiLevel(@,3)[-1]
```

TABLE 8.2 RSI Trend (3-Day Trailing Stop)

Asset	Profit	# Trades	# Days	Max Draw	MCL	P:MD	%W	P:L
ES	(55,105)	193	6	(60,000)	9	N/A	25.91	1.49
CL	61,930	179	7	(14,950)	7	4.14	40.22	2.20
NG	67,640	185	6	(40,940)	10	1.65	37.30	2.07
GC	14,100	189	6	(26,210)	11	.54	32.80	2.33
ZS	20,875	160	6	(17,437)	12	1.20	40.62	1.88
ZN	8,733	172	7	(11,607)	8	.75	43.02	1.53
EU6	(6,940)	169	6	(33,045)	8	N/A	33.73	1.87
JY6	8,882	163	7	(27,787)	7	.32	44.79	1.36
SB	(4,471)	185	6	(11,955)	12	N/A	33.51	1.75
Total:	115,644	1,595	6	(55,207)	15	2.09	36.74	1.92

Notes: Portfolio summary includes data from January 1, 2000, to December 31, 2009, and assumes $10 round-turn deductions for slippage and commissions.
Source: CQG, Inc. © 2010. All rights reserved worldwide.

Although RSI Trend as showcased here enjoyed a respectable risk-adjusted rate of return, by lengthening the trailing stop from a 3-day to 10-day high and low, performance improves dramatically (see Figure 8.3). While some aspects—such as average profit to average loss ratio and percentage of winning trades—remained similar, our portfolio's profit to maximum drawdown ratio increased from 2.09 to 7.08. In this example the trade-off for improved performance was a lengthening of average trade duration from 6 to 18 trading days (see Table 8.3).

Using CQG, the programming code for RSI Trend system with a 10-day high and low trailing stop is written this way:

```
Long Entry:

RSI(@,9)[-1] > 65

Long Exit:

LoLevel(@,10)[-1]

Short Entry:

RSI(@,9)[-1] < 35

Short Exit:

HiLevel(@,10)[-1]
```

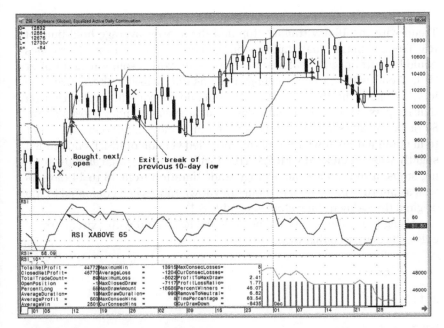

FIGURE 8.3 Equalized Active Daily Continuation Chart for CME Group Soybean Futures Using RSI Trend with 10-Day Stop

Note: Trade summary includes data from January 1, 2000, to December 31, 2009, and assumes $10 round-turn deductions for slippage and commissions.

Source: CQG, Inc. © 2010. All rights reserved worldwide.

TABLE 8.3 RSI Trend (10-Day Trailing Stop)

Asset	Profit	# Trades	# Days	Max Draw	MCL	P:MD	%W	P:L
ES	(29,800)	105	17	(30,955)	9	N/A	34.29	1.39
CL	86,430	99	18	(22,250)	5	3.88	44.44	2.17
NG	139,520	98	19	(62,970)	7	2.22	44.90	2.03
GC	3,880	110	17	(24,020)	8	.16	37.27	1.70
ZS	44,772	89	19	(18,585)	8	2.41	46.07	2.08
ZN	21,533	92	20	(13,116)	6	1.64	50	1.43
EU6	43,775	95	19	(19,457)	6	2.25	41.05	1.92
JY6	26,457	93	18	(29,992)	8	.88	37.63	2.14
SB	5,287	103	17	(9,910)	9	.53	37.86	1.86
Total:	341,854	884	18	(48,281)	13	7.08	41.29	1.97

Notes: Portfolio summary includes data from January 1, 2000, to December 31, 2009, and assumes $10 round-turn deductions for slippage and commissions.

Source: CQG, Inc. © 2010. All rights reserved worldwide.

Is there a happy medium between the improved performance of RSI Trend with the 10-day trailing stop and the shorter average hold time of RSI Trend with the 3-day trailing stop? Of course, a wide array of variables could be introduced to achieve a best of both worlds solution, and I offer "RSI Trend with extreme readings exit" as one possible alternative. The idea is to keep the 10-day trailing stop but add an exit-with-profit criterion that triggers whenever the nine-day relative strength index closes above 80 or below 20 (see Figure 8.4). As seen in Table 8.4, although the profit to maximum drawdown ratio of this modified version of RSI Trend eroded slightly when compared with RSI Trend with the 10-day high and low trailing stops, it did reduce the average trade duration from 18 to 14 days as well as improve profit to maximum drawdown ratio when compared to the original three-day trailing stop (see Table 8.4).

Using CQG, the programming code for RSI Trend with extreme readings exits is written this way:

```
Long Entry:

RSI(@,9)[-1] > 65

Long Exit:

LoLevel(@,10)[-1] OR RSI(@,9)[-1] > 80

Short Entry:

RSI(@,9)[-1] < 35

Short Exit:

HiLevel(@,10)[-1] OR RSI(@,9)[-1] < 20
```

Ichimoku Crossover Systems In 1969, a Japanese journalist, Goichi Hosada, designed a trend-following method known as the *Ichimoku Kinko Hyo*, which translates as "one-glance balanced chart." Nowadays, the indicator is commonly known as *Ichimoku clouds* because of the uniqueness of its cloud feature. The indicator has four main components:

1. Tenkan Line: (highest high + lowest low) / 2 calculated over the last 9 bars
2. Kijun Line: (highest high + lowest low) / 2 calculated over the last 26 bars
3. Senkou Span B: (highest high + lowest low) / 2 over the past 52 bars, sent 26 bars ahead
4. Senkou Span A: (Tenkan line + Kijun line) / 2 plotted 26 bars ahead

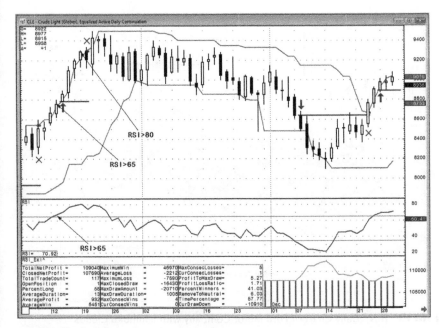

FIGURE 8.4 Equalized Active Daily Continuation Chart for CME Group Crude Oil Futures Using RSI Trend with Extreme Readings Exit
Note: Trade summary includes data from January 1, 2000, to December 31, 2009, and assumes $10 round-turn deductions for slippage and commissions.
Source: CQG, Inc. © 2010. All rights reserved worldwide.

TABLE 8.4 RSI Trend (Extreme Readings Exits)

Asset	Profit	# Trades	# Days	Max Draw	MCL	P:MD	%W	P:L
ES	(27,382)	117	14	(31,427)	9	N/A	33.33	1.53
CL	109,040	117	13	(20,710)	5	5.27	41.03	2.46
NG	93,620	112	14	(45,640)	10	2.05	41.07	1.93
GC	20,430	117	14	(22,620)	7	.90	39.32	1.82
ZS	27,242	107	13	(18,215)	8	1.50	44.86	1.61
ZN	16,607	108	15	(16,042)	6	1.04	49.07	1.33
EU6	29,122	114	13	(20,590)	6	1.41	39.47	1.82
JY6	54,345	108	13	(21,745)	8	2.50	44.44	1.90
SB	(3,944)	120	13	(11,179)	9	N/A	38.33	1.47
Total:	319,080	1,020	14	(48,249)	12	6.61	41.18	1.85

Notes: Portfolio summary includes data from January 1, 2000, to December 31, 2009, and assumes $10 round-turn deductions for slippage and commissions.
Source: CQG, Inc. © 2010. All rights reserved worldwide.

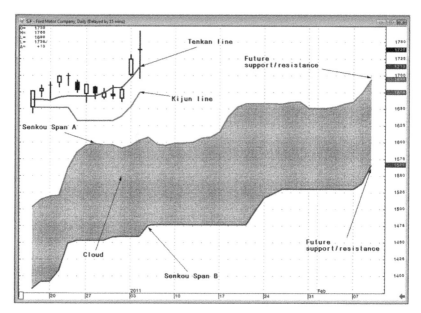

FIGURE 8.5 Daily Chart of Ford Motor Company with Ichimoku Clouds
Source: CQG, Inc. © 2010. All rights reserved worldwide.

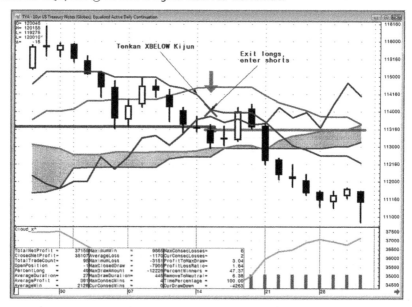

FIGURE 8.6 Equalized Active Daily Continuation Chart for CME Group 10-Year
U.S. Treasury Note Futures Using Ichimoku Crossover
Note: Trade summary includes data from January 1, 2000, to December 31, 2009,
and assumes $10 round-turn deductions for slippage and commissions.
Source: CQG, Inc. © 2010. All rights reserved worldwide.

The Tenkan and Kijun lines are traditional, trend-following moving average crossover tools. By contrast, the difference between Senkou Span A line and Senkou Span B lines forms a cloud that offers support or resistance levels over the coming 26 periods (see Figure 8.5).

Although the Ichimoku clouds offer trend-following traders a wide array of possible trading system alternatives, they can also be used to create a simple Tenkan/Kijun trend-following crossover model (see Figure 8.6).

Using CQG, the programming code for the Ichimoku crossover system is written this way:

```
Long Entry:

Imoku1(@,9)[-1] > Imoku2(@,26)[-1]

Long Exit:

Imoku1(@,9)[-1] < Imoku2(@,26)[-1]

Short Entry:

Imoku1(@,9)[-1] < Imoku2(@,26)[-1]

Short Exit:

Imoku1(@,9)[-1] > Imoku2(@,26)[-1]
```

TABLE 8.5 Ichimoku Crossover System

Asset	Profit	# Trades	# Days	Max Draw	MCL	P:MD	%W	P:L
ES	(10,200)	105	25	(46,287)	15	N/A	33.33	1.82
CL	129,160	89	29	(31,390)	3	4.11	46.07	2.28
NG	163,380	97	27	(67,220)	5	2.4	43.30	2.00
GC	(6,230)	105	25	(45,300)	6	N/A	42.86	1.25
ZS	23,655	117	22	(29,807)	8	.79	38.46	1.94
ZN	37,159	95	27	(12,226)	6	3.04	47.37	1.82
EU6	60,475	115	23	(37,740)	10	1.60	41.74	1.96
JY6	33,095	108	24	(23,157)	10	1.43	42.59	1.75
SB	1,592	123	21	(12,101)	13	.13	35.77	1.86
Total:	432,086	954	25	(92,771)	16	4.66	40.99	1.98

Notes: Portfolio summary includes data from January 1, 2000, to December 31, 2009, and assumes $10 round-turn deductions for slippage and commissions.

Source: CQG, Inc. © 2010. All rights reserved worldwide.

Next, we will make the simple Tenkan/Kijun trend-following crossover model more robust by incorporating the clouds. Specifically, long entry now requires bullish Tenkan/Kijun crossovers to occur above the clouds, and short-entry bearish crossovers must occur below the clouds. Also, open positions are exited whenever a reversal crossover occurs or the close is no longer above or below the cloud (see Figure 8.7).

Using CQG, the programming code for the Ichimoku Clouds crossover system is written this way:

```
Long Entry:

Imoku1(@,9)[-1] > Imoku2(@,26)[-1] AND Close(@)[-1] >
Imoku3(@,52)[-27] AND Close(@)[-1] > Imoku4(@,9,26,Sim,1)
[-27]

Long Exit:

Imoku1(@,9)[-1] < Imoku2(@,26)[-1] OR Close(@)[-1] <
Imoku3(@,52)[-27] OR Close(@)[-1] < Imoku4(@,9,26,Sim,1)
[-27]

Short Entry:

Imoku1(@,9)[-1] < Imoku2(@,26)[-1] AND Close(@)[-1] <
Imoku3(@,52)[-27] AND Close(@)[-1] < Imoku4(@,9,26,Sim,1)
[-27]

Short Exit:

Imoku1(@,9)[-1] > Imoku2(@,26)[-1] OR Close(@)[-1] >
Imoku3(@,52)[-27] OR Close(@)[-1] > Imoku4(@,9,26,Sim,1)
[-27]
```

Although the original Tenkan/Kijun crossover model's portfolio enjoyed a higher total net profit as well as a larger percentage of winning trades, overall performance was less robust because of significantly higher maximum drawdowns endured and inferior average profit to average loss ratio when compared with the Ichimoku clouds crossover (see Tables 8.5 and 8.6). This comparison confirms the old poker cliché: "It's not how many pots you win, but how big the pots are when you win them."

Bollinger Band Breakout System   Bollinger Band breakout was introduced in Chapter 3 and is the simplest mechanical trading system I ever developed. Like RSI Trend, it is another model capitalizing on losses

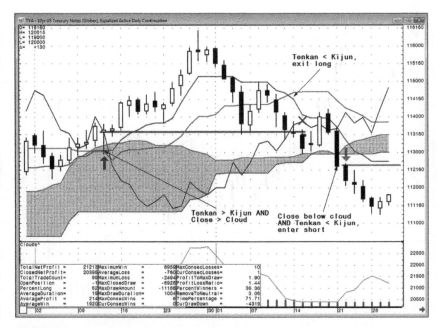

FIGURE 8.7 Equalized Active Daily Continuation Chart for CME Group 10-Year U.S. Treasury Note Futures Using Ichimoku Clouds Crossover

Note: Trade summary includes data from January 1, 2000, to December 31, 2009, and assumes $10 round-turn deductions for slippage and commissions.

Source: CQG, Inc. © 2010. All rights reserved worldwide.

TABLE 8.6 Ichimoku Clouds Crossover

Asset	Profit	# Trades	# Days	Max Draw	MCL	P:MD	%W	P:L
ES	1,302	106	19	(29,547)	13	.04	28.30	2.57
CL	111,870	98	20	(33,060)	7	3.38	30.61	4.38
NG	124,690	98	20	(88,690)	8	1.41	37.76	2.39
GC	(4,750)	113	16	(31,290)	8	N/A	29.20	2.28
ZS	15,317	12	18	(29,925)	7	.51	36.27	2.06
ZN	21,213	99	19	(11,188)	10	1.90	36.36	2.53
EU6	61,252	111	17	(25,785)	9	2.38	32.43	3.25
JY6	28,785	109	17	(16,790)	12	1.71	33.94	2.65
SB	8,986	115	16	(10,847)	11	.83	30.43	2.95
Total:	368,665	951	18	(73,546)	14	5.01	32.70	2.89

Notes: Portfolio summary includes data from January 1, 2000, to December 31, 2009, and assumes $10 round-turn deductions for slippage and commissions.

Source: CQG Inc. © 2010. All rights reserved worldwide.

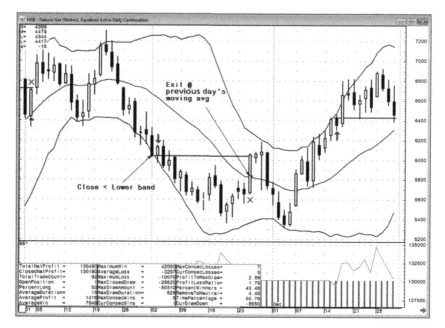

FIGURE 8.8 Equalized Active Daily Continuation Chart for CME Group Natural Gas Futures with Bollinger Band Breakout System

Note: Trade summary includes data from January 1, 2000, to December 31, 2009, and assumes $10 round-turn deductions for slippage and commissions.

Source: CQG, Inc. © 2010. All rights reserved worldwide.

TABLE 8.7 Bollinger Band Breakout

Asset	Profit	# Trades	# Days	Max Draw	MCL	P:MD	%W	P:L
ES	(24,082)	102	11	(26,622)	10	N/A	31.37	1.61
CL	59,860	92	13	(24,960)	12	2.40	39.13	2.42
NG	130,490	92	15	(50,310)	7	2.59	43.48	2.29
GC	(10,440)	101	13	(25,080)	9	N/A	32.67	1.76
ZS	42,155	87	14	(14,705)	10	2.87	45.98	2.26
ZN	18,796	86	15	(11,680)	7	1.68	43.02	1.95
EU6	29,280	82	14	(23,572)	8	1.24	37.80	2.22
JY6	(9,552)	84	13	(31,582)	10	N/A	36.90	1.68
SB	6,902	96	13	(6,962)	7	.99	34.37	2.37
Total:	243,409	822	13	(77,073)	16	3.16	37.78	2.21

Notes: Portfolio summary includes data from January 1, 2000, to December 31, 2009, and assumes $10 round-turn deductions for slippage and commissions.

Source: CQG, Inc. © 2010. All rights reserved worldwide.

suffered by those hoping for mean reversion. Bollinger Bands are two standard deviations above and below a 20-period simple moving average and are traditionally used to capitalize on the market's propensity to mean reversion. By entering long positions when the market closes above the upper band (and short positions when it closes below the lower band), trend-followers can play breakouts and use the 20-period moving average as a simple yet robust trailing stop (see Figure 8.8).

Using CQG, the programming code for the Bollinger Band breakout system is written this way:

```
Long Entry:

Close(@)[-1] > BHI(@,Sim,20,2.00)[-1]

Short Entry:

Close(@)[-1] < BLO(@,Sim,20,2.00)[-1]

Long Exit and Short Exit:

MA(@,Sim,20)[-1]
```

Mean Reversion Systems

The main disadvantage of most throwaway trend-following systems is their poor winning percentages. By contrast, mean reversion systems typically enjoy high winning percentages. Generally speaking, this improvement in winning percentage of trades comes at the cost of a deteriorating average profit to average loss ratio.

RSI Extremes System RSI Extremes is a throwaway system featured in my first book, various articles, and trading courses over the years because it combines a mean reversion oscillator (relative strength index) with a long-term trend-following indicator (a 200-period simple moving average). By combining these two indicators, RSI Extremes forces traders to wait for markets to become extremely overbought or oversold and then allows entry only in the direction of the longer-term trend. The version shown here buys when the market is above its 200-period simple moving average and the 9-period RSI is below 35 or sells when the market is below its 200-period simple moving average and the 9-period RSI is above 65. We exit with profits from long positions whenever the long-term trend reasserts itself and the 9-period RSI generates a reading above 65, and we exit shorts when the 9-period RSI drops below 35. In addition, the system includes a fail-safe stop loss exit of $7,500 per contract (see Figure 8.9).

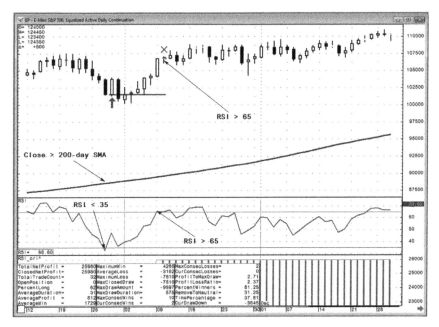

FIGURE 8.9 Equalized Active Daily Continuation Chart for CME Group E-Mini S&P 500 Index Futures with RSI Extremes System

Note: Trade summary includes data from January 1, 2000, to December 31, 2009, and assumes $10 round-turn deductions for slippage and commissions.

Source: CQG, Inc. © 2010. All rights reserved worldwide.

TABLE 8.8 RSI Extremes

Asset	Profit	# Trades	# Days	Max Draw	MCL	P:MD	%W	P:L
ES	25,980	32	31	(9,597)	2	2.71	81.25	.55
CL	33,140	35	24	(43,170)	5	.77	65.71	.85
NG	11,110	46	18	(66,850)	6	.17	47.83	1.16
GC	17,460	37	27	(14,890)	1	1.17	70.27	.67
ZS	(11,850)	35	36	(23,742)	2	N/A	60	.55
ZN	(3,539)	32	32	(16,494)	2	N/A	59.37	.59
EU6	11,745	33	23	(15,020)	3	.78	66.67	.58
JY6	(3,732)	32	28	(17,235)	2	N/A	62.50	.53
SB	8,875	32	34	(6,720)	2	1.32	75	.62
Total:	89,189	314	28	(79,012)	10	1.13	64.65	.64

Notes: Portfolio summary includes data from January 1, 2000, to December 31, 2009, and assumes $10 round-turn deductions for slippage and commissions.

Source: CQG, Inc. © 2010. All rights reserved worldwide.

Using CQG, the programming code for RSI Extremes is written this way:

```
Long Entry:

RSI(@,9)[-1] < 35 AND Close(@)[-1] > MA(@,Sim,200)[-1]

Long Exit:

RSI(@,9)[-1] > 65 OR OpenPositionAverageEntryPrice
(@,ThisTradeOnly) - Dollar2Price(@,7500) / OpenPositionSize
(@,ThisTradeOnly)

Short Entry:

RSI(@,9)[-1] > 65 AND Close(@)[-1] < MA(@,Sim,200)[-1]

Short Exit:

RSI(@,9)[-1] < 35 OR OpenPositionAverageEntryPrice
(@,ThisTradeOnly) - Dollar2Price(@,7500) / OpenPositionSize
(@,ThisTradeOnly)
```

As expected, the mean reversion system enjoyed a superior percentage of winning trades as well as a deterioration of average profit to average loss ratio when compared with various trend-following systems such as Bollinger Band breakout, Ichimoku cloud crossover, and so on.

RSI Extremes System with Volume Filter   Since electronic trading has eliminated the problem of lagging volume data on exchange-traded futures contracts, I include a modified version of the original RSI Extremes system with a volume filter that allows entry only if volume decreases as the market achieves its extreme RSI reading (see Figure 8.10).[2]

Using CQG, the programming code for RSI Extremes with volume filter is written this way:

```
Long Entry:

RSI(@,9)[-1] < 35 AND Close(@)[-1] > MA(@,Sim,200)[-1] AND
Vol(@)[-2] > Vol(@)[-1]

Long Exit:

RSI(@,9)[-1] > 65 OR OpenPositionAverageEntryPrice
(@,ThisTradeOnly) - Dollar2Price(@,7500) / OpenPositionSize
(@,ThisTradeOnly)
```

Short Entry:

```
RSI(@,9)[-1] > 65 AND Close(@)[-1] < MA(@,Sim,200)[-1] AND
Vol(@)[-2] > Vol(@)[-1]
```

Short Exit:

```
RSI(@,9)[-1] < 35 OR OpenPositionAverageEntryPrice
(@,ThisTradeOnly) - Dollar2Price(@,7500) / OpenPositionSize
(@,ThisTradeOnly)
```

Although the volume filter did not dramatically improve our mean reversion system, we did enjoy fairly consistent, moderate improvements when compared with the original version in terms of profit to maximum drawdown ratio as well as average profit to average loss ratio (see Tables 8.8 and 8.9).

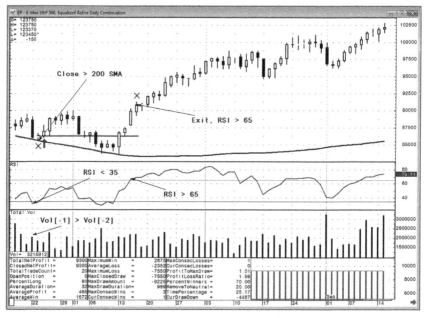

FIGURE 8.10 Equalized Active Daily Continuation Chart for CME Group E-Mini S&P 500 Index Futures Using RSI Extremes with Volume Filter

Note: Trade summary includes data from January 1, 2000, to December 31, 2009, and assumes $10 round-turn deductions for slippage and commissions.

Source: CQG, Inc. © 2010. All rights reserved worldwide.

TABLE 8.9 RSI Extremes with Volume Filter

Asset	Profit	# Trades	# Days	Max Draw	MCL	P:MD	%W	P:L
ES	10,100	20	32	(9,145)	1	1.10	70	.74
CL	23,480	26	24	(35,180)	4	.67	73.08	.63
NG	36,830	43	17	(45,130)	4	.82	51.16	1.19
GC	13,390	25	29	(17,050)	1	.79	64	.98
ZS	(13,750)	15	26	(27,665)	3	N/A	60	.45
ZN	(8,078)	25	34	(16,128)	2	N/A	56	.52
EU6	21,160	24	22	(14,390)	2	1.47	66.67	.75
JY6	1,535	24	26	(20,117)	3	.08	58.33	.75
SB	11,630	22	29	(5,331)	1	2.18	86.36	.78
Total:	96,297	224	27	(75,901)	8	1.27	64.29	.72

Notes: Portfolio summary includes data from January 1, 2000, to December 31, 2009, and assumes $10 round-turn deductions for slippage and commissions.
Source: CQG, Inc. © 2010. All rights reserved worldwide.

Combining Noncorrelated Systems

A quick glance at the Totals row of Tables 8.1 to 8.9 suggests that trading a diversified portfolio of assets makes many positive expectancy models more robust. Although asset class diversification is the most common form seen in trading, this section introduces readers to trade system diversification. In general, trade system diversification capitalizes on the principle that markets can do only two things, trend or trade in a range; therefore by simultaneously executing both trend-following and mean reversion models, we can improve our risk-adjusted rate of return. Since both models enjoy positive expectancy overall and capitalize on different types of market behavior, it is reasonable to assume that when a trend-following model experiences its equity drawdown because of choppy markets, the mean reversion model's ability to capitalize on this same choppiness will temper the severity of the drawdown (and vice versa for trending markets).

Although any of the trend-following and mean reversion models shown in Table 8.10 could be used to illustrate trade system diversification, Table 8.11 combines two of the most robust throwaway models shown in this chapter, RSI Trend with a 10-day stop and RSI Extremes with the volume filter. As expected, the profits of the two models are additive, but the worst peak-to-valley drawdown in account equity is not. Therefore, the profit to maximum drawdown for the combination of these two models is superior to either model as a standalone system. In addition, although the combined performance of the models still experienced less than 50 percent winning trades, the addition of our mean reversion model did increase the

TABLE 8.10   Comparisons of Mechanical Trading Systems

System	Profit	# Trades	# Days	Max Draw	MCL	P:MD	%W	P:L
RSI Trend10	341,854	884	18	(48,281)	13	7.08	41.29	1.97
RSI Trend3	115,644	1,595	6	(55,207)	15	2.09	36.74	1.92
RSI Trend exits	319,080	1,020	14	(48,249)	12	6.61	41.18	1.85
BB Break	243,409	822	13	(77,073)	16	3.16	37.78	2.21
Ichi Xover	432,086	954	25	(92,771)	16	4.66	40.99	1.98
Ichi Clouds	368,665	951	18	(73,546)	14	5.01	32.70	2.89
RSIx Volume	96,297	224	27	(75,901)	8	1.27	64.29	.72
RSIx	89,189	314	28	(79,012)	10	1.13	64.65	.64

Notes: Portfolio summary includes data from January 1, 2000, to December 31, 2009, and assumes $10 round-turn deductions for slippage and commissions.
Source: CQG, Inc. © 2010. All rights reserved worldwide.

TABLE 8.11   Combining RSI Trend and RSI Extremes with Volume Filter

System	Profit	# Trades	# Days	Max Draw	MCL	P:MD	%W	P:L
RSI Trend10	341,854	884	18	(48,281)	13	7.08	41.29	1.97
RSIx Volume	96,297	224	27	(75,901)	8	1.27	64.29	.72
Combo	438,151	1,108	20	(46,892)	9	9.34	45.85	1.60

Notes: Portfolio summary includes data from January 1, 2000, to December 31, 2009, and assumes $10 round-turn deductions for slippage and commissions.
Source: CQG, Inc. © 2010. All rights reserved worldwide.

percentage of winning trades from 41.29 percent for RSI Trend as a stand-alone to 45.85 percent for the combined portfolio (see Table 8.11).

NONMECHANICAL MODELS

Although many of the indicators used in classical technical analysis, such as trendlines, retracements, divergences, and so forth, are difficult to incorporate into mechanical trading models, they are still quite robust and can be used to develop rule-based positive expectancy models.[3] A key in developing robust trading models using these indicators is recognizing that the indicator is not a complete stand-alone trading system and must therefore be augmented with rules of risk management as well as exiting with profits. Although the spectrum of possibilities regarding exit for classical indicators is virtually limitless, I focus on regret minimization techniques introduced in Chapter 6.

Fibonacci Retracement Models

Despite lacking a universally objective answer regarding which cyclical highs and lows to measure from, speculators are attracted to models incorporating retracement theory because they participate in the dominant, longer-term trend during pullbacks, thereby identifying low-risk/high-reward trading opportunities.

Although Charles Dow published his concepts of buying or selling into retracements within the major trend around 1900, most speculators nowadays use retracement levels introduced by Ralph Nelson Elliott in the 1930s, which are based on Fibonacci number sequences. The most popular—and therefore commonly used—of these Fibonacci retracement levels are the 38.2 percent, 50 percent, and 61.8 percent retracements.[4]

Figure 8.11 shows how Fibonacci retracement levels allow discretionary traders to objectively quantify entry levels, risk, and reward. As stated earlier, retracement traders should ask, "Do I want more trading signals and more false positives or fewer, higher quality signals with fewer false positives?" For example, aggressive traders (who fear missing the trade) could sell cash U.S. dollar–Japanese yen (USD–JPY) at the 38.2 percent retracement level of 91.17, placing a protective stop loss order above

FIGURE 8.11 Weekly Chart of Spot USD-JPY with Fibonacci Retracement Levels
Source: CQG, Inc. © 2010. All rights reserved worldwide.

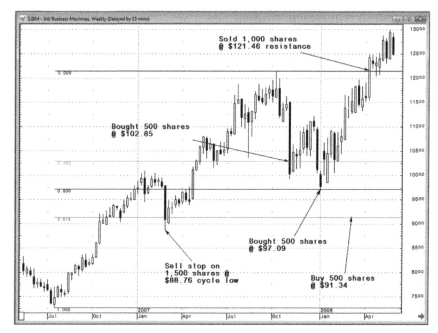

FIGURE 8.12 Weekly Chart of IBM Inc. with Fibonacci Retracement Levels
Source: CQG, Inc. © 2010. All rights reserved worldwide.

the 61.8 percent retracement level of 95.10, and exit with profits at previous cycle lows of 84.82. By contrast, more risk-averse traders (willing to risk missing the trade) might wait to sell at the 50 percent retracement price level of 93.13, placing a protective stop loss order above the 61.8 percent retracement level of 95.10, and exit with profits at previous cycle lows at 84.82. Finally, the most conservative traders could accept the highest probability of missing the trade by waiting to sell at the 61.8 percent retracement level of 95.10, placing a stop loss order just above 95.10, and exit with profits at previous cycle lows at 84.82 (see Figure 8.11).

Finally, remember that as long as we do not violate prudent rules of risk management, we can incorporate the regret minimization techniques described in Chapter 6 to ensure partial participation in retracements by staggering our limit entry orders at various retracement levels (see Figure 8.12).

Divergence Models

Another popular type of market behavior traders exploit to build positive expectancy models is based on the concept of divergence. The rule of thumb for divergence models is that the indicator is right and the price is wrong. The two most commonly employed types of divergence models are volume divergence and oscillator divergence. In both instances, traders are looking for divergence to signal trend reversal, so the key to success is complementing the signals with stringent rules of risk management as well as a willingness to accept multiple consecutive small losses so as to participate in the early—and often most profitable stage—of the new market trend.

Although it sounds obvious, it is worth mentioning that divergence models—along with other reversal methods—attempt to capitalize on trend reversals and success is therefore predicated on a pre-existing trend to reverse from. In other words, reversal models should signal trade entry only after a clearly identifiable trending period, or as I like to say, you can't reverse from sideways.

RSI Divergence Trade: Home Depot Inc. On November 5, 2010, Home Depot made a new intraday price high of $32.29 per share (its highest high since June 17, 2010) along with a new nine-day RSI high. The accompaniment of the new high in RSI in early November confirmed the health of the bullish price move. By contrast, on November 16, 2010, the stock took out its November 5, 2010, highs but RSI recorded a lower high. This divergence between the RSI oscillator and price signaled a low-risk/high-reward trading opportunity.

As a result, divergence traders sold the next day's opening price of $31.66 and placed a protective buy stop at the previous day's high of $32.82. Looking at recent cycle lows, they simultaneously placed a limit order to buy back 50 percent of the short position at October 18, 2010, cycle lows of $30.18. They could use a one-day trailing buy stop (see Figure 8.13) to let profits run on the remainder of the position. In this particular trade, the one-day trailing stop was triggered on the following day's open at $30.60 (see Figure 8.14).

RSI and Volume Divergence Trade: CME Group Crude Oil Futures Next we will incorporate two complementary technical indicators to confirm the validity of divergence signals. In this example, we choose volume and the nine-day RSI oscillator and take trades only if both indicators show divergence from price action. Looking at Figure 8.15, notice how August 2008 CME Group crude oil futures made new highs, which were not confirmed by the RSI oscillator making higher highs. If we looked only at RSI, this would be a divergence trade. However, by adding a second divergence criterion, volume, we see a significant increase in daily volume as the market made new highs and therefore filtered out this suboptimal divergence signal (see Figure 8.15).

FIGURE 8.13 Daily Chart of Home Depot Inc. with RSI Divergence
Source: CQG, Inc. © 2010. All rights reserved worldwide.

FIGURE 8.14 Daily Chart of Home Depot Inc. Trade Showing Exit on Trailing Stop
Source: CQG, Inc. © 2010. All rights reserved worldwide.

FIGURE 8.15 August 2008 Daily Chart of CME Group Crude Oil Futures Contract Showing RSI Divergence and Volume Confirmation as Contract Makes New Highs
Source: CQG, Inc. © 2010. All rights reserved worldwide.

By contrast, the new price highs on July 3, 2008, were accompanied by both RSI and volume divergence. This divergence was obviously occurring on a daily basis leading up to the ultimate highs of July 3, 2008, and it is only after RSI drops from its peak that we can be certain the oscillator will validate its divergence.[5] RSI gives evidence of its top with a lower reading on July 4, 2008, so we sell the July 7 open at $144.27, placing a protective buy stop at the July 3 high of $145.85. Our initial profit target for 50 percent of the position is recent cycle lows at $131.75. Unfortunately, before reaching these lows, our one-day trailing stop was triggered on July 10, 2010, at $138.28 (see Figure 8.16).

Interestingly, crude oil again made new highs on July 13, 2008, and again the highs were accompanied by divergence in volume and RSI. The violent down day on July 15 brought RSI off its cycle highs, confirming the divergence and triggering a sell signal for divergence traders on the open of July 16 at $138.77. Protective stops were placed at the July 13 cycle high of $147.27, and our initial profit target for 50 percent of the position at recent cycle lows of $131.75 was achieved on July 17. Also, our one-day trailing stop was triggered on July 21 at $132.04 (see Figure 8.17).

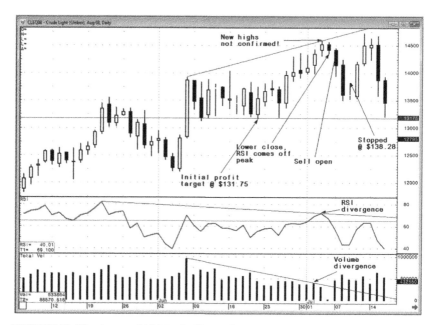

FIGURE 8.16 August 2008 Daily Chart of CME Group Crude Oil Futures Contract with RSI and Volume Divergence Trade

Source: CQG, Inc. © 2010. All rights reserved worldwide.

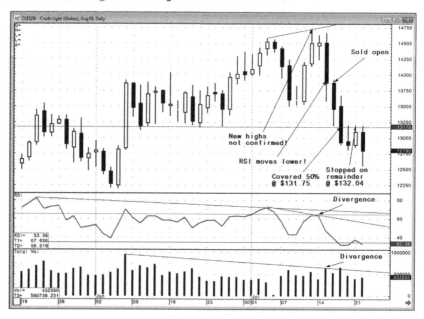

FIGURE 8.17 Second Divergence Trade in August 2008 CME Group Crude Oil Futures

Source: CQG, Inc. © 2010. All rights reserved worldwide.

Classical Technical Models

Trendlines and horizontal support, or resistance breakouts, are also commonly used by technicians to build positive expectancy trading models. Just as we saw with divergence models, trendlines, along with horizontal support and resistance levels, are merely indicators that must be augmented with risk management criteria to build comprehensive trading methodologies.

Trade: Coca-Cola Co. During the October 2008 credit crisis, Coca-Cola Co. rebounded to $47.53 per share. That high formed a horizontal resistance level that went unchallenged until the week of May 18, 2009. Recognizing $47.53 as a psychological pivot, long-term trend-following traders bought there in May 2009, placing sell stops at the March 2009 cycle low of $37.44. As the new bull trend matured, old resistance at $47.53 not only became new horizontal support, but also acted as trendline support. Traders continued tracking this up trendline until it broke on a closing basis during the week of January 4, 2010. As a result of its close below the up trendline, speculators sold shares at the open of the following week at $55.15 (see Figure 8.18).

FIGURE 8.18 Weekly Chart of Coca-Cola Co. with Horizontal Resistance, Support, and Trendline

Source: CQG, Inc. © 2010. All rights reserved worldwide.

Combining Technical Indicators

Most traders using nonmechanical models combine a wide array of the aforementioned indicators. They also typically complement these indicators with fundamental analysis such as government reports, weather, geopolitics, central bank interest rate decisions, and so forth. Although the variety of combinations is virtually limitless, a simple example is included next.

Trade: McDonald's Corporation   A significant uptrend line can be drawn on the daily chart of McDonald's Corporation from cycle lows on July 30, 2010, to subsequent lows on September 30 and October 12. When the market closes below its up trendline on November 16, 2010, this is our cue to watch for RSI divergences. That divergence occurs on December 7, 2010, when new highs in the stock are not confirmed by new RSI highs. Following this divergence, we wait for evidence that the market has completed its uptrend. This evidence occurs on December 8 when the stock gaps below the dominant up trendline and RSI falls from its December 7 peak.

As a result, we sell the December 9 open at $79.20, placing a protective buy stop at the December 7 high of $80.94 or at $79.91 (which is just above the broken up trendline). The old September 2010 resistance level of $76.26 should act as initial support and is therefore a logical price to cover shorts. This $76.26 support level was breached on December 27, 2010 (see Figure 8.19).

EQUITY TRADING MODELS

The global dominance of electronic trading has been an indisputable boon for speculative traders, resulting in lower commissions and greater liquidity. Nevertheless, the demise of open outcry exchange-traded futures destroyed two previously viable positive expectancy day trading models, namely opening range breakouts and gap trading.[6]

Twenty-four-hour markets means that, generally speaking, the only remaining gaps occur between the North American Friday afternoon close and Australia's Monday morning open. Also, 24-hour price discovery in electronically traded futures and foreign exchange markets has eliminated pent-up buying and selling pressure, thereby lessening the significance of price discovery on the open in the asset's primary market venue.

The only significant exception to this rule regarding gaps and opening ranges is in equity trading. Because U.S. equities close at 4 P.M. EST and open at 9:30 A.M. EST, they still experience pent-up buying and selling

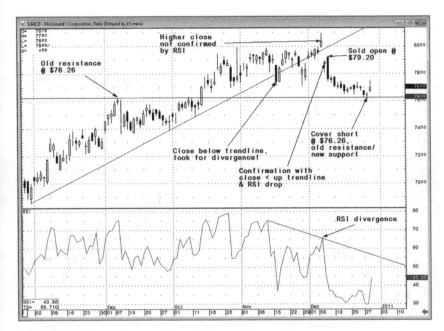

FIGURE 8.19 Daily Chart of McDonald's Corporation with Trendlines, Horizontal Resistance, Support, and RSI Divergence
Source: CQG, Inc. © 2010. All rights reserved worldwide.

pressure on the 9:30 A.M. EST open as well as gaps between the 4 P.M. EST close of the previous day and the 9:30 A.M. EST open of the following day (see Figure 8.20).

Opening Range Breakout

When I started trading on the floor of the New York Futures Exchange in 1987, day trading models based on breakouts from the opening range were extremely popular among some of the most successful speculators. As explained earlier, these models worked based on the concept that breakouts following the establishment of the day's opening range tended to follow through more often than breakouts during subsequent time intervals because the opening range incorporated pent-up overnight buying and selling pressures. Of course, each trader tailored this general concept to fit his individual hold time, risk appetite, and reward criteria. Short-term traders used the first five minutes as their opening range, whereas longer-term day traders defined the opening range as the first hour of trading. Irrespective of which timeframe traders used for the opening range, they would take

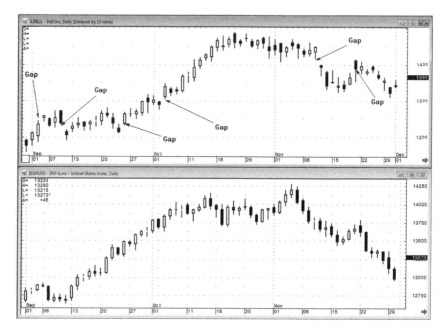

FIGURE 8.20 Comparison of Daily Charts of Dell Inc. and Spot Eurocurrency–U.S. Dollar Shows Gaps in Equities

Source: CQG, Inc. © 2010. All rights reserved worldwide.

trades in the direction of the breakout from the high or low of that range, placing stops at the opposite end of the range.

Trade: Intel Corporation   On December 29, 2010, Intel shares opened at $20.94, which was a gap above their $20.88 closing price from December 28. Although this set a bullish bias for the day, conservative traders waited for the establishment of the high and low of the opening range. As stated earlier, the opening range needs to be defined by each individual trader's personality. In this particular example, we define the opening range as the first 15 minutes of trading. Consequently, the high of the opening range was $20.98 and the low was $20.90, so breakout traders place buy stops at $20.99 and sell stops at $20.89. During the 10:00 A.M. EST candlestick, our buy stop was triggered at $20.99. Our original sell stop order at $20.89 now serves as our risk management stop in case of a false breakout.

   Although there are virtually limitless ways of exiting this trade, I personally favor quick, opportunistic trade management for day trading where a limit order to sell half the position is placed one tick above the high of the breakout bar and the remainder of the position uses a trailing stop set to

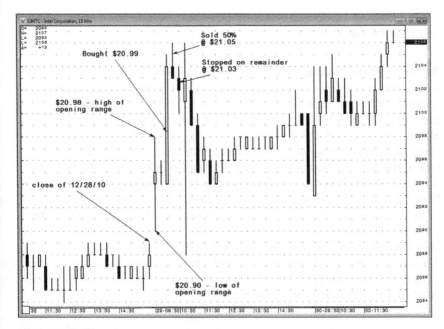

FIGURE 8.21   Fifteen-Minute Chart of Intel Corporation Showing Opening Range Breakout Trade

Source: CQG, Inc. © 2010. All rights reserved worldwide.

the previous bar's low. By managing the position this way, we took profits on half the trade during the 10:15 A.M. EST candlestick at $21.05 and were stopped out of the remainder during the 10:30 A.M. candlestick at $21.03 (see Figure 8.21).[7]

Gap Trading

Careful examination of Figure 8.21 showed a bullish gap up from the previous day's close. In fact, gap trading and opening range breakout trading typically go hand in hand for many day traders. Gaps are the difference between the previous day's closing price and the next day's open. Technicians divide gaps into two categories: filled and unfilled gaps. Filled gaps are typically antithetical to successful opening range breakout traders. Instead day traders buy or sell breakouts from the opening range and place risk management stops at the high or low of the gap opening (as shown in Figure 8.21).

Many day traders will add a second confirming criterion to their gap trades. Common additional criteria include requiring the gapping opening range breakout be accompanied by increasing volume or a break of the previous day's high or low.

Trade: Altria Group Inc. Throughout December 29, 2010, Altria Group Inc. held support at $24.70 per share. Because the December 30 open gapped below that support, we sold at $24.67. Our initial risk management buy stop would be just above the old support–new resistance level of $24.70. However, after the 15-minute opening range bar, more risk-averse traders could lower stops to one penny above the gap's high. Also, a break below the low of the opening range bar will confirm the validity of the down gap as well as the break below the $24.70 support level. This confirmation occurred during the 9:45 A.M. EST bar when we broke the low of the opening range and generated our profit target for 50 percent of the position one penny below $24.60 (which was the low of the breakout bar). We consequently covered 50 percent of our position during the 10 A.M. EST bar at $24.59 and began trailing our protective buy stop on the remainder of the position at the high of the previous bar. That buy stop was triggered at 10:45 A.M. at $24.62 (see Figure 8.22).

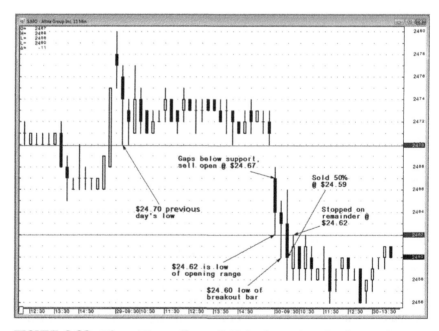

FIGURE 8.22 Fifteen-Minute Chart of Altria Group Inc. Combining Opening Range and Gap Trading

Source: CQG, Inc. © 2010. All rights reserved worldwide.

FINAL THOUGHTS

Throughout this chapter we examined a wide array of positive expectancy models. As you research and modify these models to fit your personality, remember one basic rule of thumb (which will be expanded upon in Chapter 9): *Do not second-guess the signal.* Just plan your trades and trade your plans. In general, second-guessing the signal leads to a breakdown in discipline and failure of the positive expectancy model.

That stated, successful trading is a multidimensional proposition; there consequently are notable exceptions to rigid adherence of this trade-your-plans rule. The most obvious are instances in which adherence to the plan would result in violation of risk management rules (as defined in Chapter 2). Another exception is blindly adhering to a trading plan despite a paradigm shift in the value of the asset traded (as defined in Chapter 1). Finally, short-term traders must avoid entry prior to price shock events such as government reports, interest rate announcements, and so on, as this could result in a high-risk/low-reward trading scenario.

CHAPTER 9

Anticipating the Signal

Patience is a high virtue.

—Geoffrey Chaucer

O ne of the most prevalent and destructive breakdowns in trader discipline arises from attempting to anticipate the signal. This chapter examines the allure of historically high or low prices and how focusing on price history leads speculators to abandon positive expectancy trading models. Particular emphasis is placed on the development of psychological tools to promote patience and discipline in the face of historically unprecedented prices.

ALWAYS TRADE VALUE, NEVER TRADE PRICE

You've heard it before: Buy low and sell high. Although on the surface it seems simple, logical, and self-evident, it is deceptive and has led to fantastic losses for countless traders because no one knows what a high or low price is while markets are moving to unprecedented historical price levels. When I wrote these words in 2011, 1,067.2 seemed like a low price for the Dow Jones Industrial Average, but in 1982 it was the highest level ever recorded (see Figures 9.1 and 9.2). The truth of historically high prices seeming low in retrospect (and vice versa) led me to develop my own cliché regarding high and low prices: Always trade value, never trade price.

FIGURE 9.1 Quarterly Cash Dow Jones Industrial Average Chart Breaks to All-Time New Highs in 1982
Source: CQG, Inc. © 2010. All rights reserved worldwide.

FIGURE 9.2 Yearly Cash Dow Jones Industrial Average Chart from 1982 Break of Old Highs to July 2010
Source: CQG, Inc. © 2010. All rights reserved worldwide.

FIGURE 9.3 Quarterly Rolling Front-Month ICE Cotton Continuation Chart Breaks to All-Time New Highs in 2010
Source: CQG, Inc. © 2010. All rights reserved worldwide.

Returning to our Dow Jones Industrial Average example, although 1,067.2 seemed like a historically high price in 1982, that historically high price level simultaneously represented an undervalued market level. In fact, when the market breached its resistance at 1,067.2, it entered what I call the blue-sky phase of its new bull market. When markets rally to approach various historical resistance levels, there are a wide variety of psychological selling pressures including all the price-has-memory issues discussed in Chapter 1. By contrast, after breaching those historical resistance areas, such psychological selling pressures have been satiated. Consequently, traders selling into early stages of blue-sky rallies tend to be the weakest hands since their sole rationale for selling is that prices have never before risen to these historically unprecedented levels (see Figure 9.3).

SUPPORT (AND RESISTANCE) WERE MADE TO BE BROKEN

In 2002, a significant portion of my trading was long-term trend following in cash foreign exchange markets. Another speculator asked what I thought

FIGURE 9.4 Weekly Cash Eurocurrency–U.S. Dollar Chart in 2002
Source: CQG, Inc. © 2010. All rights reserved worldwide.

of the eurocurrency vis-à-vis the U.S. dollar. I told him I was long; he asked, "From what price?" I hesitated because the question always seemed extraneous to me. What difference did it make what price I was long from? Since I am still long now, it means I would buy the current price. But I liked the guy, so I bit my tongue, answering, "I'm long from .9066."

> *He whistled, "Nice trade. Where are you getting out?"*
> *I responded, "No idea. I'll sell when it stops going up."*
> *He winced, "There's a lot of resistance on that chart."*
> *I said, "Resistance was made to be broken."*

The guy probably thought me out of my mind. Spot euro was trading at .9750 (see Figure 9.4) and there was obvious psychological resistance at 1.00 along with important historical resistance at 1.10, 1.23, as well as at the all-time highs of 1.4535 (see Figure 9.5). I wish I could say I knew the market was going to break those levels, but I honestly had no idea. Instead, it was *because* I had no idea where the market would trade in the future that I was willing to wait for evidence of a trend reversal. Without such evidence, there was absolutely no reason to sell, and without a reason

FIGURE 9.5 Quarterly Cash Eurocurrency–U.S. Dollar Chart Showing Various Levels of Long-Term Resistance
Source: CQG, Inc. © 2010. All rights reserved worldwide.

to sell, trend-following traders should remain long. Why? It was still a bull market, and long-term trend followers must be long in bull markets and short in bear markets. To do otherwise is illogical. As shown in Figure 9.6, objective evidence of a reversal—violation of long-term technical support—came in 2005 with breaking of 2004 cycle lows at 1.1761.

DON'T ANTICIPATE, JUST PARTICIPATE

Rookie traders want to buy the low tick and sell the high tick. We examined this desire to buy the low and sell the high in Chapter 6 as the perfect trader syndrome. If one could buy the low and sell the high, they would achieve the elusive goal of perfection in trading by capturing all of the market's potential profits—thereby completely eradicating regret—without enduring any emotional pain of losses or the potential for loss. Although this allure of perfection in trading is quite natural, it is also responsible for the destruction of the vast majority of fledgling trading careers.

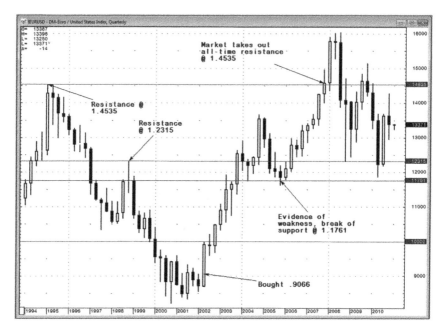

FIGURE 9.6 Quarterly Cash Eurocurrency–U.S. Dollar Chart Showing Breaking of Various Levels of Long-Term Resistance

Source: CQG, Inc. © 2010. All rights reserved worldwide.

The perfect trader syndrome represents our desire for psychological comfort and for reward without risk. By contrast, my work with traders entails training them to be comfortable with imperfections, discomfort, and risk. Successful trading requires abandonment of perfection in favor of robustness and relinquishing of comfort for even-mindedness regarding profit and loss. Although it seems counterintuitive, successful trading is not about anticipating future market direction or trend reversals. It means instead participating in the trend's current, proven direction until there is evidence of that direction's reversal; as I like to say, "Don't anticipate; just participate."

Breakout Example: Cash U.S. Dollar–Japanese Yen

In late April 2010, volatility in cash U.S. dollar–Japanese yen (USD–JPY) as measured by its 10-day average true range declined steadily. As the indicator generated its low volatility reading, clearly delineated levels of horizontal support at 92.74 and resistance at 95.00 were established. By early

May, I positioned for a breakout by placing a buy stop above recent resistance at 95.00 and a sell stop at 92.74. On May 4, 2010, we tested 95.00 and dropped, strengthening my conviction that a break of 95.00 would lead to a bull move in spot USD–JPY. May 5, 2010, saw a renewed challenge of the resistance. I was almost certain the bull trend had begun. As we moved from 94.55 to 94.65, then 94.75, I began questioning, "Why was I waiting for the inevitable break of 95.00? Wasn't I a professional trader? Didn't my job entail anticipating breakouts before they happened?"

As soon as these questions arose, I stopped and repeated the mantra: "Don't anticipate; just participate." I recognized my impatience as a caution flag. If I struggled to wait for evidence of a bullish breakout, other, less experienced traders would *not* wait for evidence. They would buy 94.60; they would be buying in anticipation of a breakout that had not occurred. Consequently, if the market did not break 95.00, instead of buying a low price in a nascent bull market, they would have bought a high price in a bear market. This is exactly what happened. The market rallied to 94.99 on May 5, 2010, and then failed, closing at 93.81.

On May 6, 2010, as the market dropped within pips of my sell stop price at 92.74, I called a long-time colleague complaining, "I'm probably flushing some money down the toilet here on dollar-yen. Just yesterday they were failing at resistance. Now they're gonna fill me at the bottom of the range and scream back up to 95." He asked, "You pulling the order?" I answered, "No, of course not. Just frustrated at how much I'm risking on this thing." After hanging up the phone, I calmed myself by silently repeating, "Don't anticipate, just participate," and reasoning, "If I'm uncomfortable selling there, everyone's uncomfortable . . . discomfort leads to profits, comfort to losses. I'm managing the risk, playing the probabilities . . . whatever happens, happens."

Around 11:30 A.M. EST, I sold 92.74. By 1:45 P.M. EST, the market had dropped violently enough for me to safely lower the protective buy stop to my 92.74 entry level. Within 15 minutes, the flash crash occurred and USD–JPY dropped to 89.87. By 2:45 P.M. EST, the market dropped to 89.00, one of the largest moves in the history of foreign exchange trading. The trade I was almost certain would be a waste of time and money was one of my biggest profits in 2010 (see Figure 9.7 and Figure 9.8).

According to trader psychology, the market action in dollar-yen made complete sense. Impatient traders saw the market approaching resistance at 95.00 and bought in anticipation of a break that never materialized. As the market dropped to its support at 92.74, even veteran traders hesitated to sell since the recent challenge of 95.00 represented a huge risk if the breakdown at 92.74 proved false. Because few traders could sell 92.74 and impatient traders were already long from the top of the trading range (around 94.60 to 94.80), the trade became a perfect storm. When many

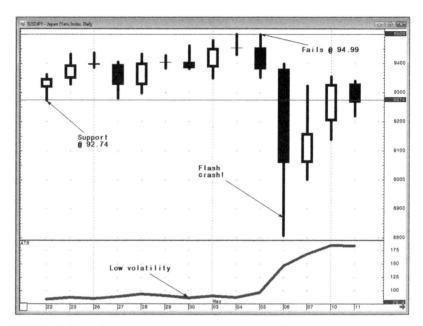

FIGURE 9.7 Daily USD–JPY Chart Showing Breakout from Low Volatility
Source: CQG, Inc. © 2010. All rights reserved worldwide.

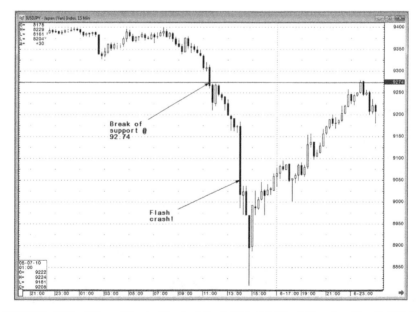

FIGURE 9.8 Fifteen-Minute Chart of Cash USD–JPY Chart Showing May 6, 2010, Flash Crash
Source: CQG, Inc. © 2010. All rights reserved worldwide.

impatient traders are wrong and very few experienced traders are right, it creates a liquidity vacuum. This is exactly what happened on May 6, 2010. Since few had sold the support at 92.74, few were taking profits. Simultaneously, many had bought in anticipation of a break higher that never materialized and when they exited, this combination of factors culminated in a quick, violent crash.

Reversal Example: CME Group Wheat Futures

The most common manifestation of traders anticipating market action instead of simply participating in what the market is currently offering is anticipating the reversal. Anticipating the reversal occurs because we are habituated to trading price instead of value. We watch prices break to new contract highs and calculate how much money would be made by merely revisiting prices experienced just last month. This return to last month's prices seems more realistic, probable, and prudent than buying new highs in hopes of selling in the future at an amorphous and unknown higher level. So we anticipate a reversal that has never materialized and sell new highs only to buy back even higher highs.

September 2010 CME Group wheat futures offer a classic example of anticipating the reversal. On July 1, 2010, September wheat futures broke to close above old contract highs at $4.86 per bushel. While trend followers bought this decidedly bullish price action, impatient, inexperienced countertrend traders focusing solely on price (instead of value) might have sold this supposedly high price. Countertrend traders with a bit more experience might have waited for oscillators like the nine-day RSI to signal an overbought reading of 80 or higher. Such traders would have sold September wheat on July 8, 2010, at $5.29 per bushel. In either case, there was no evidence of a trend reversal. The occurrence of new contract highs (or lows) means absolutely nothing. The nine-day RSI generating a reading above 80 (or below 20) also means nothing.

Although it seems counterintuitive, the only reason to sell is if there is evidence of a likely market top. Such evidence did not exist on either July 1, 2010 at $4.86 per bushel or on July 7, at $5.29 per bushel. Evidence of a probable top can occur only when prices break a technical support level. Such evidence eventually came on August 9, 2010, when the market completed a two-day reversal pattern by closing below $7.24 per bushel. Countertrend traders who sold the opening of August 10, 2010, at $7.13 per bushel did so not because of high prices or oscillator readings, but because technical action suggested a high probability that the asset was overvalued (see Figure 9.9).

Trading reversal patterns is not easy, and I specifically chose September 2010 wheat futures from countless possible reversal patterns to

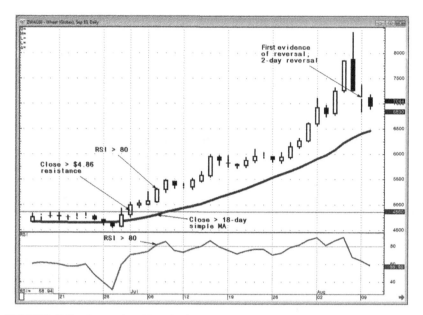

FIGURE 9.9 September 2010 Daily CME Group Wheat Futures Chart
Source: CQG, Inc. © 2010. All rights reserved worldwide.

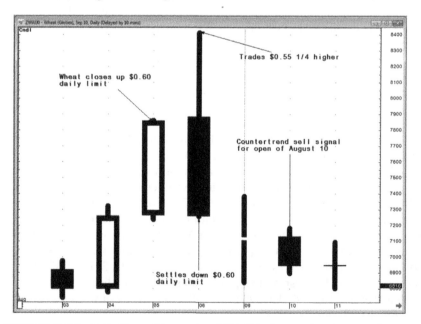

FIGURE 9.10 Daily Chart of September 2010 CME Group Wheat Futures Showing
Extraordinary Levels of Volatility
Source: CQG, Inc. © 2010. All rights reserved worldwide.

illustrate this point. Although the reversal signal generated on August 9, 2010, was valid, it simultaneously represented a high probability *and* high-risk setup. In fact, this particular countertrend trade was shown in Chapter 2 to exemplify use of management discretion in overriding high-risk trades, remember?

FINAL THOUGHTS

One of the biggest fallacies of trading is that beginners need to learn lots of tools and techniques to succeed. Ironically, the early years of a speculator's career are spent unlearning worldly wisdom gained before placing the first trade. Before that trade, you were taught to seek out bargains and buy low-priced items. Walmart became one of the largest multinational corporations in history because consumers embrace this particular philosophy. Unfortunately, worldly wisdom is antithetical to successful speculation. Cheap stocks like Enron and Lehman Brothers get cheaper, while pricey ones like Berkshire Hathaway become more expensive. Training yourself not to anticipate the trading signal is challenging because it feels unnatural and uncomfortable . . . and that is why it works.

PART III

Trader Psychology

CHAPTER 10

Transcending Common Trading Pitfalls

Everything is real and is not real,
Both real and not real,
Neither unreal nor real.
—Nāgārjuna

One of the most important ingredients for success in speculation is trader psychology. This chapter, along with Chapter 11, shows how to remove destructive biases preventing or limiting success in trading. Chapter 12 provides traders with a wide array of tools to reinforce productive trading behavior.

CHARACTERISTICS OF MARKET BEHAVIOR

What can be said about market behavior without exception or contradiction? All market behavior is multifaceted, uncertain, and ever changing. By distilling trading to these essential truths, we prune away any and all extraneous delusional trading biases that prevent or limit our success.

Multifaceted

Beginners always seek a simple solution to successful trading. Success, unfortunately, requires a robust, complex solution, which I call the *casino paradigm.* Our inability to provide novices or outsiders with a

191

simple one-line explanation of how successful speculation works stems from the complex, multifaceted nature of market behavior. I often say there is no tic-tac-toe solution to market behavior; it is instead like three-dimensional chess.

The three-dimensional chess analogy confuses beginners because speculation seems to be like a simple buy low–sell high proposition. Worse still, this illusion of simplicity is reinforced by the belief that anyone can buy a stock and sell it three hours later at a profit. When this argument is made, I remind them that while it is possible for a novice to put a golf ball into a hole in three or even two strokes, this does not mean they will beat Tiger Woods at the Masters this year. The difference is Tiger's ability to play superior golf consistently over the entire course.

In fact, it is the complexity of market behavior that allows the novice to put on a winning trade despite a lack of trading skills. Furthermore, market behavior is so complex that even my casino analogy fails to fully describe the prerequisite skills in successful speculation. Although it is true that speculators must consistently employ a positive expectancy model while managing risk on each and every trade (just like a casino), every game offered by the casino has limitations that do not exist in markets. For example, in craps, only one player rolls the dice at a time, other players cannot place bets after the dice leaves the shooter's hand, players cannot lose more than they bet, and so on. None of these limitations exist in the markets . . . no limits in risk, reward, when orders can be placed, simultaneous placement of multiple orders, and so on.

This is what I meant by the statement "Market behavior is multifaceted" and why I chose the Nāgārjuna quote to open this section on trader psychology. All beginners yearn for a simple, linear solution to market behavior but discover that everything is real and is not real, both real and not real, neither unreal nor real. This complex, multifaceted nature of market behavior leads to our superimposing of limits onto this limitless environment. Some limits, such as risk management, are essential to our survival as traders, but others such as being unwilling to trade before holidays, during lunchtime, on Fridays, during Elliot Waves A and C, and so on, are biases that can impede success or in severe cases, virtually guarantee failure.

Traders' delusional beliefs must be thrown off so they can face the multifaceted reality of market behavior without allowing its complexity to paralyze them. Although a daunting task, the key is taking it one step at a time and playing to the innate, individual strengths of each trader. For example, beginning traders typically have a propensity toward small profits and large losses, so a first step could be developing positive expectancy models that force the placement of stops upon entry or an adjustment of stops to break even as soon as positions experience a statistically significant unrealized gain while simultaneously preventing profit-taking during the first two days of the trade. Once traders have been acclimated to overcome their bias against letting winners run and cutting losses, more advanced rules allowing for taking partial profits as soon as market conditions (as defined by asset volatility) permit can be introduced. Eventually, as the trader matures, discretionary tools such as intuition can be added to augment the array of mechanical rules that were rigidly enforced throughout earlier stages of development.

Traders will often say, "*They* got my stop," or "*They* missed my limit," as if markets are an adversary. The danger in this delusional perception of markets is that it takes responsibility out of our hands. I like to call this failure to accept responsibility the "God's will or somebody else's fault" syndrome. If this amorphous "they" had not conspired to hit my stop I would have made money. Instead, mature traders recognize that markets do not conspire to do or fail to do anything. If our stop was hit and then the market went in our direction, it was because *we* placed it too close to current support or resistance levels. Acknowledging the multifaceted nature of market behavior forces us to take responsibility for our trades. If we made money, it is because we were in sync with the multifaceted nature of markets. If we lost, we were not.

Finally, markets are neither positive nor negative because each uptick or downtick is completely neutral from the market's perspective. This is evidenced by monitoring an asset that you do not trade and have no intention of ever trading. While observing the upticks and downticks you perceive their neutral, multifaceted nature because you have no emotional stake in their movement. Now compare this objectivity to your feelings as you watch movements in a market you trade. Suddenly every uptick or downtick causes emotional pain or pleasure. Obviously these emotions have nothing to do with the market per se; rather, you superimpose them onto a completely neutral, multifaceted environment. Such emotions bias our view of market behavior, preventing us from objectively perceiving the wide array of available information. Our position in the asset can bias our view of information about the markets by either blocking our ability to perceive risk (if fear of suffering losses is the dominant psychological bias) or preventing our ability to perceive opportunity for profit (if fear of evaporation of unrealized gains is the dominant bias). In either instance, the superimposition of irrational emotionalism onto a neutral, multifaceted market environment limits our ability to perceive reality objectively, thereby severely impeding our ability to trade successfully.

Uncertain

No one can say with absolute certainty whether the next price change will be an uptick or a downtick. Because uncertainty is guaranteed at all times, in every market, successful traders can never abandon risk management . . . not on any trade, not even for a single moment. Also, since market behavior is uncertain, successful traders must think in terms of probabilities. Forcing ourselves to think in probabilities is perhaps the greatest antidote to developing and concretizing of trader biases. If we admit uncertainty, we must acknowledge that any and all prices are possible, and in so doing, the vast limitless, multifaceted nature of markets begins eradicating delusional thinking.

Beginners find admission of uncertainty in future market behavior disconcerting. Instead, they seek out the sure thing in markets. Ironically, this elusive sure thing is exactly what this chapter offers (though admittedly not in the manner novice traders' demand); uncertainty *is* the elusive sure thing market behavior that all traders seek. Since uncertainty is guaranteed, it forces us to adapt to what markets are actually offering as opposed to clinging to our destructive habit of superimposing a delusional, restricting bias onto what we are willing to accept about market behavior.

Ever-Changing Markets

The only other guarantee in markets is change. Interestingly, despite the fact that the next tick is uncertain, uncertainty is not the same as randomness. If markets were truly random, then prices would form a bell-curved distribution. Instead, they display leptokurtosis (as described in Chapter 1) and so this uncertain, ever-changing market environment offers high-probability and low-risk opportunities to speculators. Despite the understanding that no one can guarantee when volatility will cycle from low to high or vice versa, we can still exploit the cyclical nature of volatility by developing positive expectancy models that capitalize on this repetitive cycle of market behavior (as detailed throughout Chapter 4).

After a string of losses, traders typically become despondent, saying, "They are killing me," "I just can't take another loss," "Trading is impossible," "Nobody can make money in these markets," "This losing streak will never end," and so on. When speculators fall into such negative emotional loops, I advise them to breathe deeply, and then calmly ask the casino paradigm questions: "Does my method enjoy positive expectancy?" and "Am I managing the risk?" If the answers to these questions are no, then they must stop trading until they have developed both a positive expectancy model and robust risk management methodology.

If, on the other hand, the answers to both questions are yes, then they should repeat the following affirmation until they are again able to view market activity in an unbiased, casino-like manner: "Market behavior is multifaceted, uncertain, and ever changing. I am employing a robust, positive expectancy trading model and am appropriately managing risk on each and every trade. Losses are an inevitable and unavoidable aspect of executing all models. Consequently, I will confidently continue trading." As the negative thought loop about markets, past losses, missed opportunities, and so on continues, keep combating it with the truth of this affirmation until confidence and objectivity return.

OBSTACLE MAKERS TO GROWTH AS A TRADER

Throughout my professional career, I have applied Buddhist cosmological archetypes to problems in trader psychology. Specifically, Buddhism speaks of four *maras*. Maras are obstacle makers. In the context of trader psychology, such obstacles impede our ability to objectively perceive opportunities in the markets. The four maras are the mara of death, the mara of the son of the gods, the mara of destructive emotions, and the mara of the five aggregates.

An essential truth regarding these obstacle makers is that although they seem to be external, objective realities of the human condition, this is illusory. For example, although uncertainty and loss (associated with the obstacle maker of death) are unavoidable and real, they are only subjectively painful and obstacles to growth and development if we are attached to certainty and cling to that which is being lost. Since obstacle makers are externalizations of inner psychological states, their conquest is accomplished through internal psychological work as opposed to dependency on external forces. That stated, most of us have concretized our destructive reactions to these obstacle makers to such an extent that the aid of a Buddha (Buddhas are awakened beings who have conquered the obstacle makers; the parallel in trader psychology is a master trader) or a guru (gurus are those who teach from experience on conquering obstacle makers; in trader psychology, the equivalent is a trading coach or books such as those listed in the bibliography) is needed to illuminate blind spots in our quest for psychological wellness (or what I call even-mindedness in trading—see Chapter 12).

Fear of Loss and Uncertainty

The two greatest obstacles to successful trading are fear of loss and fear of uncertainty (which manifests as fear of unrealized gains becoming realized losses). Both of these obstacles are personified in Buddhist psychology by the mara of death.

That loss on Wall Street is equated with death was taught to me by my father (an equity options broker) long before I ever placed a trade. I remember him motioning to the graves in Wall Street's Trinity churchyard, half-jokingly saying, "No mystery that there's a graveyard on Wall Street. New traders get buried here every day."

What does Buddhist psychology tell us about the mara of death? This particular obstacle maker is not conquered through denial, anger, negotiation, or despondency. Death will not simply go away. It cannot be avoided or overpowered by will. We overcome death as an obstacle through acceptance and integration.

Now try something: Substitute the word *losses* for death in the previous paragraph.

Elisabeth Kübler-Ross identified fives stages of grief related to loss in her book *On Death and Dying*. These stages are applicable to traders coping with the reality of losses, lack of control over markets, uncertainty, and regret, all of which could devolve into concretized trading biases preventing us from perceiving the multifaceted reality of markets. The stages are:

1. Denial: Although it sounds incredible, I have heard even seasoned traders hope that a particular methodology could lead to gain without the possibility of loss. Conscious or unconscious denial of the reality of loss and uncertainty arises to help us cope with the painful nature of reality. Unfortunately, denial of loss and uncertainty is extremely destructive because it prevents us from thinking in terms of probabilities, planning for the possibility of loss, and consequently from the necessity of consistently managing risk.

2. Anger: When we are forced to admit the reality of loss and uncertainty, the conflict between our delusional beliefs and the reality of the market's multifaceted, uncertain, and ever-changing nature causes anger. This anger is simultaneously directed outward toward the impersonal and neutral market and inward toward ourselves because we had to admit we were wrong, take losses, and so on.

   If anger helped us gain information about the nature of markets, motivated us to develop positive expectancy models, or helped us manage risk more efficiently, then I might say it was worth the expenditure of emotional energy. Although possible, anger rarely leads to any of these endeavors. Instead it typically manifests as a blind rage that cuts off our ability to coolly reason and successfully navigate solutions to various trading problems.

   One commonly experienced by-product of blind rage is revenge trading. Revenge trading is especially destructive because we no longer trade to win; instead, we trade to recover past losses. In so doing, we are demanding that markets behave in a way that eradicates past trading errors. In this way, we not only view markets as adversarial (thereby cutting ourselves off from emotionally tempered, objective solutions to speculation), but also blind ourselves to opportunities other than those which bring our trading account back to breakeven.

As opposed to these destructive behaviors, when facing the emotionally charged reality of losses, I advise traders to acknowledge the anger, deepen their breathing, release the emotion, and then calmly assess their situation.

3. Bargaining: As the cliché goes, "Desperate times call for desperate measures," and mounting unrealized losses lead to desperation and emotionally charged bargaining with a supreme deity among traders, failing to adhere to a positive expectancy model or robust risk management methodology. Perhaps even more common among such traders is a desperate clinging to a wide array of superstitious behaviors such as talismans against losses or our lack of control over market behavior.

Belief in a supreme deity might prove beneficial in a wide variety of situations; unfortunately, coping with mounting unrealized trading losses is not one of them.[1] As Aesop wrote, "The gods help them that help themselves." Counting on a supreme deity to bail us out of a losing trade is a bad bet. Of course, two things could happen, either of which is fatal for a speculator's career in the long run. The most likely result of our bargaining with a supreme deity in return for them bailing us out of a losing trade is that losses will balloon from large to catastrophic. The unlikely result is that losses diminish. If this unlikely event happens and we continue trading, it is only a matter of time until we are back at the bargaining table only to discover that blind faith is no substitute for research, methodical planning, stringent risk management, playing the probabilities, and unwavering discipline.

4. Depression: During this stage, the trader accepts the certainty of loss and their powerlessness over markets. I call this stage "acceptance with emotional attachment." Although a great leap forward from denial, anger, or bargaining, depression is a suboptimal emotional state because it allows past losses or missed opportunities to limit our ability to perceive information about the markets in the present.

The antidote to depression in the face of losses and powerlessness over the markets is the affirmation "Embrace and release." Novice traders tend to either deny their powerlessness over losses and the markets or they accept reality, but this acceptance leads to a wallowing in self-pity.

Denial of depression is almost as destructive as denial of losses (and powerlessness over markets) because it merely perpetuates the emotion. According to Carl Jung, this is because "what you resist, persists." For example, if I tell you not to think of the color yellow, it immediately comes to mind. The more you mentally berate yourself for thinking of yellow, the harder to stop such thoughts. Instead of denial of emotions, integration and maturity arise from accepting the truth of our feelings without allowing them to disable us. Successful traders acknowledge and embrace the reality of the market's multifaceted, uncertain, and ever-changing nature, while releasing any and all emotional despondency.

5. Acceptance: Embracing and releasing destructive emotions is typically a prerequisite to accepting the reality of market behavior. The environment is multifaceted, uncertain, and ever changing. Losses are always a possibility and we are powerless over our environment. Ironically, once we completely accept and integrate these truths of market behavior, we can perceive information objectively, free of delusional biases.

What does Buddhist psychology tell us about the mara of uncertainty? This particular obstacle maker is not conquered through denial, anger, negotiation, or despondency. Uncertainty will not simply go away. It cannot be avoided or overpowered by will. We overcome uncertainty as an obstacle through acceptance and integration.

Perfect Trader Syndrome

The obstacle maker of the son of the gods offers pleasure, convenience, and peace. In trading, this corresponds to the perfect trader syndrome outlined in Chapter 9. Instead of clinging to illusory hopes of trading without risk of loss or striving for the peace of being flat, successful traders train themselves to accept the discomfort of realizing losses and of letting unrealized profits run, of buying new highs and selling new lows, of fighting the consensus as opposed to following the crowd. They embrace their fears and consistently do that which is unnatural and uncomfortable.

Traders conquer the obstacle maker of the sons of the gods not with bravado or hubris but through gentle acceptance of their imperfections. They freely acknowledge the allure of emotional tranquillity inherent in being flat, but hearken to the better angels of our nature by understanding that growth comes through effort irrespective of peace. Paradoxically, through this commitment to growth despite adversity, speculators realize the calm within the storm's eye and stabilize the state of even-mindedness founded in a joy toward the process itself regardless of any particular trade's outcome.

Destructive Emotions

Pride goes before destruction, a haughty spirit before a fall.
—Proverbs 16:18

According to Buddhist cosmology, this obstacle maker manifests as six distinct destructive emotions united by a single thread, delusional egoism. The emotions are pride, jealousy, attachment, ignorance, greed, and aversion. Pride occurs when we imagine ourselves superior to others; jealousy results from desiring possessions or qualities of others; attachment arises from fear of change or fear of loss; ignorance stems from a delusional view of self and phenomena; greed results from a belief in material insufficiency; and aversion arises from believing in the inherently hostile nature of external phenomena.

1. Pride: Pride prevents traders from exiting losses quickly and from taking profits despite evidence of a reversal. Considering how our actions will be judged by others prevents us from operating effectively in the present moment. The antidote to this destructive emotion is realizing that the moment we begin considering imagined future judgments of others, we stop attuning ourselves to the current reality of the market's multifaceted, uncertain, and ever-changing truth.

   Affirmation: I attune myself to the present truth of the markets regardless of the imagined judgments of others.

2. Jealousy: Jealousy shifts our focus from the reality of the present moment to the actions of other traders by allowing their superior entry or exit levels to impede our ability to effectively operate in the markets. Remember that someone will almost always enjoy a superior entry or exit price to our own. The question remains whether we will allow their position to limit or block our own pursuit of opportunities for profit.

   Furthermore, the irony of jealousy is that we can never truly know what others possess; only what we *imagine* they possess. Wanting to possess what others have shifts us away from our own innate edge in the market. Recognizing that no two traders are alike, successful speculators stick to their own knitting regardless of what others do or do not possess.

   Affirmation: I attune myself to the present truth of the markets regardless of the imagined possessions of others.

3. Attachment: Attachment manifests in a multitude of forms, including (though not limited to) attachment to being right, to winning, to certainty, to stability, to linear thinking, to negative emotions, to rigidity,

to peace, to our perceptions, to not losing, to being perfect. The greater our attachment to deluded perceptions, the more rigid we become, constraining our ability to adapt to the ever-changing, multifaceted truth of market behavior.

Affirmation: I release preconceived biases and adapt to the ever-changing truth of the markets.

4. Ignorance: In Buddhist psychology, ignorance manifests as delusional beliefs regarding self and phenomena. Although on the surface we may admit that markets are multifaceted, uncertain, and ever changing, if we refuse to manage risk or think in terms of probabilities, our actions are in conflict with this truth.

Ignorance of the nature of self manifests as speculators identify with their trades through statements like "I lost again; I am worthless," "I got killed," "I'm a loser," "I'm such an idiot," and so on. Losses and being wrong often trigger destructive, debasing definitions of self associated with early memories of shame and punishment.

Consistently disciplined, successful trading depends on our creation of new definitions of self, success, losing, and being wrong. Trader psychology techniques do not fix the trader; they fix their trading.[2] Winning trades do not make us winners; neither do losing trades make us losers. We are not our trades; they are merely an activity in which we are engaged. This statement of *not being our trades* is in conflict with the way many of us define ourselves. Ask someone who they are, and they will tell you what they do for a living. We are not our careers; our careers are merely an activity in which we are engaged.

Who are we then? According to Buddhist psychology we are empty. Emptiness should not be confused with nothingness. This psychological framework is not denying the existence of our physical organism. It suggests instead that the self transcends limited linear thinking, that it is multifaceted and ever changing (just like the markets, as well as all phenomena).

Affirmation: I am not my trades. I release rigid, delusional notions of self.

5. Greed: Greed is fear inverted. Irrational fears of material insufficiency can manifest in a variety of destructive ways, including delusional recklessness in the face of uncertainty (instead of prudent risk management), an inability to exit with profits as well as unwillingness to move stops as unrealized profits accumulate. Greed is inexorably linked to fear of regret, which, aside from fear of loss, is the greatest force impeding a trader's performance. Fear of regret is so prevalent that Chapter 6 presented readers with a wide array of techniques to mitigate its destructive impact.

Affirmation: Realizing markets continuously offer limitless opportunities for abundance, I release regrets and fears of insufficiency.

6. Aversion: All sentient beings seek pleasure (mara of the son of the gods) and avoid pain (aversion). This pleasure-seeking/pain-avoidance behavior is why technical analysis helps in the development of positive expectancy trading models and specifically why price has memory (see Chapter 1).

Aversion manifests in a variety of forms, including (but not limited to) aversion to losses, being imperfect, thinking in terms of probabilities and uncertainty, being wrong, change, growth, and even the markets themselves. We deactivate destructive consequences of aversion through acceptance of the emotion and acceptance and integration of things that we feel aversion toward. Losses, uncertainty, and change are unavoidable realities of trading, so the more effective we are at integration and acceptance of these truths, the greater our success as speculators.

Affirmation: I accept and embrace the market's multifaceted, uncertain, and ever-changing nature.

Clinging to Delusional Ideas

The five aggregates in Buddhist psychology are matter, sensation, cognition, mental formations, and consciousness. They are considered obstacle makers because they serve as objects for attachment and delusional grasping toward a sense of self. In trader psychology, these five aggregates shift our focus away from the multifaceted, uncertain, and ever-changing nature of markets and toward some delusional subjective beliefs about how markets are affecting us.

1. Matter (Form): Matter includes both our internal physical bodies as well as the external phenomenal world.

2. Sensation (Feeling): Sensation is subjective categorizing of physical objects as pleasurable, painful, or neutral.

3. Cognition (Perception): Cognition is registering whether an object is recognized or not (such as the sound of a chime, shape of a suitcase, smell of a peach, and so on).

4. Mental Formations: Mental formations include all mental activities triggered by an object. Buddhist psychology subdivides mental formations into passive mental formations arising from external objects as well as thoughts introduced from an external source (like a book, film,

or person), and active mental formations resulting from internal form-creating faculty of mind.

Active mental formations figure prominently in trader psychology as delusional, limiting beliefs regarding the nature of markets as well as of speculators themselves. Believing we already know everything needed to succeed in trading cuts us off from the virtually infinite varieties of information available to us. Although some limitations (such as adherence to the 1 percent rule in risk management) are valuable heuristics enabling us to operate in markets more effectively, many active mental formations are based on faulty limiting beliefs regarding the nature of markets. The antidote to delusional rigid beliefs about the nature of markets is remembering that markets are multifaceted, uncertain, and ever changing.

5. Consciousness (Discernment): Consciousness discerns with five sense faculties (sight, sound, taste, touch, and smell) as well as a depth of awareness reflecting a degree of memory and recognition.

   In trader psychology, emotionally painful memories of past losses or missed opportunities can prevent us from objectively perceiving the reality of market opportunities in the present. Deactivation of painful memories occurs through embracing and releasing of emotions associated with the memories, while simultaneously affirming the multifaceted, uncertain, and ever-changing nature of markets, and employing casino paradigm principles (outlined in this book's first three chapters).

FINAL THOUGHTS

Trading biases prevent us from objectively perceiving reality, thereby limiting our ability to capitalize on various opportunities in the markets. Although the most common biases are fear of loss and of missing opportunities, these fears manifest in a wide variety of ways. Various techniques presented in this chapter sought to help us in overcoming irrational fears that impede our ability to objectively perceive opportunities in the markets. The keys to successful elimination of trading biases are gentleness, creativity (which are examined in Chapter 12), and persistence.

Once we identify a trading bias, it is psychologically healthy to seek its immediate elimination. The problem is that most trading biases are inexorably linked to our deepest fears regarding self-worth and material survival. Their eradication consequently tends to occur gradually, in stages, over time. If expectations regarding the elimination of trading biases are not immediately fulfilled, they can lead to frustration and despondency.

The antidote to expectations of immediate resolution to trading biases is gentleness. Be gentle with yourself regarding the resolution of these issues. Embrace the truth of your fears, and gently and gradually release them. A useful framework is what I call the steering wheel analogy. Imagine you are driving a car in need of a wheel alignment. You do not get angry with the car because it is habituated to veering to the right; you simply adjust the steering wheel instead so that you will not drive off a cliff. It does not matter whether you have to adjust the wheel 10 times or 10,000 times, you will make the adjustment over and over again without anger or judgment until safely arriving at your destination. In a similar fashion, acknowledge trading biases and gently, yet persistently, apply the antidotes offered throughout this chapter.

CHAPTER 11

Analyzing Performance

Know thyself.
—Inscribed at the Temple of Apollo at Delphi

In many careers, it's easy to blame a boss or coworker for a failure; in trading, you either take responsibility for failures and successes or shift the blame to the markets. This chapter explores a variety of techniques for consistently and exhaustively examining your actions so you can eliminate delusional notions and learn from your trading results. Although these techniques may seem tedious at first, they are invaluable in exposing blind spots in methodology, inconsistencies in planning, and failures in execution. You only get out of the markets what you are willing to put in. The more diligently you record your trades and answer the questionnaire, the more you will learn about yourself as a trader. The less you are willing to work through the exercises, the less you will learn.

A DUE DILIGENCE QUESTIONNAIRE

Commodity trading advisers, commodity pool operators, and hedge fund managers typically include a due diligence questionnaire in their marketing materials because it informs potential investors of the goals of the fund, risk tolerances, investment strategies, and so forth. Over the years of working with traders, I developed the questionnaire featured here to help articulate strategies as well as identify strengths and weaknesses in a comprehensive fashion. Although some questions may not apply to each reader, to get the most out of this exercise, I advise completion of the questionnaire in its entirety.

About the Trader

These questions force traders to examine their unique circumstances and how such circumstances affect their operation in the markets. Included in this section are questions regarding issues of trading time constraints, financial constraints, liquidity risk issues, and psychological trading biases.

Q: Do you have other professional time commitments?

   The answer to this question tells you time constraints on trade execution as well as practicality of executing various types of trading models. For example, if you are working a nine-to-five job in Manhattan, it is unrealistic to manually execute a scalping or day trading model in U.S. equities.

   The good news for those with other significant professional time commitments is that there is little or no bill payment–related pressure impinging on performance. Ironically, the elimination of such issues enhances the performance of most traders (this is especially true for beginners).

Q: What prevents you from giving up during drawdowns or from becoming reckless during winning streaks?

   The more comprehensive your plan for tempering cycles of emotionalism, the greater your odds of success as a trader. Include all the tools discussed thus far in the book, such as back testing of the models, risk management, and affirmations as well as those covered in the final chapter (such as visualization, relaxation techniques, meditation, and various somatic exercises).

Q: Have you deviated from your methodologies and if so, why?

   Be as specific as possible in answering this question, as it is the single most essential ingredient to improving performance. Beginners tend to deviate from their plan because of their unwillingness to accept losses or let winners run.

   By contrast, intermediate-level traders will typically adhere to their plan flawlessly until a loss or series of losses leads them to deviate from it *slightly* (moving stops too close to entry, moving stops too quickly, taking partial profits prematurely, and so forth). They could also deviate before potential price shock events, after significant winning streaks, or when trading more volatile assets.

Q: After deviating from your methodologies, what specific steps do you take to prevent deviation in the future?

Even experienced traders will deviate from their trading plan on occasion. In his book *Trading for a Living*, Dr. Alexander Elder introduced readers to parallels between alcoholism and the destructive habits of novice traders.[1] Just as the alcoholic can remain sober for weeks, months, or even years only to succumb to their addiction when certain destructive conditions arise, so, too, traders will execute a plan without deviation for months or even years only to fall off the wagon when specific types of market actions or personal problems cause them to lose focus.

After deviating from the methodology, we should have a specific plan in place to aid us in getting back to flawless execution. The first step in returning to flawless execution is forgiving oneself. Berating yourself does not help. Instead, remember my analogy of the automobile in need of a wheel alignment. The key was recognizing the car's propensity for veering to the right and continuing to adjust the wheel without berating yourself so as to compensate for the problem.

Forgive yourself but do not deny or forget. Use the experience to learn about yourself as a trader. Examine the circumstances in which the breakdown occurred (were the circumstances more market-related or due to personal problems?), the severity of the breakdown (was it a complete breakdown in risk management or a minor breakdown like prematurely moving protective stops to the breakeven level?), as well as the type of breakdown (canceling risk management stop loss orders, not placing entry orders, taking profits prematurely, and so forth). These should all be recorded and analyzed so that you can create comprehensive, rule-based adjustments to your existing methodologies to help you prevent future occurrences.

Q: What are your total assets under management?

Answers to this question help identify undercapitalization of small speculators and inappropriate levels of liquidity risk for large speculators.

Aspiring traders always ask me about the minimum capitalization required to start their careers as speculators. It is a tricky question dependent on several factors, the most important of which is whether you will need to earn a living from trading. Unfortunately, it is unrealistic to imagine that you will be successful as an independent speculator at the beginning of your career. This is why I suggest working as an assistant to a successful speculator or as a junior trader in a large corporation's trading organization. If you do decide to pursue a career as an independent speculator, ask yourself the following questions: What are my total assets under management? What is my monthly overhead (including rent, food, data vendor subscriptions, utilities, and so on) and will these expenses reduce my total assets under management?

Although the answer regarding a minimum capitalization depends on your responses to the preceding questions, as a general rule of thumb, my answer for rookies starting out (in 2011) is half a million dollars, as it allows you to learn how to trade while paying for data vendors, minimal overhead expenses, and weathering trading losses for two to three years. Although I advise traders to *have* half a million dedicated to your career, I suggest that you *trade* with only one-tenth of that amount (and then risk not more than 2 percent on any particular trade—see Chapter 2) until you have demonstrated that you can generate an average of 1 percent per month on your money for six consecutive months. It generally takes two to three years to learn how to trade successfully enough to generate a steady 12 percent per annum rate of return on capital, so if your overhead is $33,000 per year, after three years of losing $33,000 per year, you will still have around $300,000 in assets under management for trading. Intermediate-level traders should be able to generate 15 percent return on assets under management, or $45,000 per annum.

For large speculators, the answer here can show if assets traded represent inappropriate levels of liquidity risk. For example, if you have $50 million in assets under management, your ability to efficiently trade a large number of contracts in illiquid assets like CME Group Palladium is problematic when compared to a highly liquid asset like CME Group E-Mini S&P 500 Futures (see Figure 11.1).

Issues of liquidity risk are exemplified by Figure 11.2, which shows the market in both CME Group palladium as well as crude oil at 2:22 P.M. EST on January 19, 2011. If we had to sell four contracts of March palladium at the market price, we would sell two at $818.05 because only two contracts were bid at that price. The remainder of our four contract sales would occur at the next highest bid price of $818 per ounce. Keep in mind that the fair value of March palladium at the time of our sale was not $818.025 per ounce, but was instead the midpoint between the highest bid ($818.05) and lowest offer ($819.75). Fair value was consequently $818.90 per ounce and our average sale price of $818.025 per ounce represented $0.875 of liquidity risk. Now compare that to our sale of four contracts of CME

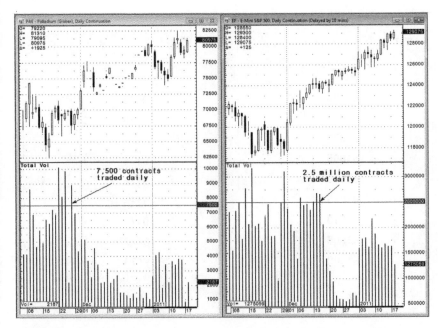

FIGURE 11.1 Comparison of Daily Continuation Charts for CME Group's Palladium and E-Mini S&P 500 Futures Highlighting Comparatively Low Liquidity of Palladium
Source: CQG, Inc. © 2010. All rights reserved worldwide.

Group crude oil. Fair value of the asset was $91.77 per barrel, and we sold all four contracts at $91.76 per barrel (because eight contracts were being bid at that price), so our liquidity risk was only $0.01 per barrel on all four contracts.

As our assets under management increase, the number of contracts traded also increases, worsening liquidity risk. Now suppose we needed to sell 200 contracts of crude oil at the market. Although our sale price would drop from $91.76 (when we were only trying to sell four contracts) to an average price of $91.73, this is still far superior to the sale price on 200 contracts of Palladium (which was so illiquid that it was not even displaying bids for 200 contracts) (see Figure 11.2).

Q: What thresholds of assets under management will impede your ability to trade specific instruments?

My solution to this issue is to create a maximum position threshold for each asset traded. For example, CME Group copper futures typically trade 30,000 contracts per day, so I cap my position size

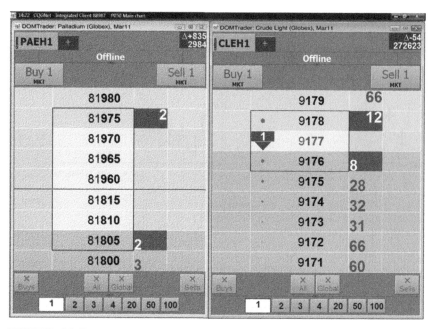

FIGURE 11.2 Comparison of Liquidity Risk in CME Group's March 2011 Palladium and March 2011 Crude Oil Futures
Source: CQG, Inc. © 2010. All rights reserved worldwide.

to 10 contracts per strategy employed irrespective of the size of assets under management. In this way, although percentage exposures to relatively low-liquidity assets like copper decline as assets under management increase, such exposures still add modestly to overall performance in addition to providing slight reductions in correlation risk through asset diversification.

For some futures contracts like CME Group E-Mini S&P 500, we measure liquidity via total contracts traded per day, while other instruments require that we measure liquidity of the actively traded front-month contract. For example, at the time this chapter was written, in agricultural markets like CME Group soybeans, wheat, and corn, actively traded front-month futures contract liquidity could be typically be estimated at around two-thirds of total volume. By contrast, for energy commodities like CME Group natural gas and crude oil, actively traded front-month futures contract liquidity could be estimated at roughly 40 percent of total volume (see Table 11.1).[2]

Q: How many strategies are you currently trading?

This question forces us to identify the type (or types) of market behavior that we are trying to capitalize on as well as acknowledge

TABLE 11.1 Position Size Limits Based on Liquidity of Front-Month Futures

Asset	Typical Daily Volume	Daily Front-Month Volume	Maximum Contracts
CME Copper	30,000	28,000	10
CME Wheat	60,000	40,000	10
CME Gold	200,000	195,000	75
CME Crude Oil	750,000	300,000	100
E-Mini SP 500	2,000,000	1,990,000	750

Note: Volumetric limit per strategy employed.
Source: CQG, Inc. © 2010. All rights reserved worldwide.

our inability to capitalize on other types of behavior. For example, if we are using a traditional trend-following system, we need to psychologically prepare for inferior winning percentages. By contrast, a countertrend trader typically needs to make her peace with inferior average profit to average loss ratios (see Chapter 3 for details on various types of trading strategies and personalities).

Q: What thresholds of assets under management will limit your ability to execute strategies currently traded?

As shown in Table 11.1, increases in assets under management severely limit our ability to diversify among low correlated asset classes. In addition to severely limiting our ability to diversify, increases in assets under management could prevent execution of specific types of strategies, including (though not necessarily limited to) many scalping models.

Q: Did you develop these models?

If we did not develop the strategies traded, are they a black box? I am cautious about trading black box methodologies regardless of their robustness because when they inevitably experience drawdowns, we do not understand why they are underperforming, and lose the confidence needed to continue disciplined adherence to the model.

Q: Does your organization follow a specific protocol in training new traders?

Although the training of new traders will vary based on the organization's edge in the markets as well as the psychological strengths of the individual, I offer the following protocol as a boilerplate template for speculative trading organizations.

First, new traders should paper trade on a demo version of your broker's execution platform. This accomplishes several things, including familiarizing traders with trade execution on the platform, encouraging testing, and development of rule-based positive expectancy methodologies as well as somewhat acclimating them to the emotional and intellectual challenges of speculative trading.

My rule of thumb for average trade duration is that the less experienced the trader, the shorter average hold time should be of their trades. When I started trading, the well-intentioned advice offered was to focus on long-term trend-following methodologies. There are many disadvantages with this approach for new traders. First, long-term trend following requires the discipline to endure multiple consecutive losses in a row, traders tend to experience more losses than wins, and the size of a typical loss is larger than those endured by shorter-term traders. Such disadvantages make adherence to long-term trend-following methodologies problematic for beginners and often even for intermediate-skilled traders.

By contrast, I suggest new traders begin their careers as scalpers or day traders. The advantage to scalping and day trading is that it forces us to become experts at trading one or two assets while continuously reinforcing the truth that winning (and by inference, success) is possible and that success is inexorably linked with stringent rules of risk management. Although scalping and day trading present their own pitfalls to inexperienced traders, including the danger of overtrading as well as the stress of making more decisions throughout the day, I nevertheless feel they compensate for innate weaknesses of beginners, including lack of patience and their inability to endure multiple consecutive losses. Finally, because scalpers and day traders execute more trades during a typical day and risk less on a per trade basis when compared to swing and long-term traders, their learning curve is usually quickened since they are experiencing more trading data points over a shorter period of time.

About the Performance Record

Although an entire chapter subsection on maintenance of trading records follows this questionnaire, the questions included next are intended to augment that material by forcing examination of potential limitations of our performance record, including use of a hypothetical track record, types of assets traded, and so on.

Q: Is your performance record real or hypothetical?

The section following this questionnaire offers readers a comprehensive trading journal for use as a template to track one's trading performance record. Many beginning and intermediate traders assume hypothetical results of a back-tested positive expectancy model can be replicated in real time. Aside from execution errors (and other operational issues), traders must account for liquidity risk as well as psychological breakdowns in discipline. Back-tested models never hesitate to execute trades following multiple consecutive losses. By contrast, in the real world, only the most experienced speculators can embody unwavering discipline when faced with multiple consecutive losses (which is why Chapter 6 introduced regret minimization techniques).

Q: What assets are currently traded?

This question forces us to examine the volatility of assets traded, position-sizing issues, liquidity risk, and correlations of assets traded.

Q: Does the typical number of trades executed change during winning or losing periods?

This question forces beginners to identify periods of revenge trading, in addition to alerting more experienced traders as to how their models are affected by bull and bear markets as well as if they are affected by the cyclical nature of volatility.

About the Methodologies

The primary purpose of questions regarding methodologies is the identification and elimination of irrational trading biases. That stated, these questions also force traders to systematically identify strengths and weaknesses of their methodologies, which often results in modifications so as to make the models more robust.

Q: How would you describe all of the various methodologies employed?

Here we force traders to define their methodologies as systematic, discretionary, trend following, countertrend, technical, or fundamental. Your answer should be comprehensive. If, for example, you are trading a systematic, technically driven countertrend methodology, is there a discretionary override of the trading signals? If there is a discretionary override, are the conditions required to trigger the override based on volatility, correlations, or other risk management considerations, or are they based on fundamentals (such as news-related event-risk issues)?

Q: Are the models used always in the market or do they allow for neutrality? If they allow for neutrality, what percentage of time are they in the markets?

Most systems that are always in the market endure larger drawdowns in account equity and experience inferior winning percentages. Systems that allow for neutrality can be sidelined for weeks or even months in a particular trading instrument. If systems traded experience a low time percentage in the markets, diversification may be critical for traders seeking consistently robust performance.

Q: Are you using the same methodologies in all markets, and if methodologies employed differ, why?

The answer here often relates to whether the methods used are driven by technicals or fundamentals (including seasonality). Technical models typically apply the same methodologies to all markets, whereas fundamentally driven models are often attuned to the unique idiosyncrasies of each market traded.

Nevertheless, a review of Chapter 8 suggests the E-Mini S&P 500 consistently underperformed on trend-following models. Although I have found stock indices underperform on throwaway trend-following models and that equities as an asset class display unique idiosyncrasies that can be exploited to enhance performance, technical models employed in real time should be robust enough to enjoy positive expectancy in all asset classes.

Q: Are trade entry and exit criteria different?

Although this seems to be a simple yes-no question, it forces us to think strategically about our methodologies. Specifically ask yourself, "Would performance be enhanced if I modified entry or exit criteria?"

Q: Do the methods work better on a specific time horizon?

If they do perform better for a specific hold period, is this because the assets traded display a greater propensity toward mean reversion or trending on that time horizon, or is improvement due to the diminished effect of commissions and liquidity risk on methodologies with longer hold times?

Q: Are the methods more robust in specific types of market environments?

Although different methods will outperform in various market environments, the most robust models will be profitable in both bull and bear markets. In addition, this question specifically highlights the advantages of trade system diversification (see Chapter 8).

Q: What are the strengths and weaknesses of the methods used?

In addition to forcing us to acknowledge and plan for periods of suboptimal performance (along with other issues, including, but not limited to, execution issues, prolonged flat periods, correlation risks, and so forth), answering this question ensures that the strengths and weaknesses of the methods used match our unique psychological skills.

Q: How frequently are changes made to the methodologies?

Changing the methodologies on a weekly (or daily) basis could indicate a variety of problems, including lack of confidence in the robustness of the models or perfect trader syndrome. Modification of positive expectancy models is an integral aspect of making methodologies more robust, but the process should be done in a systematic, rational manner through research and back testing before implementation as opposed to emotionally charged Monday morning quarterbacking.

Q: Do your methodologies capitalize on diversification?

Another trading cliché is "Diversification is the only free lunch on Wall Street." Chapter 8 illustrated the strengths of both asset class diversification as well as trading model diversification. Although it is highly problematic for scalpers to manually execute their methodologies on more than two or three assets simultaneously, for swing and position traders, diversification is usually the better part of valor. Remember that even if you are trading a robust positive expectancy model, if you only trade one or two instruments, you could wait a significantly longer period of time following a drawdown so as to achieve a new peak in account equity.

Another potential drawback in trading a single instrument is that market trends can last for years. Consequently, if you have only back tested and traded one trading instrument over the past few years and throughout that period the asset has always been in a bull or bear market, when the trend changes there is a far greater likelihood of the model's failure.

Q: How do you determine assets traded?

There are several considerations regarding trading portfolio composition, including volatility of traded instruments (to prevent overleveraging), correlations between assets traded (to ensure diversification), and liquidity of assets traded to minimize slippage. Also, there could be constraints to portfolio diversification because of the methodologies used. For example, manually executing a scalping or day trading model in U.S. equities severely limits our ability to diversify, as does trading a fundamentally driven model.

Q: How do you determine entry, exits, and stops?

Although knowing how, when, and where exits with profits will occur is not necessarily required for successful trading, it is an unequivocal prerequisite in stop placement and risk management. Also, you should know whether entry is determined solely by mechanical criteria or if there is a discretionary override.

Typical discretionary overrides include (but are not limited to) price shock events, holiday trading, lunch hour trading, and so on.

Chapter 2 discussed the three major categories of tools for stop loss order placement: mathematically derived technical stop orders, stops based on support and resistance levels, and monetary or percentage-based stops.

Q: How do you determine position size and leverage?

Here, again, our answers should incorporate volatilities of the instruments traded, correlations between the instruments held in our portfolio, and total assets under management.

Q: Do you add to or reduce exposures on winning positions? Do you reduce exposures on losing positions? And if so, how?

These questions address issues such as pyramiding, loss minimization strategies, and regret minimization strategies (which were featured in Chapter 6). The main concern here is whether modification of position sizing as the trade matures is based on predefined strategic criteria or emotionalism.

Q: Is fundamental information used? If so, does it affect risk management?

Stated simply, fundamental information should be used for defense and not offense in risk management. Beginners must be especially vigilant against using fundamentals to rationalize abandonment of prudent risk management tools. On the other hand, fundamental information is especially useful in alerting us to major paradigm shifts in the perceived value of the asset (which would supersede purely technical or quantitative risk metrics).

Q: How do you deal with price shock events?

Price shocks are short-term, news-driven events that increase volatility while decreasing liquidity. You should develop a comprehensive plan detailing how you will adapt to such events in regard to both exiting losing trades (see Chapter 2) as well as managing profitable ones (see Chapter 6).

Q: Describe the indicators used and how they form your methodologies.

Be as detailed as possible, including the types of indicators (for example, trendlines, horizontal support and resistance, oscillators, moving averages, volatility indicators, fundamentals, neural networks, statistical indicators, volume and open interest, spread relationships, seasonal and cyclical analysis) that are used to generate entry orders, stops, and exiting with profits as well as how these change over the life cycle of your trades.

Q: Do your models have long or short biases?

With the possible exception of equity trading systems, I am skeptical of methodologies with long or short biases. This chapter is dedicated to developing tools to eliminate subjective trading biases, including those toward being long or short. One of the most effective tools in training traders to eliminate their bias toward the long or short side is trading currencies because you are always long one currency and short another.

I have heard some say that shorting stocks is unpatriotic, to which I have always responded that I thought not having to pay capital gains taxes was unpatriotic. Dennis Gartman, publisher of *The Gartman Letter*, came up with one of my favorite quotes regarding long and short biases: "Trade like a mercenary guerilla." Just like the mercenary guerilla, we must train ourselves to fight without bias for whichever side (bull or bear) is paying more.

We should be mindful that bull markets have different characteristics from bear markets (except in foreign exchange as explained earlier). Markets don't crash on the upside; they crash on the downside. For example, it took more than four years for the Dow Jones Industrial Average to rally from 7,500 to 14,000, but only took 13 months for it to drop from 14,000 back down to 7,500 (see Figure 11.3). In other words, bear markets are typically quicker and more violent than bull markets; traders should therefore adjust their methodologies accordingly.

Q: Will methods or markets traded change as assets under management increase?

Increases in assets under management allow us to not only trade more volatile markets but also enable us to trade multiple contracts, thereby allowing us to employ the regret minimization techniques featured in Chapter 6 without violating rules of prudent risk management.

Q: What are your rate of return and worst peak-to-valley equity drawdown objectives?

Your answer to this question says a lot about the kind of trader you are (or aspire to be). The higher your rate of return, the greater the maximum peak-to-valley equity drawdown you will have to endure. Some traders are happier with a 20 percent annual rate of return and enduring a worst peak-to-valley drawdown of 5 percent, whereas others are willing to experience an 8 percent drawdown so they can enjoy a rate of return of 32 percent.

I encourage adapting rate of return and drawdown goals to the individual style and personality of the speculator within specific upper and lower boundaries. The lower boundaries are obviously a rate

FIGURE 11.3 Monthly Cash Dow Jones Industrial Average Chart Relative Slowness of Bull versus Bear Trends
Source: CQG, Inc. © 2010. All rights reserved worldwide.

of return exceeding the riskless T-bill rate. My personal preference regarding an upper boundary for risk is that the worst peak-to-valley drawdown should not exceed 10 percent of total assets under management. Although many might argue that 10 percent is too conservative (that is, risk averse), remember the greater one's risk appetite, the more likely one's risk of ruin (see Chapter 2).

Q: What type of instruments (cash foreign exchange, futures, options, equities, futures spreads, and so on) do you trade?

Trading of various vehicles entails specific types of liquidity risk, time constraints, volatility issues, price shock event risk, and so on. For example, because options trade at a wide variety of strike price, this necessarily fractures liquidity of all strikes traded. In addition, although holders of options are subject to theta risk, they are not subject to price shock event risk. By contrast, writers of options (as well as futures, equities, and cash foreign exchange traders) *are* subject to price shock event risk. Although a detailed exposition of the variety of risks and opportunities entailed in trading of each of these instruments is beyond the scope of this book, it is essential that traders understand the unique nuances in trading these vehicles and adapt their methodologies accordingly.

Risk Management

Questions in the following segment are intended to augment materials presented in Chapter 2. By contrast to the more universal exposition on risk management issues—for example, stop loss placement, volumetric position sizing, correlations, volatility, and so forth—found in that chapter, questions here force traders to adapt those considerations to their own unique trading methodologies.

Q: How are position-sizing limits determined?

Here we are typically looking for a position size cap of somewhere between 1 and 2 percent of total assets under management (see Chapter 2).

Q: How are you accounting for correlations between assets traded and changes in volatilities of assets?

Correlations and volatilities are used in all Value-at-Risk models. This chapter focuses on the development of tools to overcome trading biases, including biases regarding correlations among assets. When discussing trading biases, most think of long versus short biases or biases toward trend following or countertrend trading, but biases in our views regarding correlations are prevalent even among experienced speculators.

Simply stated, *correlations change all the time, and then they change again.* Although complacency or biases regarding any aspect of trading are dangerous, this is especially true for correlations because we are deluded into thinking that we have prudently managed risk. The safest way to work with correlations is to use them as risk management tools to prevent overleveraging.

By contrast, using positive correlations as a tool for generating trading signals is imprudent. In other words, if you missed a buy signal in Ford, buying General Motors is imprudent unless it, too, has triggered a buy signal irrespective of positive historical correlations between the stocks. Why? Because correlations are based on past price history and are therefore blind to current market idiosyncrasies such as Ford rising because of a strike at GM, and so on. Because correlations change all the time, and then change again, it is perhaps even more dangerous to count on negative historical correlations to help our current portfolio from becoming overleveraged (this problem was presented to readers in Tables 2.1 and 2.2 of Chapter 2).

Q: What is the maximum margin to total account equity ratio? What is the maximum at risk in any single asset class?

Generally the maximum margin to total account equity ratio is set at a lower threshold of 25 percent and an upper threshold of 50 percent. There are several reasons not to exceed 50 percent, including the increased possibility of premature trade liquidation due to margin calls as well as the prudence of keeping your powder dry in case new trading signals should be generated before model-based termination of existing positions.

The maximum at risk in any single asset class is typically set at 1 to 5 percent of total assets under management. Because of limitations of historical correlation studies discussed earlier, I personally prefer setting single asset class exposure ceilings at 2 to 3 percent of total assets under management.

Q: Does adding or reducing positions in one asset class affect the size of positions or entry orders in other instruments?

Correlation studies should help in telling us when to reduce positions in one market because of positions in other markets.

Here is an example of a robust—albeit slightly aggressive—technique used in trading highly correlated assets: If the trader is simultaneously working to sell stop-limit entry orders in both CME Group 10-year Treasury note futures and 5-year Treasury note futures, their position sizing will be smaller because of the high positive correlation between the assets. If the market weakens enough to trigger a short position in the 10-year contract and not the 5-year, they can move their protective buy stop order to just under the breakeven level in the 10-year notes and double their volumetric position size on their 5-year note sell in a stop-limit entry order. If the bear move was a false breakout, their order in the 5-year notes will not be executed and their breakeven stop will be elected in the 10-year contract. If, on the other hand, the breakdown has good follow-through, they have increased their position size in Treasury futures without significantly increasing the risk. (Disclaimer: This is not a prudent strategy to implement before the release of major news events due to the greater possibility of slippage on stop orders.)

Q: Types of stops used?

Chapter 2 discussed the various types of stop orders that could be used, including time-based stops, indicator-driven stops, price stops, volatility stops, and money management stops. Make sure the type of stops used suits your trading personality and risk tolerances.

Q: Do you adjust position size following significant profits or losses?

Chapter 2 examined Ralph Vince's fixed fractional position-sizing method of adjusting position size as assets under management increases or decreases beyond specific assets under management thresholds.

Q: Are there extreme events in which all open positions would be closed?

Although, in general, we should let our methodologies run irrespective of conditions, we should not be rigid. Severe price shock events increase volatility and decrease liquidity. In extreme cases (such as terrorist attacks), this could result in an inability to exit positions altogether. Consequently, we should predefine what would constitute an extreme price shock event, forcing liquidation of all positions.

Q: What percentage drawdown would result in closure of your account?

I personally favor a 20 percent peak-to-valley drawdown in equity as the trading account's fail-safe stop level. Although I have heard of 37.5 percent as an industry standard by setting the account's stop loss at this lower percentage, it promotes a tighter day-to-day risk management mindset.

Trade Execution Considerations

Execution considerations are especially useful in forcing traders to identify and plan for real-time implementation of the methodologies. In the back-tested environment (and even in paper trading), trades are flawlessly executed every time. Questions that follow help in acclimating speculators to real-world trading considerations—for example, trading errors, futures contract rollover issues, order execution in 24-hour traded markets, and so on—opaque to the research and development process.

Q: Do you execute trades 24 hours a day?

The advantage of trading stocks is that you avoid trade execution problems of 24-hour, 6-day-a-week markets. By contrast, futures and cash foreign exchange traders need to address a wide array of issues inherent in the trading of 24-hour markets.

The simplest and most common solution used by small speculators is artificially limiting one's trading hours. This solution is especially well suited to scalpers and day traders. The problem for swing traders and position traders is that it eliminates many trading opportunities or forces a premature end-of-day exiting of trades before reaching profit targets. The common fix for swing and position traders is artificially limiting trade entry to *your* trading hours and then using "one cancels all" or bracket orders to ensure overnight risk management as well as one's ability to exit with profits while simultaneously preventing double fills.[3]

Another possible solution to trading 24-hour markets is the formation of a partnership with other speculators who are all committed to the execution of the same methodologies. This solution is commonly used by large proprietary desks and hedge funds. Issues here are ensuring that everyone with trading privileges completely understands and is committed to disciplined implementation of the methodologies.

Finally, some traders develop and implement automated entry order programs to execute their models 24 hours a day, 6 days a week. Important considerations in the execution of automated models are the robustness of the model, programming glitches, and price shock events. Generally speaking, mechanical models tend to underperform rule-based models augmented by trader discretion. Traders opting for automated order entry programs must weigh what will be lost in performance versus the advantages of automated 24-hour execution. Also, before real-time implementation of the automated order entry program, the models should be beta tested in a simulated trading environment to ensure the absence of programming errors. Finally, purely automated execution systems by definition have no discretionary override to protect against price shock event risk or paradigm shifts (unless this, too, is automated, which can prove problematic since most automated shutdowns are based on violation of volatility thresholds as opposed to news-driven price shock events or paradigm shifts).

Q: How do you select contract maturities for exchange-traded futures positions?

Although there is no absolute right or wrong answer, the first step I take in an approach of futures contract rollovers occurs about two weeks before the rollover, when I begin monitoring volume in what will become the new actively traded front month so that I know when most speculators are rolling over. I then decide which contract month to trade according to the liquidity of various contract maturities in relationship to the typical hold time of the methodologies traded.

For example, February 2011 CME natural gas futures expired on January 27, 2011. Consequently, around January 15, 2011, although I still traded the active February futures, I also began to monitor the March contract. On January 19, 2011, the volume in the February 2011 futures contract was around 115,000 contracts and the March 2011 futures contract traded around 81,000 contracts. If the typical hold time for a methodology was two trading days, I would still buy or sell the more actively traded February 2011 futures contract. On the other hand, if the typical hold time was four trading days or longer, I would trade the March 2011 futures contract so as to avoid the risk of needing to roll out of the expiring February 2011 contract.

Q: What types of orders are used for entry, exiting with profits, and exiting with losses?

Although a comprehensive discussion of the pros and cons of the entire universe of order types is beyond the scope of this book, traders should completely understand the advantages and disadvantages of the various types of orders, including market, stop, stop limit, limit, stop close only, market if touched, one cancels other, brackets, and so on.

While I am fairly flexible about using various kinds of entry and exit with profit orders, I am quite inflexible regarding risk management orders. Specifically, I feel the only robust risk management order is a stop, because it ensures exit of the position at the next available market price (see Chapter 2).

Q: Are your orders executed electronically? Is order entry manual or automated?

Manual order execution through an electronic trading platform has many advantages, including lowest commissions, speed, efficiency, and so on. That stated, speed and ease of order placement also means it is much more susceptible to execution errors. I advise writing the orders on a piece of paper before placement. Also, I always use the electronic brokerage platform's fail-safe order integrity mechanisms before making the order live.

If an erroneous position does occur, exit it immediately. Trying to trade out of a mistake is always a terrible proposition. Since you had no intention of taking this position, you have not developed risk management criteria, exit with profit criteria, and so on.

Research and Development Considerations

Although novice speculators are especially susceptible to weakness in research and development, intermediate-level traders can also allow moderate levels of success to devolve into complacency in this area. Questions in this section force readers to face the reality of how much (or little) time and resources are presently dedicated to the research and development process.

Q: Describe your research and development process, including the process for modification of methodologies.

Imagine you were shipwrecked in the Atlantic Ocean and are drowning. Seeing a life preserver floating on the waves, you put it on without hesitation because it represents the difference between life and death. In a similar fashion, when most speculators begin their careers, they typically do so without a positive expectancy model or rules of risk management. Consequently, once they discover a positive expectancy model and combine it with a robust risk management methodology, they naturally cling to them unflinchingly (just as you would the life preserver) because they represent the difference between life and death in their career.

But what are the odds of the first positive expectancy model discovered not only being the most robust version of that model, but also perfectly matching your unique personality as a speculator? This is why research is so essential for the growth and maturation of the speculator. Returning to our shipwreck analogy, thanks to the life preserver, we are no longer drowning and can calmly scan the sea until we notice a lifeboat floating in the distance. Naturally, we swim to it. But if, after swimming to it, we see it is riddled with holes and therefore unable to support our body weight, we would cast it aside and continue scanning the ocean. On the other hand, if it were in good condition, we would use it until rescued. In a similar fashion, we continue doing research after our initial discovery of a positive expectancy model because we need to find a more robust version of that model or one that better fits our unique trading personality.

Finally, we are rescued by the Coast Guard. After we are safely aboard their ship, we naturally abandon the life raft as well as the life preserver because, unlike the Coast Guard's rescue ship, these were not the long-term solutions to our problem of being shipwrecked. That stated, we might not abandon our life raft until we were absolutely certain that the ship actually was the Coast Guard and not a pirate vessel in disguise. In a similar fashion, we do not abandon our positive expectancy model in real-time trading until we are absolutely certain (through extensive research, back testing, optimization studies, forward testing, paper trading, and underleveraged trading[4]) that this new model is more robust and a superior fit for our trading personality.

Q: How much time and money do you dedicate to research each month?

Although answers to this question depend on the types of methodologies used, at a minimum, traders should dedicate 10 to 20 hours to research each month and should subscribe to a data vendor that offers back testing and optimization studies.

In addition to the due diligence questionnaire, maintenance of a trading journal is an important part of analyzing your performance. Read on for just how to use a trading journal in your everyday trades.

TRADING JOURNAL

Maintenance of a trading journal tells us more about our methodologies than what is shown in account statements. Also, reading account statements is a passive act. By contrast, maintaining a trading journal forces active inputting and updating of our trading activity, grounding our daily decision-making process in reality therapy. This is an especially powerful tool for beginners, as it forces detailed analysis of adherence to our plan, risk management, discipline, winning percentages, number of trades, average hold time of winning and losing trades, worst peak-to-valley drawdown in equity, and so on.

In addition to the spreadsheets shown further on, traders should maintain notes on every trade executed. These notes will answer the following questions:

Why did I enter the trade?
Where was my initial stop loss order?
Why did I exit?
Did I follow my positive expectancy model?
Did I adhere to rules of risk management?
If I deviated from the casino paradigm, how did I rationalize my actions?

Although maintenance of a trading journal might seem tedious, hedge fund managers, commodity pools operators, commodity trading advisers, commercial traders, proprietary trading desks, and market-making entities keep detailed records of their trading activity. If we are still resistant to the idea of maintaining the journal despite its maintenance by our competitors, we need to examine the reason for our resistance. Is there a flaw in our methodology that we are unwilling to face? Are we violating the 1 to 2 percent rule? Are we overtrading? Do we hold on to losers too long? Are we exiting profitable trades prematurely? We need to honestly assess the reality of these shortcomings in our methodologies or find a different career. Over the long run, trading problems do not magically resolve themselves. Instead, modification of behavioral trading problems occurs through a process of identification, recognition, and admission . . . all of which are aided through the maintenance of a trading journal.

Monthly Performance Record

My daily trade-by-trade activities are initially recorded and tracked in a monthly performance record. This spreadsheet is the building block for the longer-term performance analysis spreadsheet that I call Monthly Summary Totals. Each individual monthly performance spreadsheet will be labeled as the unique calendar month and year combination to track performance. The monthly performance record is composed of either 21 or 23 columns of track record data (if you are recording the time of entry and time of exit, your spreadsheet will have 23 columns of data; if not, it will have 21).

The columns are as follows:

1. Asset—This is the asset traded and should include month and year of expiration for futures (along with strike and type—put or call for options).

2. Position—Long or short. Although in generally we should not see a bias toward either the bull or bear side, the caveat here is that trend followers should be long in bull markets and short in bear markets.

3. Entry Date—I suggest using the time and date stamp used by your broker (as opposed to whatever your particular time zone is).

4. Entry Time—The shorter your hold time, the more important tracking trade entry and exit times becomes. Scalpers and day traders learn a lot about performance and probability of success based on time of trade execution. For swing traders, tracking of columns 4 and 8 might still prove instructive, though it is usually not helpful for long-term position traders.

5. Volume—Number of contracts or shares traded. Again, watch out for trading biases such as trading heavier volumes in certain assets, long or short biases, and so forth.

6. Entry Price—Remember to average entry prices on split price fill orders.

7. Exit Date—In general, hold time on winning trades should be longer than on losing trades.

8. Exit Time—See column 4.

9. Exit Price—If you use the regret minimization techniques described in Chapter 6, parse out the volumes accordingly and show unique line items for each exit price.

10. Gross P/L—This shows profit and loss before deductions for commissions.

11. Cash Actions—Use this column to record deposits and withdrawals to the trading account.

12. Commissions—Unless you are executing scalping or day trading methodologies, commissions should represent a small percentage when compared with average gross profits shown in column 10.

13. Net P/L—This shows profits and losses after deducting for commissions.

14. Days—This shows the number of calendar days with an open position in the market. In general, we should see higher numbers for winning trades and smaller numbers on losing trades.

15. MTM Drawdown—The column shows the worst intramonth peak-to-valley drawdown in equity. In general, we want to see this number below 5 percent of total assets under management. Drawdowns in excess of 10 percent are problematic and above 20 percent would trigger the account's closure because of the triggering of its fail-safe stop loss.

16. Winning Trades—If we are using the regret minimization techniques described in Chapter 6, you will record percentages of the winning trade in this column.

17. Losing Trades—The total number of losing trades can be larger than the number of winning trades as long as they are small (this is especially common to long-term trend-following models).

18. Profits—Record all partial and full profits in this column.

19. Losses—Work on keeping the numbers in this column smaller than the numbers in the profits column.

20. Model—If you are simultaneously executing two or more methodologies, use this column to record which methodology was employed on each particular trade.

21. W Trades—If you are using the regret minimization techniques described in Chapter 6, you should add the partial profits of each complete winning trade together in this column. (Note: We do not need L Trades column since it would be identical with the Losses column.)

22. W Time—Use the exit time (number of calendar days) of the longest portion of the profitably exited trade as the winning trade time for winning trades.

23. L Time—This is the number of calendar days of your losing trades.

Table 11.2 is an explanation of asset symbols used in Tables 11.3 to 11.7.

TABLE 11.2   Explanation of Asset Symbols Used in Performance Tables

Asset Symbol	Asset Description
RBU10	CME Group Sept 2010 RBOB Unleaded Gasoline Futures
RBV10	CME Group Oct 2010 RBOB Unleaded Gasoline Futures
ZLZ10	CME Group Dec 2010 Soybean Oil Futures
CTZ10	ICE Dec 2010 Cotton Futures
EMDU10	CME Group Sept 2010 E-Mini SP 400 Mid Cap Futures
KCU10	ICE Sept 2010 Coffee Futures
GLD	SPDR Gold Trust ETF
EURUSD	Cash Euro–U.S. Dollar
GBPUSD	Cash British Pound–U.S. Dollar
AUDUSD	Cash Australian Dollar–U.S. Dollar
USDCAD	Cash U.S. Dollar–Canadian Dollar
USDJPY	Cash U.S. Dollar–Japanese Yen

Source: CQG, Inc. © 2010. All rights reserved worldwide.

Multi-Month Performance Record

Close examination of the SPDR gold trust ETF trade (symbol GLD) entered on August 30, 2010, illustrates the limitation of our monthly performance record and why it is augmented with the multi-month performance record. We entered our trade in GLD on August 30, 2010, and were marked-to-market on the trade for the month of August at the settlement price of $120.91 per share. However, this was merely our end-of-month mark-to-market settlement price. To best know how the trade was terminated, we must look at the multi-month performance record, which shows the trade entry information on August 30, 2010, as well as trade exit data on September 1, 2010 (see Table 11.8). Also, the multi-month performance record is also used to track intermonth peak-to-valley equity drawdowns as well as the time required to achieve new highs in account equity.

When the problems of intermonth performance issues have been explained, traders sometimes ask why we bother tracking monthly performance at all. The answer is that hedge funds, CTAs, CPOs, and so forth use monthly performance records to track end-of-month performance statistics. Even speculators who do not aspire to managing money are advised to maintain both monthly and multi-month track records because your end-of-year mark-to-market account value will be used for tax purposes (as opposed to the more informative multi-month performance record).

I use the same columns in the multi-month performance table as shown in the monthly tables with the exception of the cash actions column. Although cash actions are important to monitor, this is already being tracked in the monthly performance tables. By contrast, the multi-month table is only concerned with tracking our *trading* performance results.

TABLE 11.3 Monthly Performance Table—August 2010, Part I

Asset	Position	Entry Date	Entry Time	Volume	Entry Price
N/A	Deposit	8/1/2010		N/A	N/A
RBU10	Long	8/2/2010		1	2.1519
EURUSD	Short	8/5/2010		200,000	1.3161
RBU10	Long	8/2/2010		1	2.1519
GBPUSD	Short	8/6/2010		200,000	1.5897
USDCAD	Long	8/9/2010		100,000	1.0274
USDCAD	Long	8/9/2010		100,000	1.0274
USDJPY	Long	8/11/2010		200,000	85.43
EURUSD	Short	8/11/2010		100,000	1.3177
ZLZ10	Short	8/11/2010		2	42.23
AUDUSD	Short	8/11/2010		100,000	0.9136
AUDUSD	Short	8/11/2010		100,000	0.9136
EURUSD	Short	8/11/2010		100,000	1.3177
CTZ10	Short	8/11/2010		1	81.13
EMDU10	Short	8/11/2010		1	744.3
CTZ10	Short	8/11/2010		1	81.13
EMDU10	Short	8/11/2010		1	744.3
KCU10	Long	8/16/2010		1	1.7865
KCU10	Long	8/16/2010		1	1.7865
RBV10	Long	8/18/2010		2	1.8999
EURUSD	Long	8/18/2010		200,000	1.2884
USDCAD	Long	8/20/2010		100,000	1.0496
GBPUSD	Long	8/24/2010		200,000	1.5512
USDCAD	Long	8/20/2010		100,000	1.0496
GLD	Long	8/26/2010		1,000	121.38
EURUSD	Long	8/27/2010		200,000	1.2713
GBPUSD	Long	8/27/2010		200,000	1.5529
GLD	Long	8/30/2010		1,000	121.45
Aug 2010 Totals					

Notes: All performance table results are excerpted from hypothetical trading results and reproduced solely for educational purposes. Since hypothetical back-tested results were derived from daily charts, the column for "Entry Time" is blank.

Source: CQG, Inc. © 2010. All rights reserved worldwide.

Performance by Asset Record

Although breaking down performance on an asset-by-asset basis is not an absolute prerequisite for understanding and eliminating trading biases, I personally find generating a performance-by-asset table helpful. The performance-by-asset table should contain the same 22 columns shown in the multi-month performance table. The key points for analysis

TABLE 11.4 Monthly Performance Table—August 2010, Part II

Asset	Exit Date	Exit Time	Exit Price
N/A	N/A		N/A
RBU10	8/3/2010		2.1745
EURUSD	8/5/2010		1.3159
RBU10	8/5/2010		2.175
GBPUSD	8/6/2010		1.5965
USDCAD	8/10/2010		1.0301
USDCAD	8/11/2010		1.0389
USDJPY	8/11/2010		85.1800
EURUSD	8/11/2010		1.3048
ZLZ10	8/11/2010		42.2100
AUDUSD	8/11/2010		0.8999
AUDUSD	8/11/2010		0.8931
EURUSD	8/12/2010		1.2826
CTZ10	8/12/2010		80.3300
EMDU10	8/12/2010		728.0000
CTZ10	8/12/2010		80.9600
EMDU10	8/13/2010		741.5000
KCU10	8/17/2010		1.7895
KCU10	8/17/2010		1.7870
RBV10	8/18/2010		1.8709
EURUSD	8/18/2010		1.2886
USDCAD	8/23/2010		1.0516
GBPUSD	8/24/2010		1.5464
USDCAD	8/26/2010		1.0572
GLD	8/26/2010		120.6700
EURUSD	8/30/2010		1.2715
GBPUSD	8/30/2010		1.5531
GLD	8/30/2010		120.9100*
Aug 2010 Totals			

Notes: All performance table results are excerpted from hypothetical trading results and reproduced solely for educational purposes; *Mark-to-Market settlement price on open position at end of month. Since hypothetical back-tested results were derived from daily charts, the column for "Exit Time" is blank.
Source: CQG, Inc. © 2010. All rights reserved worldwide.

here are identification of any asset class biases in regard to long or short directional biases as well as irrational risk management biases.

Performance by Trading Model Record

If you are simultaneously trading multiple methodologies, this table compares the track records of both models. The performance by trading model table should also contain the same 22 columns shown in the multi-month

TABLE 11.5 Monthly Performance Table—August 2010, Part III

Asset	Gross P/L	Cash Actions	Commissions	Net P/L	Days	MTM Drawdown
N/A	N/A	200,000.00	N/A	N/A	N/A	N/A
RBU10	949.2		−5	944.2	2	
EURUSD	40		−5	30	1	
RBU10	970.2		−5	965.2	4	
GBPUSD	−1360		−10	−1370	1	
USDCAD	270		−5	265	2	
USDCAD	1150		−5	1145	3	
USDJPY	−500		−10	−510	1	
EURUSD	1290		−5	1285	1	
ZLZ10	24		−5	14	1	
AUDUSD	1370		−5	1365	1	
AUDUSD	2050		−5	2045	1	
EURUSD	3510		−5	3505	2	
CTZ10	400		−5	395	2	
EMDU10	1630		−5	1625	2	
CTZ10	85		−5	80	2	
EMDU10	280		−5	275	3	
KCU10	112.5		−5	107.5	2	
KCU10	18.75		−5	13.75	2	
RBV10	−2436		−10	−2446	1	
EURUSD	40		−5	30	1	
USDCAD	200		−5	195	4	
GBPUSD	−960		−10	−970	1	
USDCAD	760		−5	755	7	
GLD	−710		−10	−720	1	
EURUSD	40		−5	30	4	
GBPUSD	40		−5	30	4	
GLD	−540		−5	−545*	N/A	−3641
Aug 2010 Totals	8723.65		−160	8538.65	2.1	−3641

Note: All performance table results are excerpted from hypothetical trading results and reproduced solely for educational purposes.

*Mark-to-Market settlement price on open position at end of month.

Source: CQG, Inc. © 2010. All rights reserved worldwide.

performance table. The key points for analysis here are ensuring the robustness of each model as a stand-alone.

Monthly Summary Performance Totals

Monthly summary totals tables offer a comprehensive view of longer-term performance statistics. The spreadsheet includes 22 columns of track record data.

TABLE 11.6 Monthly Performance Table—August 2010, Part IV

Asset	W	L	Profits	Losses	Model
N/A	N/A	N/A	N/A	N/A	N/A
RBU10	0.5		944.2		Trend
EURUSD	1		30		MR
RBU10	0.5		965.2		Trend
GBPUSD		1		−1370	MR
USDCAD	0.5		265		MR
USDCAD	0.5		1145		MR
USDJPY		1		−510	MR
EURUSD	0.5		1285		MR
ZLZ10	1		14		Trend
AUDUSD	0.5		1365		MR
AUDUSD	0.5		2045		MR
EURUSD	0.5		3505		MR
CTZ10	0.5		395		MR
EMDU10	0.5		1625		Trend
CTZ10	0.5		80		MR
EMDU10	0.5		275		Trend
KCU10	0.5		107.5		Trend
KCU10	0.5		13.75		Trend
RBV10		1		−2446	MR
EURUSD	1		30		MR
USDCAD	0.5		195		Trend
GBPUSD		1		−970	MR
USDCAD	0.5		755		Trend
GLD		1		−720	Trend
EURUSD	1		30		MR
GBPUSD	1		30		MR
GLD	1			−545*	Trend
Aug 2010 Totals	14	5	15099.65	−6561*	

Notes: All performance table results are excerpted from hypothetical trading results and reproduced solely for educational purposes.

*Mark-to-Market settlement price on open position at end of month. "Trend" is notation for trend-following model; "MR" is notation for mean reversion model.

Source: CQG, Inc. © 2010. All rights reserved worldwide.

The columns are as follows:

1. Month—This column displays both month and year.

2. Gross P/L—This shows total monthly profit or loss before deductions for commissions.

3. Commissions—This shows total monthly commissions. Unless you are executing scalping or day-trading methodologies, commissions should

TABLE 11.7 Monthly Performance Table—August 2010, Part V

Asset	W Trades	W Time	L Time
N/A			
RBU10			
EURUSD	30	1	
RBU10	1909.4	4	
GBPUSD			1
USDCAD			
USDCAD	1410	3	
USDJPY			1
EURUSD			
ZLZ10	14	1	
AUDUSD			
AUDUSD	3410	1	
EURUSD	4790	2	
CTZ10			
EMDU10			
CTZ10	475	2	
EMDU10	1900	3	
KCU10			
KCU10	121.25	2	
RBV10			1
EURUSD	30	1	
USDCAD			
GBPUSD			1
USDCAD	950	7	
GLD			1
EURUSD	30	4	
GBPUSD	30	4	
GLD			N/A
Aug 2010 Totals	15,099.65	2.7	1

Note: All performance table results are excerpted from hypothetical trading results and reproduced solely for educational purposes.

Source: CQG, Inc. © 2010. All rights reserved worldwide.

represent around 1 to 2 percent of average gross profits shown in column 2.

4. Net P/L—This shows total monthly profit or loss after deducting for commissions.

5. Number of Trades—This column alerts us to overtrading tendencies. Although scalpers and day traders will have higher numbers, in general, the smaller your number of monthly trades, the better.

TABLE 11.8 Comparison of Monthly versus Multi-Month Results for GLD Trade

Tables	Exit Date	Exit Price	Gross P/L	Commissions	Net P/L	Days
Aug 2010	8/30/2010	$120.91*	−$540.00*	−$5.00*	−$545.00*	N/A
Multi-Month	9/1/2010	$122.51**	$530.00	−$5.00	$525.00	2
Multi-Month	9/1/2010	$121.47**	$10.00	−$5.00	$5.00	2

Note: All performance table results are excerpted from hypothetical trading results and reproduced solely for educational purposes.
*Mark-to-Market settlement price on open position at end of month.
**Exit price on 500 shares (50 percent of total volumetric position).
Source: CQG, Inc. © 2010. All rights reserved worldwide.

6. Worst Draw—This is the largest intramonth and intermonth peak-to-valley drawdowns in dollars. Use an asterisk to denote intermonth peak-to-valley drawdowns in equity.

7. Start Acct Bal—This shows the account balance at the beginning of the month.

8. ROR %—This shows the rate of return for the month and is Net P/L from column 4 divided by the Start Acct Bal in column 7 (unless intramonth deposits and withdrawals occurred that month).

9. Cash Actions—This column shows all deposits and withdrawals to the trading account.

10. EOM Acct Bal—This shows the account balance at the end of month and will also be used as the following month's Start Acct Bal amount.

11. W—This column is the total number of winning trades for the month.

12. L—This column is the total number of losing trades for the month.

13. Avg Profit—This column shows average profit on all winning trades.

14. Avg Loss—This column shows average loss for all losing trades.

15. %W—This column shows the percentage of winning trades for the month and is calculated by taking column 11 and dividing it by column 5. Although most traders find it easier to stick with methodologies enjoying higher winning percentages, some very successful long-term trend traders consistently experience less than 50 percent winning trades. The key to their success is very robust P:L Ratios (see column 17) and W/L Times (see column 22).

16. Time—This shows the number of calendar days with an open position in the market.

17. P/L Ratio—This shows the ratio of average profit to average loss and is calculated by taking column 13 and dividing it by column 14. In general,

TABLE 11.9 Monthly Summary Totals, Part I

Month	Gross P/L	Commissions	Net P/L	# of Trades	Worst Draw
Aug 2010	8,723.65	−160.0	8,563.65	19	−3,641
Sep 2010	10,556.00	−197.5	10,358.50	21	−1,810
Total:	19,279.65	−357.5	18,922.15	40	−3,641

Note: All performance table results are excerpted from hypothetical trading results and reproduced solely for educational purposes.
Source: CQG, Inc. © 2010. All rights reserved worldwide.

traders want this ratio to be significantly above 1.0, unless their %W (see column 15) is significantly greater than 50 percent.

18. % Draw—This is the largest percentage intramonth and intermonth peak-to-valley drawdowns. It is calculated by dividing the largest dollar amount drawdown shown in column 6 by the total account equity before the beginning of that drawdown. Use an asterisk to denote an intermonth peak-to-valley drawdown in equity.

19. Days Draw—This shows the longest intramonth or intermonth drawdown. Remember that the longest drawdown is not necessarily the largest. Use an asterisk to denote an intermonth peak-to-valley drawdown.

20. Monthly P:MD—This measures how much net monthly profit was generated vis-à-vis how much risk was endured to generate that profit. The higher this number, the more robust the methodologies traded. It is calculated by dividing Net P/L from column 4 by Worst Draw of column 6.

21. P:MD—This measures how much total (multi-month or multiyear) net profit was generated vis-à-vis how much risk was endured to generate that profit. Because this number is cumulative net profits and the worst peak-to-valley drawdown will not necessarily change over time, this

TABLE 11.10 Monthly Summary Totals, Part II

Month	Start Acct Bal	ROR %	Cash Actions	EOM Acct Bal	W	L
Aug 2010	200,000.00	4.28	200,000	208,563.65	14	5
Sep 2010	208,563.65	4.97	N/A	218,922.15	16	5
Total:	N/A	9.46	200,000	218,922.15	30	10

Note: All performance table results are excerpted from hypothetical trading results and reproduced solely for educational purposes.
Source: CQG, Inc. © 2010. All rights reserved worldwide.

TABLE 11.11 Monthly Summary Totals, Part III

Month	Avg Profit	Avg Loss	% W	Time	P:L Ratio	% Draw
Aug 2010	1161.51	−1093.50	73.68	1.80	1.06	1.72
Sep 2010	1059.57	−919.17	76.19	2.77	1.15	0.87
Total:	1106.90	−1116.60	75.00	2.33	0.99	1.72

Note: All performance table results are excerpted from hypothetical trading results and reproduced solely for educational purposes.
Source: CQG, Inc. © 2010. All rights reserved worldwide.

TABLE 11.12 Monthly Summary Totals, Part IV

Month	Days Draw	Monthly P:MD	P:MD	W/L Time
Aug 2010	12	2.35	2.35	1.71
Sep 2010	6	5.72	5.20	2.97
Total:	12	N/A	5.20	2.44

Note: All performance table results are excerpted from hypothetical trading results and reproduced solely for educational purposes.
Source: CQG, Inc. © 2010. All rights reserved worldwide.

number should increase significantly over time when compared to the Monthly P:MD.

22. W/L Time—Here the total average holding time of all winning positions is divided by the total average holding time of all losing positions. In general, traders strive to make this number larger as their skills improve.

Monthly Summary Performance Totals by Trading Model

If you are simultaneously executing multiple trading models, it is helpful to break down performance by each trading model, as this alerts us to strengths and weaknesses of each model as a stand-alone as well as how simultaneous implementation enhances overall performance. The spreadsheets are composed of the same 22 columns used in the monthly summary totals table.

FINAL THOUGHTS

People tend to have unrealistic beliefs about the growth and development process in trader psychology. We imagine the removal of trading biases as a yes-no, bias or no bias proposition. Think instead of emotional growth and development like a spiral of musical notes in a scale. Our psychological development (in most instances) is not linear; we instead experience stronger and weaker octaves of the same emotions such as fear, greed, pride, jealousy, and so on. For example, as we continue working on ourselves as traders, it might appear that we have completely eradicated associations of emotional pain with losses. This belief could even be validated by enduring a loss without any association of emotional pain whatsoever. However, in most instances what has happened is resolution of a stronger octave of associations of emotional pain with loss, and when a larger-than-average-sized loss or a string of consecutive losses occurs, emotional pain resurfaces at these weaker octaves.

Comparing the C sharp note to the emotional pain experienced by traders enduring losses, as beginners we feel a stronger C sharp note, whereas intermediate-level traders feel the same C sharp note but it is a weaker, less destructive octave of this same pain of losing. Finally, even master traders feel this same C sharp note of emotional pain after losses, but they have trained themselves to embrace and release the emotion almost instantaneously. By realizing that the resolution of trader biases occurs in stages, we are emotionally prepared for their recurrence on these weaker octaves. Consequently, when recurrence does arise, instead of frustration or despondency, we recognize this weaker octave of emotion for what it is, evidence of our maturation from being emotionally crippled by losses to a tempered acceptance of this weaker octave, which still requires resolution to shift us from the octave of competent trader to that of master trader.

Other, more ideological, trading biases also tend to be resolved in stages. For example, a beginning speculator might display a bias toward going long or short, trading on quiet days as opposed to days when government reports are released, or Fridays versus Mondays. Intermediate traders could have resolved such strong biases but could still display biases toward trading ICE Brent Crude Oil versus CME Group WTI Crude Oil. Even advanced traders who have resolved such intermediate-level biases might still display biases toward trend following as opposed to countertrend trading.[5]

Finally, trading biases correspond to developmental stages of speculators. Beginning traders display extremely destructive biases such as biases against admitting that they are wrong as well as biases toward small profits and large losses. These biases are so destructive to traders that they lead to emotional breakdown and failure, which forces us to acknowledge the realities of the market's multifaceted, uncertain, and ever-changing nature. It is at this developmental stage—following an account blowup—that we have the potential to learn the reality of being stuck between the proverbial rock (of not wanting to lose) and a hard place (of regretting missed profit opportunities). According to Sun Tzu, "Do not press an enemy at bay (*because*)...if they know there is no alternative, they will fight to the death."[6] In other words, by recognizing that fear of loss leads to regret over missed opportunities for profit and participation so as to minimize regret over missed opportunities leads to fear of losses, we are sufficiently motivated to develop and adhere to a casino paradigm method irrespective of the outcome, adopting a "whatever happens, happens" attitude. Ironically, it is oftentimes our pairing of this attitude with the casino paradigm methodology that marks the transition from novice to intermediate-level trading skills.

Remember, adoption of this "whatever happens, happens" attitude is not a reckless disregard for risk. We instead manage the risk, acknowledging our fear of loss, but we feel that fear and execute the casino paradigm method anyway (see Chapter 12). We acknowledge the possibility of loss, but have sufficiently matured as traders so that we recognize acceptance of this possibility as the price paid to minimize the regret of missing opportunities for profit.

The transition from beginner to intermediate trader is unparalleled throughout the career of the speculator because it represents our shift from failure to success. A common problem among intermediate-level traders is allowing moderate degrees of success and achievement of initial financial goals to devolve into complacency and risk aversion. Complacency and risk aversion typically arise from laziness or an irrational clinging to suboptimal methods due to an erroneous belief that the only alternative is a return to previous experiences of emotional chaos and financial ruin. If the issue is complacency leading to irrational levels of risk aversion, the antidote is refocusing on probabilities and committing to specific, cutting-edge performance goals. By contrast, if the problem is an irrational fear of failure, the antidote is research, including development, back testing, and optimization of mechanical trading systems. The more time dedicated to research and testing of other positive expectancy models, the more easily irrational biases regarding our model can be eliminated. Researching other models fosters an attitude of open-minded inquisitiveness that promotes modification of our own methodology in accordance with our unique trading personality.

The transition from intermediate to advanced trader is often marked by incorporation of intuitive skills—which come from experience—to augment purely mechanical methods.

Advanced traders also use internal irrational emotionalism as a barometer to access intuition regarding consensus mentality (which is almost always wrong). For example, whenever a parabolic move in my favor occurs and I imagine cataclysmic events that could push the market to new all-time highs, I calmly *notice* the euphoria and immediately exit

TABLE 11.13 Overview of Trader Skills

Skill Level	Methodology	Risk Management	Discipline	Challenge
Beginner	None	None	None	Develop casino paradigm method
Intermediate	Rule based	Stop losses, position sizing	Adheres to rules with rare, minor breakdowns	Complacency, risk aversion
Advanced	Rule based, augmented by intuition	Risk management pyramid	Near-flawless to flawless	Develop new models, refine existing models

Note: These categories are offered for illustrative purposes only and should not be thought of as hard and fast delineators of beginner, intermediate or advanced trading skill levels.

50 percent of the position, while raising my stop on the remainder. More often than not, emotionally charged daydreams of cataclysmic events, all-time new highs, and so forth, mark the peak or trough of a market move.

Advanced traders hone self-awareness to such an extent that they can distinguish hoping from intuition. The easiest way to differentiate hoping from intuition is an internal monitoring of emotions. Wishing is an emotionally charged superimposition of our subjective beliefs onto the market's behavior. By contrast, intuition is an emotionally neutral, objective perception of the market's truth.

Finally, although I have tried to delineate basic characteristics and tendencies of traders at various developmental stages of their careers, part of what distinguishes the advanced, or master, trader from intermediate or beginners is an ongoing commitment to growth and refinement of skills. They recognize that there is no static plateau of mastery in trading, that it is a fluid process of refinement, and that success in trading, as the cliché goes, "... is a journey, not a destination." Whereas intermediate-skilled traders struggle to get back into their old groove of successful trading after a setback, master traders realize there is no idealized past to return to, that you can never step into the same river twice (because rivers, like the markets, are multifaceted, uncertain, and ever changing). They therefore view so-called setbacks as opportunities to perceive previously unconscious blind spots in their skills and use them to achieve new heights of success in trading (see Table 11.13).

CHAPTER 12

Becoming an Even-Tempered Trader

He who binds to himself a joy
Doth the winged life destroy.
But he who kisses the joy as it flies,
Lives in eternity's sunrise.

—William Blake

T raders cannot afford rigid beliefs. While beginners are susceptible to extremely destructive biases such as exiting profits quickly, letting losers run, and so on, even experienced traders can improve performance by overcoming subtler trading biases. For example, although experienced traders realize that they cannot be rigidly bullish or bearish, their flexibility often falls apart when it comes to modification of positive expectancy models or risk management methodologies. This chapter examines a wide array of psychological and somatic tools and techniques, including even-mindedness, meditation, visualization, and research to aid in tempering emotionalism, promoting creativity, and overcoming various trader biases.

THE "I DON'T CARE" GUY

While dining with some childhood friends (who are not in the industry) one asked what I taught traders. After explaining it, another replied, "I get it, you're the 'I don't care' guy." Although a humorous simplification of trader psychology, in many ways his response was right. Emotionalism in trading does not work. As long as you are not reckless about risk management

241

while executing a positive expectancy model, you should not be emotionally attached to the results of your trades. If you do care, then you either haven't done enough research to be certain that it is a positive expectancy methodology, you're not managing the risk, you're letting previous negative trading experiences sabotage your edge, or you're addicted to the gambler's mentality of needing to win as opposed to knowing you will succeed.

This is the only industry in which individuals destined to experience 10,000 to 1,000,000 data points (or trades) over the course of their careers obsess over the results of a single data point. The cliché about only being as good as your last trade is both untrue and psychologically destructive. The antidote is remembering that throughout your career you will experience everything from profits when the market missed your stop loss by one tick, to losses when your stop was the high or low price. If you cling to each of these experiences, you will ride the emotional roller coaster of euphoria and depression ad infinitum. The roller coaster is exhausting, demoralizing, and leads to career burnout (especially in electronically traded, 24-hour markets).

But there is an alternative. Instead of obsessing over past losses, premature profitable exits, and so on, focus on market opportunities offered in the present moment with emotional even-mindedness while simultaneously learning from past errors so that you trade more effectively now and in the future. What is even-mindedness? It means trading without attachment to winning or aversion to losing on any single trade. I often compare master traders to actuaries who pore over statistical tables so as to better determine probabilities and risk. When the unlikely loss does occur, they do not imagine themselves as failures and abandon the profession; they instead recognize it as a cost of doing business. Even-mindedness techniques strive to temper emotional reactivity to the results of a single trade. Instead of obsessing over the outcome of *this* single trade, realize that as long as you are managing the risk and adhering to a positive expectancy model, a year from now you will not even remember this trade. As opposed to defining success or failure based on whether a single trade was a profit or a loss, focus on the casino paradigm process and measure success by the degree to which you demonstrated disciplined adherence to the positive expectancy model and rules of risk management.

Even-mindedness means consistently operating in the middle ground of tempered emotionalism. Typically, beginning (and to a lesser extent intermediate-level) traders cycle from extremes of greed-driven recklessness in which prudent risk management rules are abandoned and panic in which fear of loss sabotages their ability to successfully execute the positive expectancy model by either preventing them from placing entry orders, setting stop loss orders too tight (too close to entry price levels), or moving stops from loss to breakeven levels prematurely (see Table 12.1).

Becoming an Even-Tempered Trader   **243**

TABLE 12.1   Emotional Spectrum of Trading

Paralysis	Fear	Even-Mindedness	Reckless After Entry	Blind Recklessness
Unable to initiate positions	Adjusting stops prematurely; Premature profit-taking	Flawless execution of model	Deviating from model— adding risk after entry	Not quantifying risk with stops; Overleveraging

After a trade, irrespective of whether it was a profit or loss, traders must fight tendencies toward fearfulness or recklessness. Following a winning trade, fearfulness can manifest as an unwillingness to give back profits. Some speculators stop trading altogether once they achieve their monthly profit target so they do not lose it all back. The antidote to this tendency is remembering each trading opportunity is unique and unrelated to previous or subsequent opportunities. Just because you are up 10 percent on the month has absolutely no bearing on whether the next trade will be profitable. Remember, the market is unaware of whether you are up 10 percent or down 5 percent. It is instead continuing to offer opportunities to participate in your positive expectancy model. It is up to you whether you superimpose artificial ceilings on performance merely because you have not yet turned the calendar ahead to a new month.

On the other hand, recklessness can arise from euphoric delusions of invincibility as well as traders imagining they can abandon disciplined adherence to risk management or the positive expectancy model since they are now playing with the house's money. The antidote here is remembering that there is no such thing as the house's money and that as soon as the market generates a profitable mark-to-market, those profits are yours. That the profits are yours is reflected by your brokerage statement. It is consequently just as irrational and irresponsible for you to be more reckless after profits as it is for fear to derail your continued adherence to a positive expectancy model after losses.

After losing trades, fearfulness can manifest as paralysis preventing the placement of entry orders, setting stop loss orders too tightly (that is, too close to entry price levels), or moving stops from loss to breakeven levels prematurely. The antidote is remembering that the model enjoys positive expectancy and our fear is therefore irrationally tied to memories of previous losses and is counterproductive. Reckless abandonment of the model or risk management can also arise after losses from our desire to recuperate quickly. The antidote to recklessness after losses is patience and remembering that markets offer opportunities for profit more quickly and more frequently than we imagine after suffering a loss. The specific anti-dote for losses depends on whether we executed our positive expectancy model while successfully managing the risk. Remember, there are always four possible trading outcomes: winning from a good bet, winning from a bad bet, losing from a good bet, and losing from a bad bet. Consequently, if our loss was due to a mistake in modeling, risk management, or discipline, we need to learn from such errors so we can operate more effectively in the future. However, if the losses occurred despite our flawless execution of the casino paradigm, we merely need to accept such losses as an un-avoidable aspect of our profession and continue our disciplined execution of the positive expectancy model.

As opposed to recklessness or fearfulness, even-mindedness means re-maining centered despite emotions accompanying cycles of profit and loss, and not allowing such emotions to be projected onto a multifaceted, un-certain, and ever-changing future. As stated throughout Chapter 10, a key to mastery of even-mindedness is embracing and releasing the emotions accompanying profits and losses. Embrace and acknowledge the truth of your resistance to tempered emotionalism when faced with losses, then re-lease the resistance, accepting its momentary truth while realizing the im-permanence of that emotion, releasing and allowing your mind to expand and perceive a wider spectrum of possibilities than habituated emotional responses.

As stated in Chapter 4, one of the few guarantees in markets is the cyclical nature of volatility. The subjective experience of low volatility is often marked by boredom, lack of concentration, and distraction, which can lead to abandonment of our positive expectancy model. By contrast, high-volatility environments are typically accompanied by tumultuous market-moving events that trigger emotional reactivity such as greed or panic, which can also result in loss of focus and abandonment of our model. Even-mindedness entails adherence to rule-based, positive expectancy trading irrespective of where the market is in its cycle of volatility.

THE MASTER TRADER

What distinguishes master traders? They realize the key to even-mindedness is practice. Like the Olympic swimmer who tirelessly trains for years so as to more effortlessly swim flawless laps, they constantly hone their craft by practicing flawless execution of their casino paradigm method. Although master traders remain unconcerned with the outcome of any particular trade, they consistently challenge themselves to stretch beyond their comfort zone by achieving detailed trading goals. They are willing to predefine risk without irrational fear because they trust in their edge. Despite their recognition of each opportunity's uniqueness, they realize their positive expectancy model works because it consistently skews probabilities in their favor. Master traders quickly disassociate past losses from present opportunities so as to minimize distractions while simultaneously acknowledging mistakes without self-flagellation. They are meticulous risk managers who know that by playing great defense, the offense usually takes care of itself. They acknowledge imperfections and therefore can leave money on the table, manage risk, and avoid chasing missed opportunities. They have learned the antidote for concern over missed opportunities is patience and knowing new opportunities will arise in the future. They are opportunistic and flexible, having learned to lose their opinions and not their money. After a loss, they simply move on to the next trading opportunity without trying to recuperate lost capital. They recognize recuperating previous losses as a trading-to-break even mentality as opposed to trading to win. They personify even-mindedness by focusing on the process as opposed to thinking about the money (see Chapter 5).

Advanced traders master the paradox of embodying unwavering discipline without being rigid. They superimpose rules onto the limitless nature of markets and are unwavering in adherence to risk management criteria while simultaneously remaining flexible so as to attune to the ever-changing nature of market behavior. They change when the market changes by maintaining objectivity and consistent discipline irrespective of winning or losing streaks. They hope when afraid and remain vigilant when euphoric. They embrace, accept, and integrate emotionalism of gain and loss without allowing it to subvert their goals. They participate in high-probability setups irrespective of suboptimal entry levels. They realize that being right and sitting tight makes up for a multitude of minor mistakes.

Master traders consistently stretch beyond their comfort zone, while simultaneously capitalizing on opportunities that play to their innate strengths. For example, if they are only comfortable trading on fundamentals, they paper trade on technical indicators; if their comfort zone is trading high-tech stocks, they paper trade agricultural futures; if they are comfortable implementing a countertrend scalping model, they paper trade a long-term trend-following system. They recognize the importance of expanding beyond any rigid beliefs regarding markets and realize it takes conscious effort in the form of research and experimentation to transition beyond their innate comfort zone.

Advanced traders have mastered the paradox of remaining confident in their positive expectancy models without allowing that confidence to degenerate into rigidity or complacency. After a loss (or a series of losses), instead of second-guessing their edge, they continue to accept probabilities and manage risk. They know that unless the market proves them wrong by taking out support or resistance levels and triggering stops, they are right, and traders with the opposite position have incorrectly assessed the market (since it failed to violate support or resistance levels) and must therefore exit. This incorrect assessment by those who are wrong gives master traders the confidence and patience needed to let profits run. The market has proven they are right by increasing their account balance and so they stay with the trade until evidence of a reversal appears in the form of a statistically significant (for example, 1 percent) decrease in their trading account.

Master traders execute each and every positive expectancy opportunity offered without hesitation or bias and accept small, manageable losses as the price paid to enjoy outsized profits. This gives them the prerequisite mindset to be right and sit tight. They are okay with being wrong, but not okay with staying wrong and therefore augment price-driven risk parameters with time-driven criteria such as not holding losing positions longer than 24 hours and so forth. They have relinquished perfectionism in favor of flexibility, robustness, and a continuous commitment toward honing their craft.

Some traders imagine embodying even-mindedness of the master trader as the acquisition of unnatural psychological skills. The universal innate capacity for even-mindedness is instead evidenced by specific instances in which we instinctively enter a state of emotional calm despite experiencing a highly stressful situation. This suggests that, as opposed to acquiring an unnatural skill, we simply need to access this inner calm by deactivating habituated reactions of destructive emotionalism. Although it is challenging to make your peace with prematurely exiting with small profits, moving stop loss orders too soon, pulling the trigger after multiple consecutive losses, and learning from past errors without falling prey to self-flagellation, not only is it possible, but this prerequisite skill is key in abandoning the emotional roller coaster of euphoria and despondency.

How do master traders consistently access this inner calm state that promotes sustained and focused awareness irrespective of extreme stress due to periods of high volatility or extreme boredom during cycles of low market volatility? The key is accessing what is known in Eastern spiritual traditions as witness consciousness. Witness consciousness allows master traders to objectively observe their behavior, thereby aiding in deactivating emotionally destructive cycles of egocentricity (for example, obsessing over what losses will mean to us emotionally, how premature profit-taking will affect our status, and so on) in favor of an objective (as opposed to subjective) view of market opportunities. The development and maturation of witness consciousness allows them to consistently access what Buddhist psychology calls *jñāna*, or wisdom awareness. This state of jñāna is juxtaposed to *vijñāna*, or divided wisdom. Master traders have learned that consistent success is sustained not through repression or denial of the disparate aspects of vijñāna mind-seeking expression, but instead to channel their expression harmlessly within the emotionally tempered context of even-mindedness.

Just like the fad dieter who has learned to chew gum or do sit-ups as a harmless outlet for expression of their binging, midnight fridge-raiding vijñāna mind, so, too, the master trader creates harmless methods of expression such as analytical research for the vijñāna mind when it seeks destructive expression through abandonment of rule-based trading due to boredom or emotionalism. Generally speaking, these habituated destructive reactions to emotionalism or boredom can be deactivated through conscious effort by way of various techniques examined throughout the remainder of this chapter, including flexibility, creativity, meditation, visualization, affirmations, rest, and somatic exercises.

REPROGRAMMING THE TRADER

The original working title of my first book was *Reprogramming the Trader with Mechanical Trading Systems.* I liked the title because it suggested success in trading was a learned technique (as opposed to random luck or an inborn talent) achieved through adherence to a rule-based methodology, and that the process of adhering to such rules could aid in both eliminating destructive behavior and reinforcing positive psychological traits. The myth of trading is that speculators fail because positive expectancy trading models do not exist. The reality is that many traders fail because they lack the discipline to adhere to rule-based positive expectancy models. Like the dieter who cannot stick to a diet and then complains that it doesn't work, so, too, the addicted gambler trades a positive expectancy model only to abandon it after enduring three consecutive losses. In both instances, it was not that the method was unworkable; it was that the individual was unwilling to work the method.

There are many reasons why gamblers fail to adhere to rules of positive expectancy models. In addition to the problem of vijñāna mind (as outlined earlier), among the most common are self-worth issues. Some of these issues can be traced to beliefs about money and how it is earned, along with self-imposed limits regarding what we deserve. The key to resolution of these issues is deactivating destructive beliefs. We not only need to know that success is possible, but also that we deserve it. In general, disciplined adherence to a positive expectancy model remains problematic until inner conflicts regarding trading have been resolved. The good news is that deactivation of self-sabotaging beliefs is not predicated on resolution of each and every subconscious childhood trauma. We merely need instead to identify specific self-sabotaging behaviors, accept and embrace their reality, and then release them by recognizing them as an impediment to our success as traders. Until we commit to self-evaluation and correction of self-destructive behavior, trading errors, missed opportunities, and removing stop loss orders, artificial self-imposed success thresholds will continue to impede performance.

Another popular delusional belief associated with self-worth issues is poverty consciousness. Poverty consciousness is the belief that our environment is unable to provide necessities for survival or that such provisions are only attainable through exertion of superhuman effort. Also, poverty consciousness typically manifests as a belief that your material enrichment can occur only at the impoverishment of others. These beliefs are especially prevalent in trading whereby one person profits when another loses. Poverty consciousness is particularly destructive for traders because it fosters self-sabotaging behavior and reinforces self-imposed ceilings on performance. Poverty consciousness is an irrational fallacy. For example, how many people were impoverished by the development of the polio vaccine compared to the billions who benefit from it? Advancements such as modern plumbing, dentistry, information technology, and so on, enrich humanity in general. The antidote to poverty consciousness is remembering that markets are multifaceted, uncertain, and ever changing. Although trading is among the most challenging professions, it simultaneously offers virtually limitless opportunities for enrichment as long as we attune ourselves to what the market is offering and do not superimpose artificial limits upon these opportunities.

FLEXIBILITY AND CREATIVITY

As stated in Chapter 11, among the greatest challenges for intermediate-skilled traders is overcoming complacency and irrational risk-averse behavior. This intermediate stage of the trader's career is typically marked by achievement of initial financial goals, and consequently, as assets under management increase, so too can biases toward irrational risk-averse behavior. The antidote to financial conservatism and risk aversion is continuing to think in terms of probabilities, irrespective of monetary gains or losses, as well as formulating concrete, ambitious performance goals. The key to achievement of these goals is a commitment to learning, creativity, and flexibility.

The danger with consistently mediocre levels of success is that it leads to complacency and settling for status quo performance. Complacency is often accompanied by believing we already know everything needed to succeed, which artificially limits or creates internal resistance to perceiving new information or perceiving it in more opportunistic ways. Success in trading is difficult, and it is therefore quite common to take a rest-on-my-laurels approach after achievement of hard-fought success. The problem is that unless we push beyond our comfort zone, complacency can imperceptibly devolve into stagnation. Instead, by consistently emphasizing learning, flexibility, adaptability, and creativity, we commit to the growth and development required to transition from competence to mastery in trading.

The amazing thing about mind is its creativity. By asking open-ended questions that force us to look and think outside our comfort zone, new solutions arise. Among the most valuable exercises to hone trading skills is constantly asking the following questions:

How can I be more flexible in viewing the markets?
> This is among the most powerful tools to overcome internal resistance to growth and development. Since market behavior is multifaceted, uncertain, and ever changing, our view of the markets can always be more flexible. The greater our commitment to adaptability and to honing our skills, the more robust our performance will be.

Is this a low-risk/high-reward opportunity with probability in my favor?
> By asking this question about every opportunity in the market, you train yourself to consistently identify your edge and think in terms of probabilities.

How can I risk less? How can I make more?
> Although either question forces you to hone skills and be innovative, it is important to repeat both questions together to better develop a creativity that is balanced in its consideration of risk as well as reward. Also, ask these questions with details in mind, including the tightening of stop losses, trailing of stop orders more aggressively, reducing position size on positively correlated assets, taking partial profits, and so forth.

What am I doing right?
> Unsuccessful traders often already possess much of what is required to succeed. Nevertheless, when we fail to achieve desired results, it is easier to simply capitulate, saying, "Trading is impossible" as opposed to committing to what we do well while identifying and modifying specific behaviors that are undermining or limiting success.

Another effective technique for promoting creativity and flexibility is modeling your behavior after a master trader. In so doing, it is not sufficient to hypothetically wonder, "What would Trader XYZ do here?" We need instead to develop all the prerequisite tools, including positive expectancy models, risk management rules, and principles of trading discipline and then ask, "Is this how Trader XYZ would handle model development, testing, implementation, and risk management?" "Would they take this type of trade setup?" "Would they simultaneously execute three positively correlated trades with 2 percent stop losses in each?" Also, after developing a positive expectancy method and rules of risk management, we can use our own successful trades as the indwelling master trader on which to model our behavior.

MEDITATION

The practice of meditation is invaluable for traders because it lets us access a state of relaxed, alert alpha brain wave activity. The meditative state allows us to release emotional attachment, making it easier for us to adhere to rule-based trading regardless of what type of market environment we are faced with. Meditation, along with other relaxation techniques, offers a powerful tool to combat emotional reactivity to markets. By quieting the mind and slowing our breath until relaxed and alert, we are able to quiet the vijñāna mind and access witness consciousness.

Seven-Point Posture

One of the commonly used supports for aiding the mind to access this state of alert relaxation is known as the seven-point posture. The posture is not a prerequisite for achieving the meditative state; it is instead a skillful method of habituating the mind to the practice. Just as we habituate our mind to driving a car by buckling seat belts, depressing the brake pedal before shifting the car into reverse, and then checking the rearview mirror, so too the seven-point posture is used to habituate the mind to accessing this calm and alert state of witness consciousness.

The first of the seven aspects of the posture is to have your legs in either a full lotus, half-lotus, or crossed position. If it is difficult for you to sit comfortably in any of those postures, simply sit in a chair with feet planted firmed on the floor. The second of the seven aspects is to have your hands be folded together, palms up with right on top of the left. According to Drikung Kyabgon Chetsang Rinpoche's *The Practice of Mahamudra*, the right palm should be four finger widths below the navel.[1] The third posture is the spine, which should be straight. This is said to be the most important aspect of the physical posture in meditation and is key to promoting relaxed breathing as a support for the mind in meditation. Another aid in promoting relaxed breathing is the fourth aspect of the posture, the setting of shoulders back so that the chest opens up. Fifth, the chin is slightly lowered, and sixth, the tongue is held upward toward the front teeth and the mouth is opened slightly in order to relax tension in the jaw. The seventh point is the eyes, which, according to Tibetan Buddhist meditation, are slightly open with a downward gaze just beyond the tip of the nose. This final point differs from other meditation traditions that typically suggest meditation with eyes closed so as to minimize distractions. If you find meditating with eyes open too distracting, begin with eyes closed and once you are in the relaxed, alert, meditative state, open your eyes. The advantage to meditation with eyes open is that it promotes integration of ordinary waking consciousness with this relaxed, alert witness consciousness state. In this manner, we train to easily access the meditative state whenever stressed or emotionally reactive.

Mind in Meditation

The misconception is that while resting in the nature of mind there are no thoughts or emotions. Eastern meditation masters tell us that as long as we have a mind, there will be thoughts and emotions, and furthermore, that thoughts and emotions are the natural radiance of mind. In shamata, or calm abiding meditation, when thoughts and emotions arise, we allow them to dissolve of their own accord. As the great meditation master Dudjom Rinpoche said to his student Sogyal Rinpoche, "Be like an old wise man watching a child play."[2] Just like the wise old man through the practice of meditation, we train witness consciousness to watch thoughts and emotions without engaging them.

Of course, we will become distracted as thoughts and emotions arise. When this occurs, watch your breath, allowing it to be a focal point for centering the distracted mind. In so doing, thoughts and emotions will naturally dissolve of their own accord. Bring the mind back to your breath without judgment or disappointment. Remember instead the analogy of the car in need of a wheel alignment and apply the antidote of focusing on the breath as distractions arise. In this manner, our witness consciousness gradually strengthens and becomes accessible whenever distracted from even-mindedness in trading.

VISUALIZATION

Visualization techniques use creative mental imagery to reinforce productive behavior. Mind creates all the time. Sometimes its creations are positive, sometimes negative, and sometimes neutral. Although mind's creativity can be proactive, it is often reactive. In other words, the environment generates stimuli, and our creativity reacts to that stimuli. When the environmental stimulus is positive, our creative reactivity tends to be positive; when negative, our reactivity often mirrors that negativity. By contrast, conscious visualization takes mind's creativity out of this reactive mode and into proactive creativity. Now you decide the kind of mental imagery to generate and in so doing you begin subtly changing the way reality is perceived.

How do we want to perceive ourselves, the markets, and our actions in the markets? Our goal is to perceive the markets as multifaceted, uncertain, and ever changing and our activity within the markets as focused, disciplined, and opportunistic without rigidity. Of course, these are abstract concepts and we want our visualizations to be as concrete and detailed as possible. For example, visualize the release of the U.S. monthly unemployment report and see how witness consciousness watches the emotional reactivity to a profitable scenario, a losing scenario, and a neutral scenario. Visualize witness consciousness objectively observing how the body feels in the seat, the breathing, the feelings in your gut, your thoughts regarding the news, and so on.

Next, go through a detailed visualization of a successful trade. See witness consciousness noticing the analytical process that preceded trade initiation, including how it looked on the chart, the news, market sentiment as well as how the body felt, and your emotions and thoughts at that moment. Feel how each of these elements (charts, news, sentiment, your body, emotions, and thoughts) change as the markets went in your favor, retraced, went further in your favor, and so on until you exited. Now ask yourself the following questions: Would earlier or later entry have enhanced profitability? Would earlier or later exit have enhanced profitability? Would regret minimization techniques (as described in Chapter 6) have enhanced profitability?

Compare the chart, news, market sentiment, how your body felt, and your emotions and thoughts throughout the process of a losing trade and compare it to the successful trade. Now ask yourself: Did I follow the rules of my positive expectancy model? Did I adhere to rules of risk management? Did my emotions or thoughts clue me in to something different about the losing trade?

Visualization techniques can prevent open positions from distorting our objective perception of the market's truth. Through these techniques, we learn to step outside of ourselves, imagine ourselves flat (as opposed to thinking with our position), and visualize all possibilities from any particular trade, including what the trade would look like if things went well, poorly, or disastrously. One technique to help traders see the reality of the market despite their bull or bear position is visualizing the exiting of that position, and then asking, "Is the market going higher or lower?" In this manner, we train ourselves to view market action objectively as opposed to justifying beliefs based on our positions.

SOMATIC EXERCISES

What I am after is more flexible minds, not just more flexible bodies.
—Moshé Feldenkrais

According to the work of Moshé Feldenkrais (developer of the Feldenkrais Method, which seeks to improve human functioning by increasing self-awareness through movement), changes in our ability to move are inseparable from changes in conscious perception of self, and so somatic exercises are consequently beneficial in maintaining psychological as well as physiological health. By increasing somatic flexibility and moving our bodies in nonhabituated ways, our minds become more flexible as well. Since psychological flexibility is one of the key attributes distinguishing beginner (and intermediate) traders from advanced, somatic exercises can aid in our transition from competence to mastery in speculation.

Different somatic exercises are particularly well-suited for resolution of various destructive mental states. For example, Hatha Yoga (commonly known as *Yoga* in the West) is especially valuable for relieving mental exhaustion, anxiety, and mental stagnation. In Sanskrit, *ha* means sun (and is associated with masculine and active somatic energies), *tha* is moon (and is associated with feminine and passive energies), and *yoga* translates as union, so Hatha Yoga is the balance achieved through the union of masculine and feminine somatic energies. A key element in the practice of Hatha Yoga is coordination of the various *asanas* (or postures) with deep, relaxed breathing.

Because aerobic and anaerobic exercise increases the release of serotonin and endorphins, they are extremely effective in the treatment of mild forms of depression commonly experienced by traders enduring losses. Walking is among the most valuable tools in overcoming mental stagnation, commonly known as trader burnout. This issue of burnout is especially controversial in trader psychology. In working with traders, I usually take the position that the only way out (of trader burnout) is through because around 20 percent of all trades typically account for 80 percent of our profits. It is therefore better to keep trading so as not to miss outsized profits and to rest while trading instead through a combination of mental gentleness, including affirmations, rest, sleep, massage, and somatic

TABLE 12.2 Antidotes for Destructive Mental States

Problem	Antidote
Anxiety	Meditation, Breathing Exercises, or Yoga
Mental Stagnation	Yoga, Walking, Research
Boredom	Research, Affirmations
Mental Exhaustion	Sleep, Meditation, Massage, Underleveraged Trading, Yoga
Depression	Aerobic and Anaerobic Exercise, Affirmations

exercises (including Hatha Yoga, exercise, and walking). Rest, sleep, and walking are particularly powerful tools for mental rejuvenation because they allow the subconscious to provide feedback and alternative perspectives on trading problems. Also, underleveraged trading (for example, trading one-tenth your typical volumetric position size) is sometimes another useful technique for alleviating burnout while keeping you in the game (see Table 12.2).

FINAL THOUGHTS

When I started trading in 1987, every six months or so a graduating son or daughter of my parents' friends, unsure of a career path, would come to see me and ask about a career in trading. Nowadays, it is the children of our friends who pilgrimage to Florida to learn about the career of speculation. For more than 20 years, my response has remained monotonously unchanged: "Don't do it." If you are anticipating a career in trading because you cannot figure out what to do with your life, it is highly unlikely that professional speculation will work for you. Inevitably, you will be facing your fourth consecutive loss accompanied by a 10 percent drawdown in equity and will capitulate. Why? Because you will compare speculative trading to alternative career paths and will correctly think, "Why am I putting myself through this? This is the only business in the world where you work all day long only to walk away with less money at the day's end."

This is why I always ask aspiring traders the same question: "Why do you want to trade?" If they have no answer beyond making money, when the inevitable losses come, they will abandon trading for easier professions. If, however, their answer is to temper emotionalism or a love of research and problem solving, when losses come, it only strengthens their motivation to succeed. My own reason for sticking with speculation during the losing years was a desire to achieve unwavering discipline and tempered emotionalism. Various hermetic texts state, "As above, so below," or for our purposes, "As in trading, so in life." In other words, many of the important concepts discussed in this book, such as self-worth, discipline, probabilities, and even-mindedness, not only help us as traders, but also help us navigate through life in general more successfully.

Successful trading teaches poise under pressure. Tempering emotionalism, even-mindedness, and witness consciousness are skills that are practiced through trading and can translate into poise during crises of life. Just as trading teaches that although we cannot control the markets, we can control our emotional reactivity to them, so too are we unable to control the occurrence of various crises of life or how others will react to such events. Nevertheless, we do have absolute control over our own reactivity as well as how we choose to emotionally interpret such events (for example, empowering, disabling, and so on). Furthermore, our ability to temper emotionalism typically has a calming effect on those around us, just as one tuning fork will mimic the oscillating frequency of its neighbor.

Successful trading is the art of acclimating ourselves to that which is uncomfortable and unnatural through repetition until it becomes second nature. Fear is a part of trading just as it is a part of life in general. Fear serves an extremely valuable purpose in our lives, in part by alerting us to danger. Successful traders cope with dangerous situations by developing positive expectancy models and pairing them with stringent rules of risk management. Fear that remains despite our reduction of danger to improbable levels arises from habituated clinging to previous painful experiences and superimposing them onto an unknown future. The antidotes to these irrational fears are the various psychological techniques covered in these final two chapters.

Feeling fear despite the reduction of danger to improbable levels is not a problem. The problem occurs when we let these fears derail the implementation of our positive expectancy model. Imagine a hiker moves to a new area and decides to walk through the local forest. They have no preconceived notions regarding the area and love hiking in nature so their attitude is carefree. While hiking, she comes across a rattlesnake. Suddenly alert to the danger, she carefully avoids the snake and picks up a makeshift walking stick for protection throughout the remainder of the walk. Before the next hike, she brings anti-snake venom along with her walking stick for protection. It makes sense to take these precautionary measures against a known danger, but it does not make sense to abandon an activity one enjoys merely because of the existence of an improbable and manageable risk. Just like our hiker, the master trader protects himself against danger but continues pursuing his goal despite lingering fears. The key to the tempering of lingering fears is repetition of the activity along with research and underleveraged trading.

That the tempering of irrational fear (that is, fear associated with previous negative experiences as opposed to significant present danger) occurs naturally over time through repetition of the fearful activity is well illustrated by the analogy of a horror movie. Think back to the first time you saw the movie *The Exorcist*. Because you had never before seen the film, the first time you saw Linda Blair's head spin around, you were probably terrified. However, after the twentieth viewing, the same stimulus produces a different response in most people . . . namely, laughter. Repetition of the stimulus has desensitized you to that which was originally terrifying because we now know exactly what will happen next. Repetition, research, and underleveraged trading deactivate one of our greatest fears, fear of the unknown. Although we cannot know the outcome of a particular trade in the markets with the same certainty as that of a horror film, repetition of the execution of uncomfortable positive expectancy trade setups can nevertheless deactivate our fear of the unknown outcome, gradually replacing it with confidence in our edge.

Immature traders imagine everything will be perfect in their professional lives once they rid themselves of this last imperfection, this solitary remaining irritant to flawless trading. By contrast, mature traders realize their trading is robust despite the imperfection that they are currently working on mitigating. They recognize the imperfection is like a grain of sand that, despite being a source of irritation for the oyster, produces a pearl. In summary, I have tried to fill this book with a variety of grains of sand (such as trading the money, lack of discipline, regret, the perfect trader syndrome, anticipating the signal, and so on) that I have struggled to turn into pearls (for example, risk management pyramid, regret minimization techniques, casino paradigm, and so on) over the years through conscious effort, research, and even-mindedness. My sincere hope is that these pearls yield growth, flexibility, and transformation in both your trading and your life, and more than this, my hope is that they inspire you to discover unique, previously uncharted psychological irritants and turn them into pearls for the betterment of both your own trading as well as the lives of all you touch.

Notes

PREFACE

1. Although numerous authors have addressed the concepts collectively known throughout this book as the *casino paradigm*, one of the most comprehensive and lucid expositions of this paradigm is *Trading in the Zone*, by Mark Douglas (Prentice Hall, 2001), pages 101–106.

CHAPTER 1 DEVELOPING POSITIVE EXPECTANCY MODELS

1. See *Devil Take the Hindmost* by Edward Chancellor (Plume, 2000) pages 14–20.
2. See the *Forbes.com* article "Inside the Semgroup Bust" by Christopher Helman (July 28, 2008).
3. See "Prospect Theory: An Analysis of Decision under Risk" by Daniel Kahneman and Amos Tversky, in *Econometrica* 47(2) (March 1979): pages 263–291.
4. See the *Oil Marketer* article "Crude Prices Rise Despite Oil Inventory Gains in US," by Elaine Frei (April 29, 2009).

CHAPTER 2 PRICE RISK MANAGEMENT METHODOLOGIES

1. See *A Tract on Monetary Reform*, by John Maynard Keynes (Prometheus Books, 2000).
2. Slippage, or liquidity risk, is the difference between assumed and actual entry or exit prices.
3. Parameters and programming code for all mechanical trading systems presented throughout the book are detailed in Chapter 6.
4. Worst peak-to-valley drawdowns in equity are the most robust risk metric since they measure a portfolio's mark-to-market from its ultimate high water mark to its most severe nadir in assets under management (as opposed to merely calculating closed-out losses).

5. See page 181 of *Market Wizards* by Jack Schwager (Marketplace Books, 2006).
6. On page 260 of *Trading for a Living* (John Wiley & Sons, 1993), Dr. Alexander Elder offers risking 2 percent of assets under management on a single trade as a valid alternative position-sizing ceiling for those with a greater risk appetite.
7. See Ralph Vince's *Portfolio Management Formulas* (John Wiley & Sons, 1990).
8. See page 170 of my first book, *Mechanical Trading Systems* (John Wiley & Sons, 2004).
9. See page 189 of *Market Wizards* by Jack Schwager (Marketplace Books, 2006).

CHAPTER 3 MAINTAINING UNWAVERING DISCIPLINE

1. See pages 153–154 of Nassim Taleb's *Fooled by Randomness* (W.W. Norton, 2001). Although Taleb uses the urn analogy to illustrate success despite negative expectancy, it is (obviously) equally adaptable to problems of failure despite positive expectancy.
2. *Fading* occurs when speculators do the exact opposite of a particular trading strategy.

CHAPTER 4 CAPITALIZING ON THE CYCLICAL NATURE OF VOLATILITY

1. The only exception to this rule of volatility's cyclical nature is a paradigm shift, which results in an asset no longer being traded, such as bankruptcy of a company, delisting of formerly publicly traded companies, and so on.
2. The Chicago Board Options Exchange Market Volatility Index, or VIX, is a popular measure of implied volatility of S&P 500 Index options. It consequently has an inverse relationship to stock market prices and is often referred to as a fear index. Because the VIX is a directional indicator, traders sometimes mistakenly think that volatility indicators can be used to determine market direction.
3. See J. Welles Wilder Jr.'s *New Concepts in Technical Trading Systems* (Trend Research, 1978).
4. The three series of months closest to expiration are used to dampen the effects of volatility backwardation as expiration approaches.

CHAPTER 6 MINIMIZING TRADER REGRET

1. An interesting aside: Although all experts agree that undercapitalized traders are at a disadvantage (as discussed in detail throughout Chapter 2), there

is some debate regarding the relative advantage of large (more than $10 million in assets under management) versus intermediate-sized (between $200,000 and $10 million in assets under management) traders. Admittedly, many of the sources citing the advantage of large traders were written during the era preceding the information revolution of instantaneous dissemination of news, electronic trading, and deep discount brokerages. Before such innovations, perhaps large traders did have an advantage; nevertheless, I would argue that this is no longer the case. Nowadays, the advantage is clearly with intermediate-sized accounts. Larger accounts are subject to levels of liquidity risk that do not affect intermediate-sized players. Such risks manifest in a variety of ways, including partial fills or unfilled profitable limit orders as well as severe slippage on stop loss orders.

2. Interest rate futures contracts are priced in 32nds and notated as 126'02.5 (for example), meaning the asset is priced at 126 and 2.5 thirty-seconds. In this example, the U.S. 10-year Treasury note futures are valued at $126,078.125.

CHAPTER 7   TIMEFRAME ANALYSIS

1. Wilder's Relative Strength Index is calculated as follows:

$$RSI = 100 - 100/(1 + RS)$$

where RSI = Average number of x days up closes/average number of x days down closes. RSI is consequently a percentage oscillator and is bounded, meaning its readings cannot go above 100 or below zero. It therefore offers technicians a mathematically objective answer to the question "What is the trend?" since readings above 50 suggest bullishness, and readings below 50 are bearish.

CHAPTER 8   HOW TO USE TRADING MODELS

1. Since my first book, *Mechanical Trading Systems* (John Wiley & Sons, 2004), discussed issues like portfolio composition, equalized active continuation charts, optimization, curve-fitting, and so on, instead of rehashing those considerations here, I will assume familiarity with these issues and refer interested readers to that text.

2. In 2003, when I wrote *Mechanical Trading Systems* (John Wiley & Sons, 2004), although some futures markets were electronically traded, most were still dominated by open outcry. Consequently, final reported volumes of exchange-traded futures contracts always lagged by one trading day. As a result, the book did not include volume indicators in its mechanical trading systems.

3. Although it is beyond the scope of this book, Tom DeMark has been a trailblazer in mechanizing many traditionally subjective technical tools such as trendlines, retracements, and so on. For readers interested in DeMark's work, I refer you to the Bibliography.
4. See John Murphy's *Technical Analysis of the Financial Markets* (New York Institute of Finance, 1999).
5. Compare this chart to the Home Depot trade in which we did not wait for RSI to drop because of the stock's weak close its day of divergence.
6. Although electronic trading ended the viability of these day trading models, I refer readers interested in day trading models applicable to any or all asset classes to the timeframe confirmation and timeframe divergence methods outlined in Chapter 7.
7. See Mark B. Fisher's *The Logical Trader* (John Wiley & Sons, 2002).

CHAPTER 10 TRANSCENDING COMMON TRADING PITFALLS

1. Prayer can prove beneficial in trader psychology if our focal point is even-mindedness or unemotionally charged prayers for clarity.
2. See pages 151–152 of Brett Steenbarger's *The Psychology of Trading* (John Wiley & Sons, 2003).

CHAPTER 11 ANALYZING PERFORMANCE

1. See pages 28–38 of Dr. Alexander Elder's *Trading for a Living* (John Wiley & Sons, 1993).
2. The exception to these percentages occurs when actively traded front-month futures roll forward to what will be their new front month.
3. An example of a *double fill* is when stop orders result in our exiting of a position, and then limit orders are executed, resulting in unintended open market positions. Orders like "one cancels other" prevent double fills by canceling the limit after the stop is executed (or vice versa).
4. Underleveraged trading is the testing of research ideas in real market conditions without putting significant capital at risk. If a typical trade risked 1 percent of assets under management, an underleveraged trade might risk one-tenth of 1 percent.
5. These biases are offered for illustrative purposes only and should not be thought of as hard-and-fast delineators of intermediate as opposed to advanced trading skill levels.
6. See page 110 of Sun Tzu's *The Art of War* (Oxford University Press, 1963).

CHAPTER 12   BECOMING AN EVEN-TEMPERED TRADER

1. See pages 37–39 of Chetsang Rinpoche's *The Practice of Mahamudra* (Snow Lion, 1999).
2. See page 78 of Sogyal Rinpoche's *The Tibetan Book of Living and Dying* (HarperOne, 2002).

Bibliography

Chancellor, Edward. *Devil Take the Hindmost: A History of Financial Speculation*. New York: Plume, 2000.

DeMark, Thomas R. *New Market Timing Techniques: Innovative Studies in Market Rhythm & Price Exhaustion*. New York: John Wiley & Sons, 1997.

DeMark, Thomas R. *The New Science of Technical Analysis*. New York: John Wiley & Sons, 1994.

Douglas, Mark. *The Disciplined Trader*. New York: New York Institute of Finance, 1990.

Douglas, Mark. *Trading in the Zone*. New York: Prentice Hall, 2001.

Dowd, Kevin. *Beyond Value at Risk: The New Science of Risk Management*. New York: John Wiley & Sons, 1999.

Elder, Alexander. *Come into My Trading Room: A Complete Guide to Trading*. Hoboken, NJ: John Wiley & Sons, 2002.

Elder, Alexander. *Trading for a Living: Psychology, Trading Tactics, Money Management*. New York: John Wiley & Sons, 1993.

Feldenkrais, Moshé. *Awareness Through Movement: Easy-to-Do Exercises to Improve Your Posture, Vision, Imagination, and Personal Awareness*. New York: HarperOne, 1991.

Fisher, Mark. *The Logical Trader*. Hoboken, NJ: John Wiley & Sons, 2002.

Frei, Elaine. "Crude Oil Prices Rise Despite Oil Inventory Gains in US." *Oil Marketer* April 29, 2009, www.oilmarketer.co.uk.

Helman, Christopher. "Inside the SemGroup Bust." *Forbes.com*, July 28, 2008, www.forbes.com.

Kahneman, Daniel. and Amos Tversky, "Prospect Theory: An Analysis of Decision under Risk." *Econometrica* 47 (1979).

Keynes, John Maynard. *A Tract on Monetary Reform*. Amherst, NY: Prometheus Books, 2000.

Kiev, Ari. *Trading in the Zone*. New York: John Wiley & Sons, 2001.

Kiev, Ari. *Trading to Win*. New York: John Wiley & Sons, 1998.

Kroll, Stanley. *The Professional Commodity Trader*. Greenville, SC: Traders Press, 1995.

Lefèvre, Edwin. *Reminiscences of a Stock Operator*. Hoboken, NJ: John Wiley & Sons, 2006.

Lewis, Michael. *The Big Short: Inside the Doomsday Machine*. New York: W.W. Norton and Company, 2010.

Link, Marcel. *High Probability Trading*. New York: McGraw-Hill, 2003.

Murphy, John. *Technical Analysis of the Financial Markets*. New York: New York Institute of Finance, 1999.

Perl, Jason. *DeMark Indicators*. New York: Bloomberg Press, 2008.

Prechter, Robert R. Jr. *The Major Works of R. N. Elliott*. Gainesville, GA: New Classics Library, 1980.

Rinpoche, Chetsang. *The Practice of Mahamudra*. Ithaca, NY: Snow Lion, 1999.

Rinpoche, Jamgon Mipham. *Gateway to Knowledge, Volume II*. Hong Kong: Boudhanath and Esby: Rangjung Yeshe Publications, 2000.

Rinpoche, Sogyal. *The Tibetan Book of Living and Dying*. New York: HarperOne, 2002.

Ross, Elisabeth Kübler. *On Death and Dying*. New York: Touchstone Books, 1997.

Schwager, Jack. *Market Wizards: Interviews with Top Traders*. Columbia, MD: Marketplace Books, 2006.

Steenbarger, Brett. *The Psychology of Trading*. Hoboken, NJ: John Wiley & Sons, 2003.

Sun Tzu. *The Art of War*. Oxford, UK: Oxford University Press, 1963.

Taleb, Nassim. *Fooled by Randomness*. New York: W.W. Norton, 2001.

Vince, Ralph. *Portfolio Management Formulas: Mathematical Trading Methods for the Futures, Options and Stock Markets*. New York: John Wiley & Sons, 1990.

Weissman, Richard. *Mechanical Trading Systems: Pairing Trader Psychology with Technical Analysis*. Hoboken, NJ: John Wiley & Sons, 2004.

Wilder, J. Welles, Jr. *New Concepts in Technical Trading Systems*. Kingston, NY: Trend Research, 1978.

About the Author

Richard L. Weissman is a professional trader with more than 20 years of experience and has provided private consultations and training to traders and risk managers for more than 15 years. He currently serves as a senior associate with the Energy Management Institute (www.emi.org), where he teaches trading and risk courses that are cosponsored by the CME Group and the Intercontinental Exchange. He is also editor-in-chief of Weissman Signals Inc. (www.weissmansignals.com), a newsletter covering the ETF, futures, and cash foreign exchange markets. Weissman's first book, *Mechanical Trading Systems: Pairing Trader Psychology with Technical Analysis*, was published by John Wiley & Sons in 2004.

Index

Printed and bound by CPI Group (UK) Ltd, Croydon, CR0 4YY

16/04/2025

14658449-0002